I0795875

The Future Life of Trauma

The Future Life of Trauma

PARTITIONS, BORDERS, REPETITION

Jennifer Yusin

FORDHAM UNIVERSITY PRESS *New York* 2017

the modern language initiative

THIS BOOK IS MADE POSSIBLE BY A COLLABORATIVE GRANT FROM THE ANDREW W. MELLON FOUNDATION.

Fordham University Press also publishes its books in a variety of electronic formats. Some content that appears in print may not be available in electronic books.

Visit us online at www.fordhampress.com.

Library of Congress Cataloging-in-Publication Data available online at http://catalog.loc.gov.

Printed in the United States of America

19 18 17 5 4 3 2 1

First edition

for clare, in memoriam ≈ for mary, in persistere

CONTENTS

PROLOGUE: THE PLACE OF A THOUSAND HILLS

In March 2010, I traveled to Rwamagana, one of seven districts in the eastern province of Rwanda. There stands the campus of the eastern branch of the Association des Vueves du Genocide Agahozo (Association of the Widows of Genocide), or AVEGA as it is more commonly known. Formed in October 1995 by fifty genocide widows, AVEGA is a nonprofit organization that helps facilitate the economic and social reintegration of genocide widows into Rwandan society. There are four branches, located in the northern, eastern, western, and southern provinces of the country. The eastern branch features a large campus that includes a health center, a bar and restaurant, a couple of reception halls that are sometimes rented out for large functions like weddings, guesthouses, and administrative offices.

Once there, a woman—a genocide widow—who was one of the facility's principal administrators guided me on a tour of the grounds. Before becoming an administrator, she served as one of the site's trauma counselors. She had no formal training in trauma counseling. Like the other women working in a similar capacity, her knowledge and expertise was acquired through her own lived experience during the genocide.

Not long thereafter, we were in her house with two other widows. Over the next few hours, the three women talked about their experiences during the genocide in unadulterated detail and with a surprising intimacy. They related the specific ways in which particular friends and family members were killed. They showed me photos of their children—ranging from three months to sixteen years in age—and detailed the gruesome death of each child. They revealed the different forms of violence they endured and recounted the bombing of a home down the street. And there was more—much more than I could ever possibly recount. In any case, their stories are not mine to tell.

Afterward, while walking outside, I asked the widow who hosted me for the day why she and the others had shared their stories at all, let alone in such a candid way. She took me gently by the arm and pointed to the house in front of which we now stood.

"See that house," she said. "Yes," I responded. We were not far, not more than a few hundred meters from her house. "Inside that house," she continued, "lives the man who committed most of the crimes we told you about. That was the man who killed my husband, my sister, my children." "Last week," she said, "I, all of us here, all of us who survived the genocide, attended his party to celebrate his son's birthday."

Our conversation after that moment extended long in the evening hours. She spoke at length about what life after the genocide had been like for her and her one surviving daughter. If I had to identify one theme in that discussion it would be transformation. She talked about the politics of the government's ideology of a unified Rwandan identity and what it was like to live as a Tutsi during the civil war that preceded the genocide. Never once did she identify herself in any way except as transformed. In relation to herself, she only spoke of the effects of cruelty as transformative. And in response to my questions about healing wounds and attempting to restore one's life, her answer was the same: habit. It was, she said, the habits of everyday life and her decision to take up new habits that did this work.

How are we to interpret the meaning of the widow's transformation? Is it merely a demonstration of living on in time, that is, a mode of survival that shows us what does and what cannot return in repetition? And what of her mention of habit? Habit is a very interesting concept because it asserts the coincidence between being and subject and the mechanisms of daily routine. It is a particular manner and mode of being that actualizes the relation between what is prearranged and what is fashioned as a self-initiating process of synthesis. Habit, we can say, is a willed compulsion whose self-reflexive mechanism is at once active (power over mechanism) and passive (mechanical power). For the widow, is habit a purely mechanical, daily routine that helps her overcome the past in some way, and or is it an ontological phenomenon that causes or describes (or both) the transformation of her essential being?[1] What are the habit-forming effects of trauma?

These questions, to my mind, challenge us to think anew the nature of the relation between cause and effect.

Every trauma is a trace. This is a formulation with which we are familiar. The external event, whether it occurs as a form of prolonged structural oppression as in the case of racism or colonialism or as an instantaneous event like a car accident, inscribes itself in the psyche, imprints the stamp of its own brutality therein. Trace is thus taken to be a form of writing that is said to account for the violent rupture and the overwhelming impact of its effects on the psyche. This conceptual approach is shared in current dialogues between postcolonial studies and trauma studies, especially in those that seek to assess colonization and its legacies as a collective trauma that produces postcoloniality as a traumatized condition or as a post-traumatic cultural formation. However estranged the subject of trauma may be from herself, she remains who she fundamentally is even within that alienation. Despite the deeply injurious nature of trauma, there remains the understanding that even if trauma invents its subject, forms of subjectivity and survival unfold according to a flexibility and resiliency intrinsic to identity. The essential structure of the living being does not change.

It took me a considerable period of time to realize that the widow's discussion of transformation in fact resonated with a problem in the idea of trace. I can sum it up with this word: causality. In the *Critique of Pure Reason*, Kant explains that in order for a cause to be a cause, it must have a "character" that governs a particular order of events to the extent that it conditions the relations between phenomena. That is, causality characterizes the specific relation between a particular cause and its effects.[2] Another way of putting it is the idea of the finality of the nature of *a priori* necessity designates the relation (its structure and expressions) between event and wound, however contingent things in general may be. Contingency signifies that which finally happens *to* us, something other that befalls us and wounds without our being able to apprehend it and assimilate it. The event or phenomenon of trauma is thus said to consist in both its triggering and determining character as an event that is always already missed and, by accord, interminably wounding. The character of trauma has long been upheld as an experience that cannot be apprehended. When confronted with a threatening event, the only presumed escape for the self, the very core of subjectivity, is to separate from itself.

Yet the concept of cause signifies something very different from that which finally happens. Perhaps this is a banal observation. But how do we combine the predicate of that which happens and apprehend that the concept of cause is not contained within it though it necessarily belongs to it? What allows us to go outside the concept when experience cannot be called upon to help? What synthesis makes this possible?

I should say that it was not as though the widows I met that day were free from pain and suffering. Not at all. Their suffering was profound. And I would not necessarily say that they had reconciled with the man who brutalized their lives not long ago or that they had "come to terms with the past." Rather, it was as though the genocide had transformed them to the extent that they were ripped completely away from their prior selves. And then it seemed as if their daily habits of life powered another kind of transformation from within that cut them off completely from any kind of affective attachment to the neighbor. It was as though their suffering was a form of complete deprivation—like a strange indifference to suffering that was still a suffering. They were not just changed; they were transformed through and through.

Rwanda is called the land of a thousand hills. For a period of time after my first visit in 2010, I thought of it as the land of a thousand and one hills. The plus one was the accumulating surplus of the symbolic within which typological schemas of the genocide and the legacies of colonialism circulated. It was the eternal return of the absolutely irreducible other that predestines Rwanda and its people to be figural improvisations who can do nothing but delay their own death in a past that has always already come to pass. The plus one was the finality of the symbolic as that which necessarily exceeds natural, material life, conferring value to life as the sculptural care for the self. A couple of years later, as I was driving back down the Muriya hill, from the Bisesero Memorial, I remembered something as I looked upon the innumerable hills that surrounded me. While the widow and I were saying goodbye, she expressed her concerns for the "past as future." But her parting words were a call for me to remember something "very simple," as she put it. "Life," she said, "transforms itself." How to respond?

Herein lies a lesson: life has the power to transform itself from within its own energetic economies, without needing to exceed itself and without necessarily turning upon itself to disclose a sacredness hidden within it. This is the very unstable nature of life and the role of contingency in the formation of the living being. The point is that the very form and functioning of the processes of transformation inscribed within the living being reveal the ways in which it resists the production of a stereotype or range. A finite, vulnerable being includes the experience of the materiality of the event to the extent that it changes the ontological meaning of the wound and wounding in its self-differentiating movements and increasingly complex formative processes.

It is not my intent to assert that life has only a material or natural dimension, to negate the symbolic, or to suggest that the two do not oppose each other. I simply aim to show that these two domains are indissociable, and that life and the development, evolution, and transformation in the living being involve the two as a dialectical couple. I hope to uncover the conceptual status of the fundamentally shifting place between the hills of change—the place of entwinings without determinate being—that is the starting point of different processes of growth. And I hope to show that life does not need to transgress or divide itself in order to assert itself, and that the *a posteriori* can invent new relations to *a priori* schemas.

The title of this study, *The Future Life of Trauma*, may be read as an affirmation. Yes, *trauma* has *future*; yes, *trauma* has *life*, a life. The etymology of *future* affirms an inseparable, critical connection between the everyday meaning and its denotation. In the ordinary sense, *future* means the time that is still to come, what lies ahead. At the same time, it denotes the capability of enduring, since to have a future is necessarily the right to and the chance for posterity. Time is thus at once conceptual and organizing. By accord, thought of the future necessarily involves having the future. There is the time of finite life and the time of the infinite return. Here then is another affirmation: something returns. What returns in the future life of trauma? What returns of the future life of trauma? Affirmation cannot seem to avoid the problem of selection—of confirming that which has been chosen and sorted for return and for what does not return, or of operating a selection that produces its criteria in the process. What authorizes these affirmations?

Against this, I suggest that we ask instead: What *form of life* asserts itself and questions us in arriving to return? What is its destiny? What is the fate of repetition?

The Future Life of Trauma

Introduction

The Interface of Trauma

This book has but one aim. I intend to think trauma through a sustained but unconventional encounter between the psychoanalytic and postcolonial discourses of the event. More precisely, I aim to think trauma as a mutable, interactive, unstable place among the plural systems of legacy, inheritance, and memory.

Whether it is of sociopolitical, organic, or mechanized origin, trauma causes an irrevocable, unprecedented transformation of the victim's identity. It is a wound. As we will see—and as is well established—trauma is also thought of as a psychic event characterized by two coextensive factors: it involves something that emerges from within the psyche and derives from an internal cause and something that intervenes from the outside world and derives from external causes. Every trauma involves elements of surprise and fright associated with unexpected occurrences, which comprise the ways in which the psyche elaborates exteriority in the attempt to integrate it into the identity and history of the subject. This does not mean that forms of structural oppression, political violence, or prolonged scenarios of abuse are incidences of pure contingent events. Such traumas are motivated, directed, belong to genealogies of historical tendencies, and inhere in habituations that shape the exceptionality of the violent into ordinary, daily life. As a wound that results from a piercing to the body and psyche, trauma derives from the inseparable embrace between our inside and outside worlds. How can we deny that whatever form trauma takes, it involves a profound encounter between interiority and exteriority? How can we deny that such an encounter occurs as an effraction that, whether it remains constitutively inassimilable or insidiously assimilated into the very historicity of the subject, organizes and indicates itself in different ways at each of its historical occurrences?

Each of us is susceptible to the unexpected radicality of cruelty and to a suffering that profoundly and intimately cuts us from history, rendering us ontological strangers to our selves. The temporality of the undecidable future keeps us irremediably open to the absolutely surprising. As it pertains to this study, how are we to understand the meaning of the traditions and discourses that formulate life and its elaborations of modes of being as at once given by and composed within this particular notion of the temporalization of time (a logical, not empirical, time inscribed within any structure of signification), which is said to constitute the ontological horizon and direction within which being is first capable of being experienced in any kind of empirical synthesis or phenomenon? How are we to think the meaning of the psychoanalytic and postcolonial discourses that construe the dynamic histories of the living being and the subject according to the finality of absolute contingency as the necessary mode of occurring of the event? How do we approach the question of the finitude, the radical end as what arrives to accomplishment only in deferring itself, and the perilous immanence of its inverted promise in a way other than as an affirmation or confirmation of its truth?

This present work aims to develop the idea that the unstable character of the relation between repetition and life renews the conditions of the encounters with contingency, chance, necessity, and causality to the extent that we can elaborate a new experience of finitude, one which does not pertain to the meaning and matter of the existential. Generally speaking, in philosophy, the concept of finitude is the proper name for the finitude of existence. To be finite is necessary for existence, for being a living being. In the finitude of the subject—so long held to be the imperishable structure of knowledge about the subject—finitude singularly means the end; it designates only the truth and senses of the limit. However, it is possible to demonstrate that every act of repetition—from those that pertain to the general functioning of psychic life to those that indicate the traumatic effects of geographic borders—is a form of a return of repetition that unveils the mutability of the character of the relation between the subject and repetition. Insofar as the return of repetition includes experience through movements of self-differentiation, it invents a logical structure of finitude *after* the event happens, one that dismisses the divisive play of authentic time (or else, messianic time or authentic possibility and history) and the question of what is proper to the movement of life. In its processes, trauma challenges the following dominant formulations: the form and functioning of the psyche as a constellation of typological functions; the living being and subject as a repeating character; and the unilateral and definitive nature of the trace. I attempt to show how trauma unveils the loose structure of life and the living being within which the material and the symbolic operate as an unsettled dialectical couple and are not dependent upon the primacy of the other for their conditions of possibility. As an address to trauma, this book seeks to reveal within it, as its paradoxical silence, the borderlines of a concept of life that even in its trembling youth asserts itself.

Before proceeding further, let me clarify precisely what I mean by the material and the symbolic. Generally speaking, matter is what forms itself in producing its conditions of possibility. Hence the self-differentiation of matter proceeds according to its own system; there is no exteriority to the formative process. Materialism therefore refers to processes of formation and development that have no transcendental instant; it asserts the state of form in general as not transcendental. The thinking of materialism that appears in postcolonial studies generally stems from Lenin, Marx, and Engels and thereby follows the familiar dialectical teleology, which is said to explain the origin of the movement immanent to the formation of forms. This movement is regulated by an internal pull towards a teleological vision that directs the self-formative process. As Althusser shows in his analysis of Marxism in his remarkable text, "The Underground Current of the Materialism of the Encounter," the materialist tradition has been "the materialism of necessity and teleology," which is "a transformed, disguised form of idealism."[1] Against this, Althusser proposes the idea of the "*materialism of the encounter*, and therefore of the aleatory and of contingency."[2]

The contemporary significations of the term "symbolic" largely owe to Claude Lévi-Strauss, who invented the passage from symbol to symbolism in his reading of Marcel Mauss's economy of the gift.[3] He discovers the very category of the symbolic as the origin of society. In the *Introduction to the Work of Marcel Mauss*, Lévi-Strauss develops the symbolic as the structure of the various components that comprise a language, particular community, and values of society.[4]

This structure, according to him, is more precisely a structural spacing in which the spacing pertains to what he calls the "floating signifier."[5] Insofar as the floating signifier is characterized by its ability to represent an undetermined amount of signification while remaining capable of receiving an infinite plurality of meaning, it is itself utterly empty of meaning. However, it nevertheless maintains the correlation between signifier and signified. Accordingly, the floating signifier possesses a pure symbolic value, a "value zero."[6]

The symbolic thereby first refers to the symbolic domain of the symbol, which is a linguistic entity and act. It also then refers to that which has been made into a symbol, a linguistic entity, an image that represents something. The symbolic, which is different from symbolism, is thereby an order that designates the dimension of reality that has material presence but which is constitutively not material. The first appearance is always, necessarily symbolic. In its relation to that which it arranges, the symbolic is a transcendental or phenomenal instant that is necessarily in a position of exteriority. Accordingly, the symbolic is always an excess, the supplement; it is a certain fortune that happens to us and which operates to produce symbolizations that are irreducible to the material. In other words, the symbolic is a condition of possibility.

This book seeks to challenge the general priority of the symbolic. The intersections between the psychoanalytic discourse of trauma and the analytic strategies of postcolonial criticism, which ineluctably touch on contemporary continental philosophy, over the past thirty years bear witness to the hegemony of the symbolic in the insistence upon one of two presuppositions: one, that a dialectical or nondialectical breach between the material and the symbolic is that which gives rise to the necessity of materialism and therefore confers meaning upon the material; or two, that we must first go outside of any material or empirical structure of the real, that we must take leave of experience, in order to constitute our anticipatory view on the real, the horizon within which all experience becomes possible. Let us consider the subaltern in Spivak's work, Bhabha's concepts of hybridity and mimicry, the horizon of expectation in Lacan, or the Freudian pleasure principle. Whatever their project, aim, or guiding principle, these modes of critique appear according to a shared investment in the sovereignty of the primacy of the symbolic. As differentiated structures of knowledge about the contingency of the subject, these ways of reading owe the value of their radical questioning to and so serve to confirm the age-old idea in the philosophical tradition that upholds the notion of life and the flesh of the living as irremediably partitioned between its natural, material territory and its symbolic (or spiritual) realm. This is linked to the idea that existence is a human notion that only has meaning because of the human's singular capacity for imagination, thought, and language. The priority of the symbolic refers to the elaboration of modes of being as the care and protection for the self and the figural fashioning of being. The subject proceeds from and according to the determinations asserted by this structural partition of being, which is always already the closed loop of the history of being as forgetting, withdrawal, and inscription.

There is a global consistency of responses to trauma in which we can isolate the emergence of a new concept of the event that does not solely pertain to the specular resuscitation of the subject—the structure of self-consciousness or the structure of reflexivity—even if that subject arrives in the form of a deconstructed or criticized subject. Rather it is one, as I will attempt to show, that occurs in the intermediary relation between the symbolic and the material, or else history and nature, and so dismisses the classical character of the event as singularly inhering in the power of becoming an incisive point of conjunction—that is, finally happening and inscribing itself at the same time, comprising the consciousness of laws and what we call historicity (the awareness of being historical).

Today, I wonder about the absolute necessity of upholding the fixed determinisms of this partition and its concrete form and expressions of finite existence in general, and about its political legitimacies in the thinking of the conditions of the postcolonial and in the experience (not merely the exigencies) of different types of suffering. I question whether the structures of writing and trace, and thus the category of the supplement, are the proper approach to structure in general, and in particular to trauma, to memory, to the condition of suffering, and to survival. If there was ever a strict border between sociopolitical trauma and purely accidental trauma, then it is blurred and unstable at best. While forms of sociopolitical trauma, such as the prolonged structural oppression of colonialism, do not occur as unmotivated accidents, they share with traumas that derive from pure chance the disruption of the boundary between the intimate interiority of the psyche and the exteriority of the outside realm. In trauma, the difference between what is authentic or inauthentic is improbable. Trauma paradoxically dismisses the play of life and death; it dismisses the question of what is proper to this or that.

This unstable border, so intimately related to the heritage of the most essential partition, has been shifting between contemporary studies on trauma and the postcolonial for some time. To apprehend the implications of its movements, though, we must restore back to the subject the wound, and rehabilitate the capacity of life to modify and transform one's relation to repetition, and thus admit the psychoanalytic status of healing and repairing the injury. It also means attention to releasing the partition between the living being and life in order to assert the philosophical status of the power of life to free itself without needing to separate itself, and thus to transform its forms of and relations to finite existence. In order to do so, it is necessary to think the eventality of trauma through the shifting character of the synthesis that occurs between cause and effect and between contingency and necessity in order to show the dynamic interplay between determinisms and freedom that occur from within the structure of the living being. In other words, it is now time to consider trauma and the postcolonial, and the intimate intricacy of their relation as a movement of the form of posterity that challenges the primacy of the traditional law of the reversibility of difference. Such are the questions and undertakings at the core of this study.

In the first half, I undertake an analysis of the eventality of trauma in the Freudian metapsychology with a turn on the elaboration of the form of the psyche that asserts its indissociable intricacies between its symbolic and material elements. In the second half, I sustain an encounter between the postcolonial and the concept of trauma, and more broadly between the material and the symbolic, by traversing the paths opened in the processes of establishing new geographic borders during the 1947 Partition of British India and in the processes of memorialization in postgenocide Rwanda. In my closing thoughts, I question whether the structure of deconstructive responsibility is a sufficient and accurate approach to the universal urgency of memory within geopolitics today. Taken together, the chapters aim to clear the way for a new concept of life that restores back to the generations following the traumas of their histories the chance to follow along with their own lives.

Recent postcolonial critiques of trauma studies respond to the urgency to renew the ethical, political, and geopolitical importance of trauma by identifying and challenging the tendencies of the field. In particular, they point to the perpetuation of a Eurocentric bias and the assumption of an uncritical transference of the event-based model across cultures, experiences, and peoples maintained by the reliance upon the methodologies of psychoanalysis and deconstruction.[7] In his book *Postcolonial Witnessing: Trauma Out of Bounds*, Stef Craps calls for the need to reshape and resituate trauma theory in order to "foster attunement to previously unheard suffering" of disenfranchised groups of people who endure the violence of forms of structural oppression so that the field can "live up to its promise of cross-cultural ethical engagement."[8] He refers primarily to the founding work of Cathy Caruth, as well as the work of Shoshana Felman, Dori Laub, and Geoffrey Hartman, noting that their "epistemological and ethical programme" advances a modernist aesthetic of fragmentation and aporia as uniquely capable of witnessing trauma.[9] Against the "traditional individual and event-based model," Craps develops what he calls "a supplementary model of trauma which . . . can account for and respond to collective, ongoing, everyday forms of traumatizing violence" by enabling a "relational understanding of trauma" that allows us to recognize and attend to the specific types of suffering endured by others.[10] The priority of the symbolic is easily noticed in Craps's critique of trauma theory. The historical emergence of another supplementarity does not invalidate the event-based model or witnessing as performing the program of aporia since it offers for scrutiny forms of the subject and identity that formalize the effects and consequences in accordance with the logic of symbolic function. His critique therefore affirms the symbolic as the condition of possibility.

Other studies, such as those by Jenny Edkins, Ann Kaplan, and Anne Whitehead, challenge the efficacy of the poststructuralist tendencies of trauma theory by questioning, as Edkins puts it, the practice of trauma and memory "beyond what might be considered the geographical bounds of a western paradigm."[11] Through genealogical critiques of the psychoanalytic concept of trauma, both Ruth Leys and Roger Luckhurst have demonstrated what trauma owes, in its structure, to modernity.[12] These studies show that the psychoanalytic definition of trauma was elaborated within the frame of a relationship to numerous psychological and medical discourses dealing with Western experiences with war and industrialization, as a universal phenomenon common to all human communities.[13] In *The Harmony of Illusions: Inventing Post-Traumatic Stress Disorder*, Allan Young declares that the extrapolation of the psychoanalytic model of trauma into the clinical picture of post-traumatic stress disorder (PTSD), which first appeared as a concept in 1980 when it was included in the DSM-III as a diagnosable category primarily addressing the psychological suffering of Vietnam War veterans, is a universalizing discourse. "It is," he writes, "glued together by the practices, technologies, and narratives with which it is diagnosed, studied, treated, and represented and by the various interests, institutions, and moral arguments that mobilized these efforts and resources."[14]

The turn upon globalization and materiality in the elaboration of the notion of the psychoanalytic event of trauma has unveiled its normalizing power, showing itself to be a set of theoretical and practical acts of selection in the social and cultural order that creates hierarchies, forms of cultural imperialism, and engenders forms of epistemic violence. One could say that interpretations of trauma and pain that stem from the event-based model is a principle of selection that automatically sorts between what constitutes suffering and what does not and between who suffers psychological pain and who does not. In his genealogical account of the concept and practice of ethnopsychiatry, which represents an array of psychological, anthropological, and biological assumptions about the colonized subject in France, Didier Fassin shows that "the psychopolitics of otherness has become a normalized way of governing postcolonial immigrants under the auspices of the republic."[15] Further, he demonstrates that, as a product of the colonial era, ethnopsychiatry continuously inscribes cultural particularism and determinism, and colonizes by exoticizing the other.

The symbolic domain, defined here as the excess over the real, assumed in the psychoanalytic and poststructuralist concept of trauma, can thereby be seen as a program of political violence. To challenge the priority of the symbolic and its operations in the traumatic event is thus to question the ethical and political legitimacy of such a priority in general. Yet how does one think at once the character inevitable to all forms of trauma and its possible indeterminations? How does one conceptualize materiality without telos, and thus without dependence upon the transcendent economy of the symbolic? The extremely difficult problem here concerns knowing how not to identify difference in advance. Michael Rothberg identifies the dangers of what he calls "hyper-particularism" that runs the "inverse risk" of canceling any kind of comparative project that seeks to renew the global importance of trauma.[16] While Rothberg does not attend to the hegemony of the symbolic as excess—indeed his own very interesting concept of multidirectional memory inheres in it—he nevertheless helps draw our attention to the fact that many critiques turn upon critical techniques that can easily perpetuate rather than disavow the political failures.[17] It is rather striking to notice that the projects that critique the ideological tendencies of trauma studies, namely, those that deploy the analytic strategies of postcolonial critique and literary analysis, are themselves structured as the very entities they seek to critique. In their presuppositions of an irreducible gap between the symbolic and the material, such critiques ultimately serve to confirm the classical concept of life as irremediably partitioned between its natural or material aspects and its symbolic domain.

However, the gap that is opened between the plural systems of the transference of memory and legacy at the level of collective perpetuation of specificities and conditions and at the level of individual development is the paradoxical interface of trauma. As I argue, trauma must be thought as the transformability of the dynamic relations of identity and difference, and thus of the relation between the category of difference and the idea of copy—as a movement of the production of posterity in the strong sense that operates entirely from within the economies of life and the structure of the living being. At the heart of the problem of trauma, then, lies the problem of causality. Precisely how do we think the character of the relationship between cause and effect without subordinating it to the finality of the symbolic, the entire structural apparatus said to guarantee not only the possibility of experience but also in what ways the human being, because he has language, can constitute himself and endure beyond death by making for himself a whole world of the earth? This question involves the relation between the human and repetition.

Let us consider for a moment the materialist and typological strategies of postcolonial critique, captured by the work of Benita Parry and Homi Bhabha, respectively. In Bhabha's work, the concept of colonial mimicry as a strategy of subversion means that the ambivalence of colonial power is acted out through a series of parodic and permanent rituals that evoke cultural difference and other new forms of identity, which are irreducible to mimesis itself. In Parry's very interesting and widely known materialist critique of the field, she shows how the "varieties of post-Marxists now populating the field of postcolonial studies" elide the fact that their "materialist accounts of class struggle under colonialism" are "grounded in a Marxist humanism, seeking to install an ethical universality and a universal ethic."[18]

For all that Parry brings to the fore about how the materialisms on record owe themselves to Sartrean humanism, which was founded on the philosophical conceptions of the human and human reality in Hegel, Heidegger, and Husserl, never does she envisage the formations of forms of the postcolonial as fundamentally changing the very concept of the human.[19] Never does she consider that forms of human social and cultural praxis produce an entirely new notion of the subject, one that invents new relations to *a priori* structures after in acquiring its own material for its own uses. In both, we see precisely what Althusser identifies as the central problem of the materialism of necessity, which assumes the finality of contingency. "Everything," he declares, "is accomplished in advance; *the structure precedes its elements and reproduces them in order to reproduce the structure*."[20] In Bhabha, the general structure is colonial power, and in Parry, it is the structure of the very idea of the human. Nevertheless, the different analytic strategies illuminate precisely what Derrida explains in "The Ends of Man," which is that the human is what repeats itself from its destruction; it achieves itself in its erasure.[21]

I would suggest that it is in trauma that we see a profound challenge to the idea of the repeating character of the human. By their very nature, all forms of trauma have the tendency to repeat themselves. The problem here is that it becomes extremely difficult to deny that some novelty is produced in the midst of the violent turmoil. Even if we admit that the structure of the psyche undergoes changes during a traumatic event, something of its silhouette survives. Such changes would therefore seem to unfold according to and within the symbolic fabric of the gap as it is raised by symbolic function. Cathy Caruth affirms this very point in her development of figures of the death drive in her notion of the mortiferous break in life as it appears in *Unclaimed Experience* and then as "the creative act of parting" in *Literature in the Ashes of History*.[22] In the latter, there is more of an emphasis on acts of destructive creation in the positivist sense, but in both we are presented with improvisations of subjects who delay their death in the past as figural representations of a "departure into life" without return.[23] Indeed the subject of trauma is the very repeating character of, to borrow Caruth's description, "the heart of all trauma—as deferral and future repetition, as an attempted return that instead departs."[24] On its own, this particular subject of trauma cannot produce a new form of posterity; it can only come back to remind us of the effects of a past always already gone away from us.

The point here is not to challenge the law of the inclination of all traumas to repeat themselves. It is not my aim to suggest that trauma is the sculptor of living forms in any sort of positivist sense. Rather, I intend to demonstrate that the traumatized, suffering subject uncovers, in the very form of its psyche, an unstable place within the living being that can neither be automatically regulated by a program of compulsive repetition nor predetermined by the exteriority of the irreducibility of otherness—a place that is free from determinate being and is the starting point of its own formative and transformative processes. To put the idea somewhat differently, what I mean to say is that the character of the relation between the subject and repetition cannot be subordinated to finality. Life is always transforming and modifying its relation to repetition, and in its turn, the changing nature of the relation is helping life to begin itself anew. It is in this way that I mean that trauma is an interface; it is at once a structural and mutable point of interaction, a starting point for things.

From traumatic flashbacks to the legacies of colonialism during the Rwandan genocide to the institution of a new cartography in the Indian subcontinent, every type of repetition is a kind of reshaping that relates to acts of memory. Such acts nevertheless indicate a return of repetition that disrupts the synthetic value of the binding between repetition and that which it repeats. The immanent character of repetition, as I show in my reading of Freud and in my reading of the eventality of drawing borders during the 1947 Partition of British India, inheres in the uncertainty between contingency as a mode of occurring for necessity and the double of the category of necessity. In trauma, we must think afresh the determinist character of the compulsion to repeat a disturbing scenario in order to redefine, renew, and grasp the phenomenon of the death drive in contemporary, geopolitical contexts.

The concept of the event, defined as the traumatic event, brings together the postcolonial and psychoanalysis. However, the discussions that challenge the universalizing tendencies of the psychoanalytic approach to trauma in context indicate a more fundamental need to undertake a transformation in the very concept of the event in order to elaborate a new relationship between trauma and the subject and new ideas about the urgency of memory so that we can think anew the meaning of response. Rather than merely oppose the Freudian theory of trauma, it is necessary to loosen the partitioned structure of the living being and the psyche so that we grasp the meaning of trauma and its impacts on individuals and communities with a novel importance in contemporary geopolitical contexts. Such a task, to my mind, consists in showing the different ways the event assembles and asserts the coincidence between the symbolic and the organic, material dimensions of life without proceeding from pure negation. In a global time, the ethical and political urgency of repetition involves releasing, from within structures of knowing, the places dispossessed of determinate being so that we can clear the way for the mutual, free interplay between liberty and determinisms from within any framework. The reason is precisely to show that the immanent dynamic of life is the power to transform itself without transgressing itself. By organizing and indicating different ways processes of transformation occur, the concept of life unbinds itself from traditional relations that pertain to the enigma of the origin and the originary synthesis of the temporality of time.

In the *Ego and the Id*, Freud discusses the alterations of the ego as a transformation of identity.

> The experiences of the ego seem at first to be lost for inheritance; but, when they have been repeated enough and with sufficient strength in many individuals in successive generations, they transform themselves, so to say, into experiences of the id, the impressions of which are preserved by heredity. Thus in the id, which is capable of being inherited, are harboured residues of the existences of countless egos; and when the ego forms its super-ego out of the id, it may perhaps only be reviving shapes of former egos and be bringing them to resurrection.[25]

While Freud never posited alterations to the ego as effecting a total break from the accumulation of the past, he develops an ambiguous sense of transformation as that which uncovers and bears witness to a notion of primitivity as the originary form of psychic life. This concerns both particular ways of surviving and the general form of survival. Survival, for Freud, entails a succession of transformations that can be erased in order for a new form of identity to appear. For Freud and when it comes to psychic disturbances, there is always destruction and regression. Different from destruction, which concerns "what is highest in the human mind," regression aims to uncover the "most abundant links with the phylogenetic acquisition of each individual—his archaic heritage."[26] When core subjectivity is under threat, there is always the possibility of the return of the archaic, which is also the repetition of the natural in Freud. The point to underscore here is that Freud's thinking of the alterations of the ego actually indicates the very form of the psyche to be an open, interactive structure in which the transformative dynamic of identity never exceeds the economies it makes possible in the first place. At stake in this, as I will show, is the capacity of the psyche to modify the determining casual value of the unconscious.

While I would like to think transformation without constituting it in the familiar, irreducible structure of the finitude of the subject and as not dependent, in its processes, upon the transcendental economy of the symbolic, I realize that this is a redoubtable task. Indeed the semantic morphology of the term "transformation" speaks to its own symbolic power. Nonetheless, I aim to conceive of transformation as a category that includes the natural, or else material and the symbolic dimensions of life and living, and thus as a category that can and does change. I have thus taken care not to invent any idioms, so as to avoid (as much as is possible) formulating a scene of language that becomes the mode of occurring for concepts, theoretical and practical legitimacies, and the event itself. Doing so does not signal my intent to negate the symbolic but rather my aim to consider how structures of knowledge about the subject are both mutable and structural. It nevertheless may be that in the end, my attempts to develop a new idea of the event, and thus a new relationship between trauma and the wound, may not be sufficient to deconstruct the primacy of the symbolic rule of life. Notwithstanding the fact that my own work is threatened from the beginning by the programs of the very structures its seeks to critique, I am very conscious of the fact that what I propose with regard to places that are fundamentally shifting, and dispossessed of a determinate being, runs the profound danger of inventing new forms of cruelty and suffering. While I address this point in my final thoughts, what I will say here is that such is the risk that I believe is now necessary in order to develop a new relationship to otherness and to responsibility in general. Such is the immense challenge of thinking trauma in today's geopolitical contexts in order for the category of difference to produce different futures after that which finally happens.

The process of integrating the subject's innate and acquired capacities to respond to trauma to the extent that the subject takes hold of the wound, resists the loops of an interminable wounding, and clears the way for the emergence of a new identity released of accumulating pasts is also not easy. The imperishable character of psychic life presents the greatest challenge. Traces possess an indestructible, persistent character; thus nothing in the psyche can ever be fully forgotten no matter how radically the signatures of trauma may be altered by the passage of time.

In the *Genealogy of Morals*, Nietzsche discusses the notion of *aktive Vergesslichkeit*, or active forgetting.[27] The concept pertains to solving what he identifies as the "real problem regarding man," which is the idea that nature has set aside in man the paradoxical task of originating an "animal *with the right to make promises*," by making room in consciousness for man's noble functions.[28] But what is the *real* problem regarding man, regarding the human? Is it not precisely as Derrida has spelled out so remarkably in his work, and what we see in psychoanalysis, the need to overcome finitude, the wound and wounding of time? What would it look like for the human to actively forget itself? Is it possible to forget one's own finite existence without sacrificing the human's unique capacity for imagination, language, and thought? The problem here concerns not just concept of the human, but more precisely, the concept of life and the problem of the source.

Here I cannot claim to have solved this difficult challenge. Yet it begins, I would suggest, with starting a new habit: an active forgetting that includes in its process the apprehension of novel forms of death. Rather than needing to defeat finitude, we admit that in being finite vulnerable beings we have the capacity to experience the unexpected encounters with death and transform the ontological significance of wounding. To be relinquished of the first desire to resist our own transiency—this might be a way of realizing the human being. Perhaps this may be a way of freeing the capacity of life to transform itself without needing to separate from itself, and thus the capacity to welcome new forms of identity and subjectivity without expectation, without promise.

How do we, as humans, heal our most human wound? Perhaps this question is the most difficult problem that presents itself as the core of this book. As I mentioned, my goal is to think trauma. There is no way to do this except to navigate through the thicket of challenges I have laid out, to be questioned by those that I include and have invariably missed, and to be put into question by posterity. There is also, I would say, no way to undertake these elaborations without responding to the extremely fragile waves of suffering, even when those waves may not want a reply. At the heart of this book, then, is the elemental, human effort to gather the pain of the other, without assuming their place, and then let them go.

CHAPTER 1

The Problem of Trauma

A young boy, approximately eighteen months old, has recently invented a most pleasurable game. Sitting on the floor, he takes a wooden spool with a string attached and throws it into his cot and out of sight. Thrilled by this act of disappearance, the boy exclaims, "o-o-o-o!" Immediately pulling the wooden spool back towards himself, the boy joyfully hails the spool's reappearance with "da!" Over and over again, the boy gleefully throws and retrieves his wooden spool—seemingly contented by this new game. After some time has passed, the boy happens upon a full-length mirror that does not quite reach to the floor. Curious, he crouches down into the space between the mirror and the floor, realizing that when he does, his own reflection disappears from the mirror. Up and down, up and down, making his reflection disappear and return, disappear and return. A year passes. Overwhelmed by feelings of anger and abandonment when his mother leaves him to go to work, the boy defiantly throws a toy on the floor, keeping it in sight. Instead of uttering "o-o-o-o," he now yells, "All right, then, go away! I don't need you. I'm sending you away myself."[1] And the toy, animated only seconds before by the boy's emotions, now lies motionless in plain sight.

Played by his grandson, this game, *fort/da* as Freud refers to it in his 1920 work, *Beyond the Pleasure Principle*, has become an iconic example of the operation of the compulsion to repeat in psychic life. The other is the recurrence of the traumatic dream and other such intrusive phenomena. In trauma theory, the compulsion to repeat has been read as evidence of the notion of the death drive, Freud's radical postulation that calls into question the pleasure principle, and as therefore offering key insights into why the psyche is driven to repeat distressing experiences that neither pleasure nor unpleasure as categories of experience can integrate. The return to the event in traumatic nightmares and flashbacks, as Freud observes, signals the retrospective attempt to apprehend the overwhelming stimulus of the event and bind it into an experience that can be comprehended and assimilated into oneself. The *fort/da* game is similar in the sense that it is the activity by which the boy reiterates his mother's departure in the effort to understand the loss associated with her absence. Yet the game is also distinct because it presents the method of working of the repetition compulsion in a "*normal*" activity.[2]

Against ubiquitous accounts of the game as staging how the repetition compulsion in trauma adheres to and is thereby a representation or manifestation of the death drive, I read the game as staging the confrontation between the *process of representation*, which involves the binding of repetition, and the *process of representing the drive*, which entails the attempt to bind repetition. Such a confrontation proceeds by way of an elaboration of time's doubling in the context of the psychical elaboration of trauma.

As it is well known, the primary aim of Freud's seminal 1920 work is to question the principal, governing authority of the pleasure principle in the economy of the psyche. "In the theory of psycho-analysis," Freud remarks in the opening line, "we have no hesitation in assuming that the course taken by mental events is automatically regulated by the pleasure principle."[3] The underlying impressions of the pleasure principle "are so obvious that they can scarcely be overlooked"; its unicity and authority is not even contested when, under the influences of the ego's instincts towards self-preservation, the reality principle insists upon and accomplishes the effects of delaying pleasure.[4] The reality principle will replace the pleasure principle, but it does not desert its ultimate intentions. So the domination of the pleasure principle is not called into question by experiences that involve the transformation of pleasure into unpleasure by repression. Still there remains an inaccessible, obscure region, unaccounted for by any "philosophical or psychological theory," that is the site for the production of "new material," which gives rise to "fresh questions" that pose a fundamental challenge to the dominance of the pleasure principle.[5] This material consists in the "mental reaction to external danger."[6]

Specifically, Freud cites a perplexing condition called traumatic neurosis, which plagues World War I veterans and survivors of accidents and other such catastrophes "involving a risk to life," as the resource for this material.[7] He observes that in this condition, there is the compulsion to repeat, which fixates the patient to his trauma. Dreams repeatedly lead the patient back to the situation of the accident; what thus recurs in the patient's dreams is the painful experience of trauma. "We are therefore left in doubt," Freud writes, "as to whether the impulse to work over in the mind some overpowering experience so as to make oneself master of it can find expression as a primary event, and independently of the pleasure principle."[8]

Taking a cue from Freud's fourth chapter, in which he defines trauma as something that unexpectedly penetrates the "protective shield" (*Reizschutz*), trauma theory takes up the *fort/da* game as indicating how the compulsion to repeat in trauma exemplifies the characteristic deferred action of trauma (*Nachträglichkeit*).[9] The psychic apparatus does not have time to prepare itself for the sudden piercing of external excitations and discovers itself so utterly overwhelmed by the flooding of excessive amounts of stimuli that there is a "disturbance on a large scale in the functioning of the organism's energy."[10] The violence of trauma is such that it puts the pleasure principle entirely out of action because its primary function of returning to a state of quiescence is neither prepared for nor able to diminish the external excitations as they penetrate the psyche. Instead of seeking pleasure, the psyche occupies itself with the attempt to bind those stimulations in the effort to lessen and eliminate the excitations, and assimilate the effraction. So repetition and binding (*Bindung*), which consists in converting "unbound" energy into "quiescent cathexis," work together to control and tame the wild, excessive traumatic energy with the aim of returning to a state of quiescence.[11]

When Freud pursues the discovery of the "compulsion to repeat" (*Wiederholungszwang*) in the context of his analysis of the recurrence of dreams that return patients back to the scene of the accident as characteristic behavior of the condition of traumatic neurosis, he reiterates his already established conclusion that all drives are exclusively conservative in nature since they seek to return to a prior state of things.[12] As Freud notes, the life drives "are conservative in the same sense as the other instincts in that they bring back earlier states of living substances."[13] Accordingly, the death drive does not take the place of the life drives (which include the pleasure principle) in its functioning or originary status.

It would seem instead, then, that the accident dream reveals the primacy of the compulsion to repeat insofar as it operates "with a view to the psychical binding."[14] Yet the dreams of those suffering from traumatic neurosis only manage to sharpen the pain of the process of repeating rather than producing pleasure or unpleasure. Even though these dreams arise "in obedience to the compulsion to repeat," the compulsive repetition of trauma related dreams are "an exception to the proposition that dreams are fulfillments of wishes."[15] The function of the dreams therefore consist in something more originary than the fulfillment of wishes, and thus in something that is "beyond the pleasure principle."[16]

United with Freud's development of the compulsion to repeat the accident dream as coinciding with a beyond of the pleasure principle, trauma theory follows him through the next phase of his argument in chapters 5 and 6, which presents the dualism between the life drives and the death drive. The nature of the relation between processes of repetition and the dominance of the pleasure principle still troubles Freud. In an effort to resolve this problem while maintaining a logical continuity with the presentation of the compulsion to repeat, Freud tries to prove that the death drive and repetition are indissolubly linked. This is the point of separation between Freud's work and what is called trauma theory. Trauma theory remains situated in the hypothesis that the compulsive repetition of dreams that lead patients back to the scenario of the accident follows from and is a manifestation of the death drive (*Todestrieb*)—that it is beyond the pleasure principle. Freud, however, departs from this critical juncture and returns to an affirmation of the supremacy of the pleasure principle, with some additional key points. Ultimately, there is no beyond of the pleasure principle for Freud.

In the seventh and final chapter, Freud notes that, given the universal character of instincts, it is not terribly surprising that certain mental processes operate independently of the pleasure principle without necessarily contradicting it. However, this does not necessarily resolve the fundamental problem of the relation between repetition and the supremacy of the pleasure principle since "*an instinct is an urge inherent in organic life to restore to an earlier state of things*."[17] Compulsive repetition thereby illuminates the regressive character of all drives, which further reveals how, if the life drives and the death drive are amalgamated within each other, any dispersals of psychic phenomena necessarily proceed from the same logic. So Freud draws "a shaper distinction than we have hitherto made between function and tendency."[18] The distinction is as follows: "the pleasure principle, then, is a *tendency* operating in the service of a *function*" that occupies itself with the business of either entirely emptying the psychic apparatus of excitations or *maintaining the excitations within to a constant or minimum.*[19] Again, there is no beyond of the pleasure principle.

However, Freud does not actually arrive at an account of the form of the death drive, though he certainly talks about an agent for it. The distinction between tendency and function begins to elaborate an inherent relation between the processes of binding and repetition that dissolves the distinction between the death drive and the pleasure principle as simple substitutes. Trauma theory relies upon there being a discrepancy in the drives that yields alternating, operative hierarchies in order to maintain the interpretation that the compulsive repetition of the accident dream is evidence of the death drive and its subsequent ways of reading trauma as producing a victim who, over and over again, is stamped out of itself into a silhouette powerlessly and ceaselessly saturated by terrifying suffusions of a past that never passes away though it has always already passed away. *It is the relation between binding and repetition that is uniformly overlooked by current theoretical formulations of trauma.*[20] This is the source of the problem of time in trauma as both an experience of a brutal event and the conceptual apparatus that is exported into the world as a particular hermeneutics of the subject.

Although arguments concerning the repetition compulsion in trauma and its traumatizing effects consider alteration as an integral feature, the mutability of the difference between primordial temporality and lived time in repetition has not been acknowledged or investigated. We know that trauma is characterized by a happening that occurs too soon in order for it be apprehended as such and thus by the retrospective attempt to assimilate what has breached and wounded the psyche. The ruthless and vicious nature of trauma is precisely that it is an event without signification. The psychical wounds and persistent wounding to which trauma gives rise constitute, at once, a temporal rupture and a temporal irruption. The deferred action that characterizes trauma puts into action a new *attempt to bind* the traumatic stimulus. Binding in general, and particularly the attempt to bind as it is put into motion by the forced intrusion of trauma, proceeds from an irrevocable temporal difference between a more primitive state of things, which, for Freud, is neuronal or biological life, and is thus its own form of repetition. It also relies upon a preceding relation to time in which the binding of traumatic excitations may convert the "unbound" energy into "bound" energy, thereby returning to a state of quiescence. The deferred action of trauma does not stop there and merely repose in the repetitive act of sending the victim back to the scene of trauma. Given its necessary relation to binding and binding's necessary relation to the future, there can be no teleological aim to the compulsive aspect of traumatic repetitions. By its very nature, the character of compulsion is not necessarily determinist. Since we do in fact witness behaviors that reproduce and reiterate scenes of trauma that are themselves traumatizing, there must be another functioning of the deferred action that reveals another crucial process.

Generally speaking repetition in psychic life works to establish a new form of quiescence. It is an activity that functions to maintain the excitations within to a constant. This should not be read as an affirmation of familiar arguments about how one enters into a state of perpetual traumatization since it fails to account for the relation between binding and repetition. It also elides Freud's own assertion about the two defining characteristics of traumatic neurosis: "first, that the chief weight in their causation seems to rest upon the factor of surprise, of fright; and secondly, that a wound or injury inflicted simultaneously works as a rule *against* the development of a neurosis."[21] Repetition, as Freud's second characteristic suggests, is a type of reparative or restorative agent insofar as the psychic wound arises in the place of neurosis. The insistent return, the compulsion, is the mechanism, as Lacan suggests in "Tuché and Automaton," by which repetition works, on its own and by its own necessity, as the system of lived events (*Erlebnisse*) that Freud identifies, and which can be and are integrated into the psyche.[22] Repetition itself becomes a form of homeostasis in the sense that it brings about a new state of constancy that subverts the emergence of neurosis. The function of the compulsion to repeat in trauma is uncertain and unstable. On the one hand, it is the binding that forms the regime of regulating pain. On the other hand, it is the purely automatic recurrence. In both, repetition moves towards "an *old* state of things, an initial state from which the living entity has at one time or other departed and to which it is striving to return by the circuitous paths along which its development leads."[23] An external force is that which momentarily diverts this immanent movement towards this end point life seeks. The further life goes away from the prior state, the more complex these "circuitous paths" become. Life appears, it would seem, in a process of developmental complexity.

SHATTERING THE CRYSTAL, THE SHATTERED CRYSTAL, AND CRYSTALLIZING THE SHATTER: THE EVENT

The indissoluble necessity of the "protective shield," Freud's theory of "psychic reality," which is where events are translated, altered, comprised, and created, presents a conceptual enclosure that is neither avoidable nor seemingly permeable. The concept of the psychic event is thus the forefront that any analysis of trauma encounters, for it poses a fundamental opposition to the possibility of an unprecedented psychic subject who realizes the memory of what befalls it.

From his early texts like *Studies on Hysteria* to his later writings like *Beyond the Pleasure Principle*, and from his seduction theory to his analysis of war neuroses and railway disasters, the event was an ever-evolving concept in Freud's work. In the midst of its changes and developments, a constant feature in Freud's thinking of the event was the character and articulation of its synthesis between the outside and the inside, between discontinuity and continuity, and between the contingency of chance and the chance of necessity. A striking image of these syntheses occurs in *New Introductory Lectures on Psychoanalysis*. Freud presents us with a compelling metaphor of the suffering patient as a shattered crystal:

> If we throw a crystal to the floor, it breaks; but not into haphazard pieces. It comes apart along its lines of cleavage into fragments whose boundaries, though they were invisible, were predetermined by the crystal's structure. Mental patients are split and broken structures of this kind.[24]

Immediately a strict correlation between the haphazard nature of an accident and the form of breakage is presented. The crystal forms itself in producing the boundaries of its unique formation, and thus its conditions of possibility. Accordingly, breakage cannot exceed this process of formation since the crystal's structure orients and predetermines the form of breakage insofar as the shattering is itself regulated by an internal tension that pulls towards the borderlines that establish the structure. The process of shattering and the forms of the shattered pieces are accomplished in advance insofar as the structure of the crystal precedes any internal or external factors.

The metaphor of the crystal portrays the psyche itself as a materialism; it is the crystal. At the same time, however, there is also the implication of the event, the shattering of the crystal, as material that can be acquired for the psyche's own use. Although the event is an instant that seems to discover itself in a position of exteriority—namely, the unexpected effraction that breaches the protective shield and the suffering patients endure as a result—the manner of its occurrence and the elaboration of its effects are predetermined and therefore absorbed by the psyche's unique structure. While the metaphor of the crystal also clearly affirms Freud's dialectical, teleological view of the psyche (any breakage occurs according to preformed patterns) it nonetheless blurs the lines between an external event and an internal event in its articulation of the event as a kind of materiality.

Freud posits the necessary character of the synthesis between the event and the responsive behavior of the psyche. The shattered form mimes, by virtue of the pattern of jagged shards, its own shattering in the very cleavages that take place. Thus the event itself is manifested in a dynamic synthesis of the unanticipated accident and the processes that come from within that produce the internal, psychic event. In the instant the external event happens, it is detached from its own exteriority and folded into the internal dynamics of the psychic economies. It is always a doubling articulation, the crystallization of the shattering psyche as the crystallizing of the shattered psyche. Patients suffering from mental illnesses thus crystallize into visages of shattered crystals, images of cleavages and cleaving acts that, at the same time, disclose and withhold meaning. To be sure, however, the shattering of the crystal has always already happened.

For Freud, the wound caused by an unanticipated accident is secondary to the meaning of the breakage as that which reconducts us back to what is given by the psychic structure. The behavior of the psyche directly correlates to its form. Of course, Freud never diminishes the influence of unexpected occurrences, and he remains, throughout the trajectory of his work, committed to explicating the problem of trauma and the unique problems it imposes upon the ordinary trajectory of psychic life.

By the time we get to *Beyond the Pleasure Principle*, "traumatic neurosis," as Freud notes, is already a condition that has long been known.[25] As part of this general rethinking of this neurosis, which entailed discerning specificities of "war neurosis" as a pathological variant to traumatic neurosis, Freud began to undertake a serious reconsideration of psychoanalytic theory in relation to states of fright (*Erschütterung*), which "emphasizes the factor of surprise" and designates "the name we give to the state a person gets into when he has run into danger without being prepared for it."[26] At the same time, what is described as "traumatic" are "any excitations from outside that are powerful enough to break through the protective shield."[27] Therefore a "large-scale" disturbance in the functioning of the psyche ensues; again, for Freud, the crystal shatters according to its own preexisting lines of cleavage. A trauma is traumatic to the extent that it invokes a preexisting, internal conflict. Any empirical shock or event is only properly traumatic when it injures an already or previously wounded subject, that is, when it triggers and calls into existence a more prior scene. The meaning of the breakage has precisely to do with the pathogenic effects of an experience that emerge from the aggregate of the occurring as the pure result of chance and the course the internal psychic events take in response. Thus the psychic event asserts the coincidence of an external event and the mode(s) in which the accident occurs within the psyche, with the latter constituting the event as it is lived in the psyche.[28]

As an image of the shattered crystal, the traumatized patient thereby becomes the expressions of the form of the shattered crystal, the domain of lived events that comprise the symptomatic dimension. In his early 1901 work, *The Psychopathology of Everyday Life*, Freud discusses how the unique work of the psychoanalyst begins with the analysis of unanticipated acts and actions that turn out to be fortuitous coincidences that both disclose and hide their meaning. These *symptomatic acts*, as Freud names them, become a matter of both pure chance and psychic necessity that have meaning as a principal and a causal character.[29] In other words, symptoms involve a heterology and hermeneutics of chance: the *pure chance of* an event that occurs from the outside in an unanticipated manner opens the *pure chance for* the development of lived, subjective events that confer significance upon the former by means of translating into the latter as an originary, psychic event.[30] From this doubling of chance, we can see a basic double organization of the event that starts to break the line between the synthesis of the external event and the lived event, on the one hand, and the interpretive system of the originary, phantasmatic occurrence of the event, on the other. [31]

The conference of its signification marks an indissociable intricacy between the unanticipated occurrence of the outside event and its reception, which is constitutive in the sense that it gives rise to a hermeneutics within an internal fiction created and elaborated by the psyche. Repetition asserts the intimacy of this intricacy as the intersection of the phenomenal duality of chance (unexpected and opportunity). Thus the shattered crystal displays the essential life/death dualism in different ways at each time.

THE DUALISM OF THE DRIVES AND THE LIBIDO

There are three rather distinct phases of Freud's development of the theory of the drives, each of which includes a slight revision of their temporal orientations. At the same time and throughout these particular elaborations, Freud consistently asserts that psychic energy is a divided, dualist energetics that necessarily supposes a difference among its sources. Freud coins this energy as the "libido theory," though libido is not the only energy that circulates within the psyche. "Something in the nature of a theory has at last shaped itself in psychoanalysis," Freud writes, "and this is known by the name of the 'libido theory.'"[32] As Freud developed the theory of the drives, he classified the different sources of energy. First, he divided them between the ego drives, which compel the individual towards self-preservation, and the sexual drives, which compel the individual to exceed one's own limits and reproduce oneself. Then he further divided the sexual drive into the ego drive (narcissism, ego-mediated individuality in which the ego becomes an object of libidinal investment) and the object drive. In his third and final version of the theory of the drives, he divided them into the life drives, which includes all of the sexual drives, and the death drive. These three phases are reflected in his 1905 *Three Essays on the Theory of Sexuality*, his 1915 essay, "Drives and Their Vicissitudes," and the 1920 *Beyond The Pleasure Principle*, respectively.

The first model seen in the 1905 work is clearly a normative, developmental telos in which a determinist, anticipatory temporality reigns. In particular, the developmental aspect of the sexual drives concerns their objects and aims. The drives thereby yield a backward-glancing orientation. In contrast, the focus on the component of repetition in *Beyond the Pleasure Principle* plainly suggests that the unconscious is atemporal in nature, which serves as a foundational conceptual brick in trauma theory's structure with regard to the drives. The unconscious is unaware of any sort of retroactive temporality and is caught within a never-ending, uncompromising automatism of periodic iterations. So a timeless orientation seems to reign. As already mentioned, Freud also reiterated the fundamentally conservative nature of the drives in the 1920 work. The schema offered in the 1915 essay, however, settles somewhere in between the early and late works in which the drives are a kind of an amalgam of permanent and substitutable factors. On the one hand, the drives seek the absolute zero of the inorganic state, which becomes the exclusive condition and principle of the drives. On the other hand and by virtue of the contingency that inheres in their relation to their objects and aims, the drives are impressionable and pliable, and therefore change their aims and objects.

Although this may read, as Adrian Johnston suggests, like an irreconcilable inconsistency in Freud's development of the theory of the drives that reveals a contradiction inherent within the essence of the drives, I would suggest that the different articulations indicate in different ways that the structure of the drives is both mutable and structural.[33]

In the midst of Freud's evolving theory of the drives remains the libido, the constant energetic force in each and every psychic life. There are two implications to the libido as a constant, shared aspect. First, every individual, whether pathological or not, is subject to a libidinal economy and its workings. Second, and in being subjected to the economy, any and all variations of the sexual drives and their phenomenal dispersions within the psyche are therefore permutations of the libidinal force. These two implications correspond to a structural separation that organizes the libido theory. In one sense, the libido specifies the general economy within which bounded and unbounded energies circulate and the economy by which they work. This is itself a theory of the economy of energy that involves the evaluation of outcomes. In the other sense, the libido is only one among many energies, and thereby specifies the dynamic work of the sexual drives. The libido theory designates the dualist logic of the general economy of energy and the logic of the coimplication of the general economy and the energetics of the energies as including and borrowing from each other. The libido theory, we can say, is *a theory of the intricacy of the matter and meaning of psychical energy* in which the libido, the constant energetic force, includes what occurs in the interactions among energies and to the energies in the processes of exchange.[34]

While Freud clearly maintains the differential pathways along which the libido travels, there occurs in trauma a transformation in the form of the subject that does not owe itself to causal regimes implicit within libido theory. Such a transformation is not the result of the *fort/da* of narcissism whereby there is a shift into the cathexis of the ego and it becomes the large-scale basin from which the libido is cast out to objects and the site back towards and into which the libido flows from objects. Neither is it a result or form of sublimation in which both object and aim are fundamentally altered in the name of a higher social or ethical order.[35] Accordingly, such an essential alteration cannot be ascribed to a type of seduction or even to the work of the death drive as the return to a state of inorganicity. We should keep in mind that the concept of causality signifies something very different from that which finally happens and is therefore not contained within what happens even though it necessarily belongs to it. The challenge of the transformation that I propose involves the predicate of that which happens, while also apprehending causality as that which is not contained in the latter representation.

TRAUMATIC NEUROSIS

In his 1914 essay, "On Narcissism: An Introduction," Freud identifies and follows a general "antithesis between ego-libido and object-libido" to its logical conclusion whereby their value is assessed as a derivative of the libido as differentiated within itself.[36] He writes:

> The value of the concepts 'ego-libido' and 'object-libido' lies in the fact that they are derived from the study of the intimate characteristics of neurotic and psychotic processes. A differentiation of libido into a kind which is proper to the ego and one which is attached to objects is an unavoidable corollary to an original hypothesis which distinguished between sexual instincts and ego-instincts.[37]

From this point forward and as Freud then develops in greater detail a year later, in the 1915 essay, "Drives and Their Vicissitudes," the ego drives and sexual drives will no longer be strictly opposed. This distinction provides the critical frame through which Freud will, for the remainder of this work, contemplate the psychical attempt to apprehend one's own death. It is in particular, as Freud notes, the analysis of "pure transference neuroses," to which war neuroses belong, that takes him to the frontiers of the front line and compels the necessity for a new theoretical approach.

Accordingly, Freud's developing concept of narcissism suffuses his theoretical mediations on war neuroses from traumatic neuroses. Although Freud's mention of the two neuroses in *Beyond the Pleasure Principle* often leads to their conflation in the formulation of trauma theory, they are not one and the same. War neuroses are classified as "transference neuroses" (sometimes called object neuroses), which involve a movement towards a sexual object and the ego's efforts to ward off attacks waged by the sexual drives. Traumatic neuroses fall under the category of "narcissistic neuroses," which entails a turning of the ego within itself and a withdrawal from external objects. In narcissistic neuroses, there is no evidence of such a struggle because the unexpected fright and violence of the accident catches the psyche utterly unprepared. War neurosis belongs to both categories of neuroses because of an internal battle "between the soldier's old peaceful ego and his new warlike one."[38] So the patient suffers from transference neurosis and accident-related trauma.

As Freud explains in "Memorandum on the Electrical Treatment of War Neurotics," the first form of psychic trouble is the result of the conflict between the two egos in which the warlike ego emerges from within as an enemy on the front line that must be destroyed. The danger (not fright) exemplified by the soldiering ego is the same as the one posed by the libido during peacetime. The second form of disturbance does not at all answer to the aforementioned conflict in the ego.[39] "War neuroses," he writes, "are only traumatic neuroses, which as we know, occur in peacetime too after frightening experiences or severe accidents, without any reference to a conflict within the ego."[40]

In "On Narcissism: An Introduction," Freud offers for scrutiny an interesting picture of traumatic neurosis as akin to dementia, paranoia, or melancholia, which "resembles illness in implying a narcissistic withdrawal of the positions of the libido on the subject's own self."[41] This description of the libido's departure curiously returns in a different form in *Beyond the Pleasure Principle*, when Freud declares that the second of the two primary characteristics of traumatic neuroses is precisely that "a wound or injury inflicted simultaneously works as a rule *against* the development of a neurosis."[42] The first characteristic, as already mentioned, is fright. An absolutely indispensable aspect of fright is precisely that it is caused by an unpreparedness for anxiety, including the absence of hypercathexis of the frontline systems. It is caused by the absence of anxiety.[43] In fact, then, the "mechanical violence of trauma would *liberate* a quantity of sexual excitation which, owing to the lack of preparation for anxiety, would have a traumatic effect." Yet at the same time, as Freud further notes, "the simultaneous physical injury, *by calling for a narcissistic hypercathexis of the injured organ*, would bind the excess excitation."[44]

This is a remarkable moment in the text. Here Freud suggests that *inherent in trauma itself is a reparative aspect.* Both the functioning and the synthetic value of binding inheres in the *transformation*—the word that Freud consistently uses throughout his writings to describe the process—of unbounded, mobile energy into the bound energy. Accordingly, the binding of repetition in trauma works in the attempt to repair what has been breached.

What I am proposing here cannot be subsumed under the usual psychoanalytic thinking of trauma as only possessing a triggering power within certain regimes of events or even under the ontological value of creative invention. In part, I am suggesting that the very opening up of one's own death, the death of the prior self within life, which involves both the attempt to bind excitation and the binding of repetition, includes a conversion of separation from departure into transformation. In other words, it borrows from the adventure of separation.

ON THE MATTER OF BINDING AND THE BINDING MATTER OF TRAUMA

We must recall the particular work of binding in the pleasure principle. In the case of trauma, as I have already established, the psychic apparatus, having been caught completely off-guard, occupies itself with the attempt to bind the overwhelming (quantitatively and qualitatively) excitations that have penetrated the protective shield. Binding immediately jumps into the trenches in the effort to tame the wild and dangerous mobile energy. Freud brings this picture into relation with "Breuer's distinction between quiescent (or bound) and mobile cathectic energy in the elements of the psychical systems."[45] We are given to understand, as Freud consistently notes, "the binding of the energy that streams into the mental apparatus consists in its change from a freely flowing into a quiescent state."[46] Even though Freud wavers on whether or not the compulsion to repeat trauma somehow escapes the pleasure principle, a more scrupulous reading of the discussion reveals an important consideration of *the emergence of a different state of quiescence in trauma*, which takes residence in the relation between binding and repetition.

For Freud, generally speaking, the imperishable character of psychic life is a paradox. On the one side, it is the retrograde force that tries to return to and restore organic life to an anterior state of pure inorganicity. This is the basic work of the death drive. On the other side, the imperishable character of psychic life reposes in the enduring form of memory and its intrinsic capacity for reactivation and revivification. Thus the paradox of psychic life is precisely that its economies of exchange borrow from the irreversible change from a state of nonlife into life. Thus, psychic life involves a return to a more primitive form of life that is itself an interplay between the reversibility of nature and the irreversible nature of processes of self-differentiation. "By being born," Freud writes in *Group Psychology and the Analysis of the Ego*, "we have made the step from an absolutely self-sufficient narcissism to the perception of a changing external world and the beginnings of the discovery of objects. And with this is associated the fact that we cannot endure the new state of things for long, that we periodically revert from it, in our sleep, to our former condition of absence of stimulation and avoidance of objects."[47]

Insofar as the very advent of life not only consists in the transformation of the prior state of absolute quiescence, life itself also includes and acquires, in its spontaneous self-formative movements, the stimulation of excitations that are already bound as material for its own use. Psychic life is a doubling that starts repetition by disconnecting repetition itself from that which it repeats. We may dream of extinguishing the excitations of life, but the conditions of possibility for life seem to enfold the surprise of experience. By accord, then, the form of psychic life is always growing and transforming itself.

So if it is true that no living unity can escape "the most universal endeavor of all living substance—namely to return to the quiescence of the inorganic world," then instinct need be considered.[48] Enter the notion of "the binding of an instinctual impulse" as "a preliminary function designed to prepare the excitation for its final elimination in the pleasure of discharge."[49] The *attempt to bind* is an instinctual impulse that is necessarily present within every living entity. Since, as Freud makes clear, there can be no life without the stimulation of excitation, *the idea of binding the instinctual impulse to return to the prior state of absolute absence of excitation is secondary*, since a more primitive binding of energy has already occurred. As it thus follows, instinctual life is dualistic. Freud asserts:

> Two kinds of processes are constantly at work in living substance, operating in contrary directions, one *constructive or assimilatory* and the other *destructive or dissimilatory*. May we venture to recognize in these two directions taken by the vital processes the activity of our instinctual impulses, the life instincts and the death instincts?[50]

Even though the life drives and the death drive may seem to correspond to opposing actions and operate in divergent directions, they are interlocked and fused within one another as the activity of the very instinctual impulses at the heart of every living substance.

Drawing further from biology, Freud explains that the associational vitality of germ cells affords us a way of thinking how the "sexual instinct is the embodiment of the will to live" since their multicellular character becomes the means by which they prolong their life.[51] Freud writes:

> One helps to preserve the life of another, and the community of cells can survive even if individual cells have to die. . . . Accordingly, we might attempt to apply the libido theory which has been arrived at in psycho-analysis to the mutual relationship of cells. We might suppose that the life instincts or sexual instincts which are active in each cell take the other cells as their object, that they partly neutralize the death instincts (that is, the processes set up by them) in those cells and thus preserve their life, . . . and still others sacrifice themselves in the performance of this libidinal function.[52]

At first the libido is defined as an affect linked to the sexual instincts. However, the efforts of Eros—the libidinal, sexual or life instincts that are present in each cell of every living entity—consist in differentiating, multiplying relations among already existing units, establishing greater unities, and preserving life as such.[53] Accordingly, a defining characteristic of the energy of Eros—the libido—and its significance in life is its mobility, which enables it to pass freely from one object to another.[54] The libido is an energetic entity that moves through cellular and psychical barriers, entangling them in the neutralization of the regime of the death instincts in the general domain of psychoanalytic effects. It is in this sense that the life instincts are constructive and assimilatory. Thus the libido becomes the circulation of the symbolic function of the accumulating quantity of affect.

The drive of Eros is combination and production. As logic would have it, the death drive aims for the dissolution of amalgamated forms and their destruction.

Freud emphasizes the fact that more often than not, the two instincts are "fused, blended, and alloyed with each other" and that they nearly always appear together.[55] Consequently, the provinces of their respective tendencies can certainly swap roles. However and even though separating the two is an especially obstinate task, they still either work together or oppose each other. The distinction between the two drives is never erased, and neither is it a simple alternative since they begin from an original, differential "mixture" or "fusion."[56] Instead the distinction lies in the "expression of an inertia" in the latter and the "elasticity present in what is organic."[57]

In the *Project for a Scientific Psychology*, Freud establishes the *principle of inertia* (initially called the principle of neuronic inertia), which asserts that the fundamental activity of the neurons is to divest themselves of excitation. The most basic activity of the nervous system is to liquidate excitations to the lowest possible level that ensures the viability of biological survival. The principle of inertia is also, then, the principle of constancy. Accordingly, the principle accounts for the differentiation between two types of neurons—the motor and the sensory—as the mechanism that employs quantities of excitation only by getting rid of it. From its very beginning, however, the principle of inertia is disturbed by the existence of "endogenous stimuli" that originate from within the system and work to increase its internal complexity.[58] The motor and sensory neurons cannot employ endogenous excitations as a contrivance for liquidation or flight from them.[59] Within this, Freud distinguishes between the ψ (psi) neurons, which function to discharge and eliminate endogenous excitations, and the (phi) neurons, which control external stimuli.[60] He then further delineates the ψ and Φ neurons from the ω, or perceptual, neurons, which he identifies as a third system of neurons that involves the contrivance of quantity into quality.[61] I return to these neuronal systems in a later discussion. For now, though, the point to underscore is that the somatic like the neurobiological is a doubling of two different systems of production (transference and generation), through which the movements of their economies of energetics render the difference between nervous energy and psychical energy improbable.

The endogenous stimuli put pressure on the nervous system since it is incapable of employing such excitations. Accordingly, as Freud tells us in his well-known quote, "the stimulus of the drive does not arise from the external world but from within the organism itself."[62] Freud will associate this internal pressure with the drive, which demands its own space that precludes the nervous system and into which it can deter and dispose of its own excess excitations. This is both the source and the space of the psychic apparatus. The drive emerges as the force that threatens the different neuronal systems by rendering obsolete its self-regulating mechanism because it is the manifestation of the inside itself that appears from the inside. Paradoxically, however, this inside is not a space of interiority per se but more precisely the area of what Freud calls "contact-barriers," the frontier with no limit, a spatiality of self-differentiation that plays with the energies of its own outside.

The instinctual processes inherent in a living unity are tendencies towards the restoration of a prior state of things. As Freud formulates it, the drive—whether of life or of death—pushes towards the past, not towards alteration. The "final goal" towards which organic life strives is the ancient state of inanimate matter.[63] This certainly explains his rather enigmatic claim that the "*the aim of all life is death.*"[64] The initial stage of the growth and formation of psychic life occurs in the separation from and deconstitution of the state of pure inorganicity. This includes excitations that have already been bound and can no longer be altered. It is only the unbound or free energy that has the capacity to be transformed. Despite the urgency of the drive's internal pressure, it necessitates a doubling, which is also a redoubling of itself in order to put into action its work as authorizing and authoritative. At times, as Laplanche and Pontalis point out, the drive is itself presented as the "psychical representative of the stimuli originating from within the organism and reaching the mind." In other instances, it becomes "part of the process of somatic excitation, in which case it is represented in the psyche by 'instinctual representatives' which comprise two elements—the ideational representative and the quota of affects."[65]

Because the drive derives from the spatiality between the somatic and the psychic that is inseparable from their very production as an aggregate, it necessitates, according to Laplanche and Pontalis, an originarily structural doubling that produces its own surplus in order to establish the difference between itself as a "psychical representative" and an "instinctual representative." In the same moment, the drive redoubles itself from within in order to send out its emissaries. The pressure that the drive exerts on the system is both quantitative and qualitative since its former capacity involves a quantity of energy and its latter capacity entails a partitioning of the elements of instinctual representative within energy. Affect, then, is a product of the most basic activity of the nervous system. The drive can only manifest itself through representation and affect since it requires being able to attach itself to some representative or affective state in order to then utilize the representative(s) as the representation of the drive itself. The instinctual representative is thus the split within itself as a representation or group thereof that is cathected to a proportion of psychic energy and as a proportion of affect, or affective state.[66] The different representatives and affects of the drive develop in tandem with each other, always drawing from the common source of the contradiction between the psychic and the somatic.

For Freud, psychic life refuses or is incapable of overcoming this distinction. On this point he never wavers. We know from the activity of the drive that psychic life is said to produce its own symbolizations that are irreducible to the work of the nervous system. The essential work of the drive adheres to the general structure of representation, which is also the condition of possibility for the drives. This point is affirmed when Freud explains why the drive can always change its own vicissitude: "A drive can never become an object of consciousness—only the representative that represents the drive can be such an object. Even in the unconscious, moreover, a drive cannot be represented otherwise than by a representation. If the drive did not attach itself to a representation or manifest itself as an affective state, we could know nothing about it."[67] The key, however, is that the redoubling of the doubling of the drive is a transferable, mutable articulation point that arranges the interactions between the nervous system and the psyche differently at each of its instances. What thus appears to be an arrangement of economy of excess that determines the relations between its elements is instead the starting point of a self-differentiating interplay of the interactions between the different organizations of the psyche that, in a sense, make its structure follow after it as its *a posteriori* formation.

As it follows, the attempt to bind the instinctual impulse is itself a form of repetition of the more primitive binding that has already occurred. Freud himself makes this clear when he states:

> The elementary living entity would from its very beginning have had no wish to change; if conditions remained the same, it would do more than constantly repeat the same course of life. . . . Every

> modification which is thus imposed upon the course of the organism's life is accepted by the conservative organic instincts and stored up for further repetition. . . . It would be a contradiction to the conservative nature of the instincts if the goal of life were a state of things which had never yet been attained. On the contrary, it must be an *old* state of things, an initial state from which the living entity has at one time or another departed and to which it is striving to return by the circuitous paths along which its development leads.[68]

In this assessment, the death drive is immediately inscribed within the general movement of life, whereas the life drives aim to lessen the internal tensions of bounded energy or keep them constant. While pleasure always corresponds to a diminution and is the result of lowering the tension caused by a certain quantity of excitation in a given period of time, the lessening of tension itself has two significations inherent within it that pertains either to the minimum level of a given system within the living unity (equanimity) or to the death of the living unity.[69]

In a brief yet crucial moment in *Beyond the Pleasure Principle*, Freud distinguishes between these two states:

> The dominating tendency of mental life, and perhaps of nervous life in general, is the effort to reduce, *keep constant or to remove internal tension* due to stimuli (the 'Nirvana principle', to borrow a term from Barbara Low)—a tendency which finds expression in the pleasure principle, and our recognition of that fact is one of our strongest reasons for believing in the existence of the death instincts.[70]

Thus the lessening of tension associated with establishing an equanimity within life is the Nirvana principle, and those associated with the death instinct is therefore the principle of constancy. In "The Economic Problem of Masochism," Freud revisits the idea of the Nirvana principle and argues for its difference from the principle of constancy: "We must perceive that the Nirvana principle, belonging as it does to the death drive, has undergone a modification in living organisms through which it has become the pleasure principle; and we shall henceforth avoid regarding the two principles as one."[71] First, this means that the attempt to bind and the process of binding repetition that we see in traumatic experience is always, in the end, one of the functions of the pleasure principle or a phase in its work. Second, repetition in trauma is the binding of repetition itself, which leads to a new state of equanimity that is reparative in character.[72] While we can say that trauma involves the matter of binding, binding is neither, as Martin Hägglund has suggested, the condition of possibility for the pleasure principle nor the matter of trauma.[73]

Now we may return to *Beyond the Pleasure Principle* and take a closer look at Freud's challenge to the supremacy of the pleasure principle through the compulsion to repeat trauma. As already established, the psyche preoccupies itself with binding the excessive quantities of stimulus that have pierced the protective shield. The accident dream, which sends the victim back to the scene of trauma and is itself traumatizing, works with a view towards psychical binding and thereby obeys the law of the compulsion to repeat. As I have just established, the compulsion to repeat is an aspect of the instincts. Of course, these dreams do not produce pleasure. Pleasure always leads to the lessening of excitations; this is the economic outcome of binding. But pleasure can look like either the Nirvana state of equanimity or the state of quiescence towards which the death drive aims. This should not be taken as an affirmation of Jacques Derrida's notion of the bindinal economy and the logic of stricture, which, as he develops the concepts, designate binding as the condition of possibility for the pleasure principle.[74] It is the very arrangement of psychic life as involving a unicity of the natural and the symbolic and the matter of binding therein that establishes the typology in which the drives and thus the pleasure principle operate—not binding itself.

This postulation helps explain Freud's wavering on the question of whether there exists a beyond of the pleasure principle. However, what seems to be Freud's inability to resolve this question is but an affirmation of the problem of representation at the heart of the binding matter of trauma. The psychical system is a manifold that operates from within and between the different economies of energetics of life and the living being, not outside of it. More to the point, Freud's account of binding does in fact offer a clear conclusion about the relation between binding the pleasure principle that challenges the idea that the compulsion to repeat trauma necessarily corresponds with the death drive. As Freud concludes:

> We have found that one of the earliest and most important functions of the mental apparatus is to bind the instinctual impulses which impinge on it, to replace the primary process and convert the freely mobile cathetic energy into a mainly quiescent (tonic) cathexis. While this transformation is taking place no attention can be paid to the development of unpleasure; but this does not imply the suspension of the pleasure principle. . . . The binding of an instinctual discharge

> would be a preliminary function designed to prepare the excitation for its final elimination in the pleasure of discharge.[75]

While this moment may easily be read as affirming the primary function—and perhaps transcendental status—of binding, Freud immediately follows it with the resolution that "the pleasure principle, then, is a tendency operating in the service of a function whose business it is to free the mental apparatus entirely from excitation or to keep it as low as possible."[76] In trauma, binding only primes the psyche for the pleasure principle in the chronological sense since it is always preceded by the more primitive tendency.

What seems like a moment in which binding becomes the condition of possibility for the pleasure principle is instead the occurrence of an inversion in which the dominance of the pleasure principle appears to be incapacitated by something that is mysteriously beyond it. This occurrence is the opening of a new possibility in which the attempt to bind the traumatic stimulus, which works in the service of a pleasure principle, has changed its aim. Psychic life regulates itself precisely by informing itself of itself, and a new aim emerges and opens from within its own internal manifolds as the starting point of a new history and set of contingencies for the subject. This aim busies itself with binding repetition since the compulsion to repeat trauma, as deeply painful and unpleasurable it may be, nevertheless follows instinctual processes of repetition and binds the wild energy that would otherwise utterly destroy the psyche. The binding of repetition is the representative that represents the drive and repetition is the form of the representative that represents the drive. It is in the relation between binding and repetition that we begin to see how the psyche's rhetorical operations are assisting in shaping rather than constituting a particular relationship to repetition, and how that relationship, in turn, shapes the psyche.

THE MOTHER AND THE WRITER, THE DAUGHTER AND THE FATHER: THE TIME FOR (OF) REPETITION

Freud has been dwelling on the subjects of war neuroses, traumatic illnesses, and death for some time now. Five years earlier, in 1915, when all the young men in his family are fighting at the front, he writes "Thoughts for the Times on War and Death." He resolves to try to solve the problem. Can there be a beyond of the pleasure principle? Is there a form of the death drive? Is the compulsion to repeat the answer? He begins writing about how the symptoms of war neuroses resemble those of traumatic neuroses but deviate from them in the explicit absence of a gross mechanical force. The topic of traumatic neuroses is "dark and dismal" so he leaves it in favor of another that stages the same problems at the heart of the compulsion to repeat trauma: the "normal activity" of his grandson's play with his toys.[77] In particular, he pays attention to the game as it is first played with a wooden spool. Two footnotes follow his writing, and our reading. They stretch out like little cathected innervations that silently furrow the text, at once urging a reflection on the following generations and leaving something for someone else to pick up.

In the process of throwing the spool away, he notices that the child utters "a loud, long-drawn-out 'o-o-o-o', accompanied by an expression of interest and satisfaction."[78] Suddenly, and for the first and only time in *Beyond the Pleasure Principle*, a break in Freud's narrative voice occurs. He refers to himself in the third person as "the writer of this text."[79] A stranger appears before us, yet after an "and"—the three-letter conjunction that at once coordinates the terms that precede and follow it while opening into another place and time.

Who precedes and joins "the writer" in this troubling meeting? Our writer appears after "the boy's mother."[80] Unnamed, the boy's mother reappears in a brief footnote a few pages later: "When the child was five and three-quarters, his mother died. Now that she was really 'gone' ('o-o-o'), the little boy showed no signs of grief."[81] The mother was Freud's daughter, Sophie, who died towards the end of his writing *Beyond the Pleasure Principle*. A catastrophic inversion: the parent survives the child. Yet, something like a suture tugging at the texture of the text reveals within the game a new organization that makes it quite difficult to pin down the time of generations. The son comes before the mother, the daughter comes before the father. The father, the writer, is engendered by the daughter—an interruption in the order of succession. The seminal reason, the seed, is made to follow after. The game now plays with inheritance, that is, with the processes of engendering, forming, and constituting the form of posterity that makes possible different movements and effects of truth in the text.

They confer, Freud tells us, and agree upon the interpretation of the boy's "o-o-o-o" as a representation of the German word *fort*, which translates as "gone."[82] The word remains; it starts Freud's analysis of the game as an example of the challenge posed to the supremacy of the pleasure principle by the repetition compulsion. This word, which furrows within the text, authorizes the game. "Fort" appears only *in* (not simply as) the vanishing of the grammatical union of the relations. In other words, "fort" appears to us as an autonomous rhetorical figure only in dis-placing and dis-connecting from its own referents. Its referents are present only insofar as their functioning forms the spatiality of the different figures and their relations. "Fort" flies out of the boy's mouth, the writer's pen; it is thrown and throws itself in an adventure of a separated word. Out of sight, the boy pulls the spool back towards himself and hails "its reappearance with a joyful '*da*' ['there']."[83] The toy can only appear again after it has "gone" away. "This, then," Freud tells us, "was the complete game—disappearance and return."[84] Sent out as a word only to return as *da* and then as a game. The game is a doubling game of the return of repetition, which includes the play of the processes of development, evolution, and transformation. It is the game of activity and of passivity in the impure spontaneity of heritage, of lineage, of family. In the end, of course, Freud was never able to resolve whether the game was more or less about disappearance or return. Then again, texts, like inheritances, must be read by their inheritors in order to be something given.

The game plays with the interplay between the exchanges and (re)productions among systems of generations and of transmissions of memory and inheritance. It displays the unstable source and uncertainty of repetition at the general level of characteristics and at the individual level of the boy's attempt to grapple with his mother's departures and returns and then with her final disappearance. It also then reveals the memory of the death of Sophie in Freud's own way of organizing himself with the loss of his child. At the same time, there are exchanges occurring among what is being conveyed, or exchanges of exchange, which disclose, within the game itself, other new organizations that distribute meanings of "fort" differently at each instance of its textual occurrences. In each of these regimes and whether on the level of our reading or within the individual who discovers itself shattered, there is an autonomous process of the forming of a particular relationship to repetition that in its turn, shapes repetition itself and that which is being reiterated, recreated, reshaped, produced, and so on. In the interplay of the ways exchanges between different regimes of the translations and transcriptions of inheritance and memory arrange and display themselves, the symbolic and the material blend and paradoxically dismiss the play of the distinction between disappearance and return. The game plays instead with the complicitous cohabitation of necessity and chance that says something about deviation between deriving and arriving.

In the chronology of Freud's writing, Sophie was not yet gone in the first mention of "the boy's mother." It is unclear when precisely she died during the writing of *Beyond the Pleasure Principle*, but the footnote is, as the past perfect tense "had died" indicates, a posthumous entry. The fact of her death shapes the text as a knowing that suffuses the first enunciation of "the boy's mother" with the shape of a presence who follows after the shadow of "the writer." "The boy's mother" is also an arrangement of Sophie's name. Thus it is at once the form of Sophie and of her death that furrows itself in the pages. Before us, then, we have a double figure of the double of life and death whose outline of an incomprehensible silence meets us in the troubling end of the separation between the time of the living and the time of death.

The footnote that references Sophie's death follows after the text as its *a posteriori* forming. The death of the mother and daughter confers meaning upon the translation of the boy's "o-o-o-o" a few pages earlier is, in the textual chronology, yet to come. Situated in finer printed beneath the main body of the text, the footnote becomes a kind of textual burial that memorializes her death. It is also, in naming her, conferring the presence of her life. The writing of the *fort/da* game and of *Beyond the Pleasure Principle* appears as at once anticipation as mourning and mourning as anticipation. In a way, then, we are reading the yet unrecorded history of an accidental archive.

Freud himself notes that trauma is "the phenomena of life."[85] The contrary to "the phenomena of life," Freud, tells us in *Beyond the Pleasure Principle*, is the mechanical, the mechanicity and mechanism of the compulsion to repeat.[86] We know well that this machine is death, and that death is the secret mechanism working within the flesh of any and every living body. This is the self-deconstructive movement of the Real, the movement immanent to the Real in which life comes to affect the structure of anticipating death, of what Lacan calls the horizon of the encounter. For Lacan, the horizon of anticipation is the horizon of separation of the self from itself. In its barest, is not separation a transformation in the form of a relation, an action that alters a connection into a severance, a division? In the most basic regard, separation includes something of a text that survives its own destruction. However, and even before the death drive appears as an explicit problem in trauma, for example, separation takes us to what is at stake in any dualism: the power of life to invent its death. And this, more precisely, confronts us with the problem of the self-deconstructive tendency of life and the structure of the effacement of the subject from within as a tendency towards pure negation.

CHAPTER 2

The Eventality of Trauma

Let us begin by situating ourselves at the site of danger where we might least expect it, where it may be furthest from our thoughts: in the encounter with beauty. In a beautifully composed short essay, "On Transience," written during the fall of 1915, two years into the Great War, Freud recounts how, during a stroll on a peaceful summer's day through the countryside, his companion, the poet, is unable to feel any joy in the beauty of his surroundings. The poet is too disturbed by the transience inherent in the beauty, and thus by its immanent decay. Freud responds by noting that the fear of the destruction of this beauty inspires two different impulses in the mind.

> The proneness to decay of all that is beautiful and perfect can, as we know, give rise to two different impulses in the mind. The one leads to the aching despondency felt by the young poet, while the other leads to rebellion against the fact asserted. No! it is impossible that all this loveliness of Nature and Art, of the world of our sensations and of the world outside, will really fade away into nothing. It would be too senseless and too presumptuous to believe it. Somehow or other this loveliness must be able to persist and to escape all the powers of destruction.[1]

In the poet's disturbance, we see anticipatory mourning as acceptance for the immanence of decay in the surrounding environment and all that it contains, which includes, of course, those who walk within it. In Freud's reply, we see rebellion expressed as the "No!" that frees the aesthetic from any constitutive bind to nature's landscape, asserting the loveliness of nature and art as a transcendental idealism that exceeds the fact of destruction intrinsic to natural life. The "No!" maintains the absolute irreducibility of beauty. Although Freud delineates between the impulses, both are straightforwardly expressions of the finitude of the subject as a structure of knowledge about the living present as pertaining to the meaning of existence. Though they entail different affects, despondency and rejection coincide with the experience of transiency, and thus of the resistance to the fleeting nature of life. In this regard, the impulses are not constitutively different. The basis of Freud's opposition to the poet is clear enough. Any impulse convokes the essential separation of the symbolic from the natural, because for him the unconscious cannot conceptualize the concept of its own death.

The poet's impulse offers a slightly different, yet corresponding picture. The despairing poet sees the signature of finitude in absolutely everything that surrounds him, even in the aesthetic, which supposedly exceeds the physical environment in all respects. Everything must and will perish, including himself. Insofar as it stems from the lacunary functioning of an ontological lack and the immanent desire to overcome mortality, the poet's sensible relation to and experience of the transience of resplendent beauty is an amplified experience of his own finite existence. What we see in the poet's despondency is an illustration of the sensible experience of the effects of the truth of primordial temporality—that the horizon of all possibility yet to come and of all destiny is originarily opened by the originary temporality of time—as the human's first wound and perpetual wounding, and thus of the attempt to overcome one's own teleological end, one's own destruction.

The impulse of the "No!" in "On Transience" as the affirmation of the absolute irreducibility of the otherness of one's own destruction resonates with Freud's comments about the unconscious as unaware of death in "Thoughts for the Times on War and Death": "at bottom no one believes in his own death, or, to put the same thing another way, that in the unconscious every one of us is convinced of his own immortality."[2] As Deleuze argues, "Freud supposes the unconscious to be ignorant of three important things: Death, Time and No. Yet it is only a question only of time, death, and no in the unconscious."[3] The unconscious *behaves as though it were immortal* even in the face of the imperishable shadow of death. This is necessarily linked to his claim that unconscious processes are timeless and not in any way altered by the passage of time. Any reference to time is necessarily bound up with the work of the system *Cs.* (consciousness) since there is an indissoluble symmetry of thinking between the concepts of time and death.

Throughout his work, Freud acknowledges that from the beginning, the psyche is vulnerable to unpredictable events of destruction and thus bound to its own finitude. As we will see, the double organization of the ego's capacity for self-sacrifice as it yields anxiety apropos death affirms the general thinking of the temporality of the unpredictable future in psychic life.[4] However, it also shows it to be a particular phase. For Freud, it is never a question of whether or not an idea of psychic destruction exists but rather a matter of the value of the unconscious meaning of the concept of the psyche's own death as an essential part of its construction and functioning. Ultimately, he maintains that the psyche can never apprehend its own destruction. Accordingly, for Freud, the unconscious cannot and does not know time, death, or negation.

The immediate issue at hand does not only pertain to the formative role of the unconscious meaning of the psyche's own destruction and the variegated rhetorical detours in which it inheres in the general structure and functioning of the psyche. It also involves understanding precisely how the event of death can be apprehended.

TOWARD A PSYCHOANALYTIC CONCEPTION OF TIME

Time is a curious concept in Freud's writings. Although there are relatively few direct references to time, the Freudian metapsychology is a profound elaboration on the thinking of time. Is not the consideration of the meaning of death evident throughout his writings a straightforward testament to this? In the first place, and as we know from Freud's well-known assertion, the psychic unconscious knows nothing of time: "The processes of the system *Ucs.* [the unconscious] are *timeless*; i.e. they are not ordered temporally, are not altered by the passage of time; they have no reference to time at all."[5] Accordingly, any "reference to time," Freud concludes, "is bound up, once again, with the work of the system *Cs.*"[6] Generally speaking, and not without good reason, this has led to the popular assessment that the unconscious is atemporal in nature, while consciousness is temporalized. This is a logical deduction that lends support to the analytic distinction between the psychoanalytic subject as the site of permanent inscriptions and the psychoanalytic encounter as characterized by processes of remembering, regressing, repeating, dream-work, object-choice, and so forth.

Freud's insistence on the conservative nature of the drives as pushing towards the past, rather than towards change, also supports the timeless nature of the unconscious. Conversely, Freud acknowledges that drives are pliable and capable of the infinite alterability in their capacity to accept new objects and aims. At the very least, this suggests that the unconscious exhibits some temporal processes and functions. The unconscious, it thereby seems, has some *concept* of its own time even though it may not cognize time. Indeed both Laplanche's radicalization of *Nachträglichkeit* (the *après-coup* of hysterical trauma) and Lacan's notions of the *point de capiton* and temporal pulsation underscore this precise fact while demonstrating how a temporalized dynamic that shapes the unconscious is evident throughout Freud's writings.[7] Adrian Johnston has also argued for the *Trieb*, itself both timeless and temporal, as the analytic conceptual locus for the collusion between the unconscious as simultaneously atemporal and temporalized in nature.[8]

What does this mean? Is the temporalized dynamic of the unconscious a demonstration of the indestructibility of the structure of effacement? To propose an answer, let us dissect the anatomy of the psyche.

THE PERIOD OF NEURONAL MOTION

Throughout his work, Freud insisted upon the timeless character of the system *Ucs.* and, accordingly, the idea of time, as either the logic of a linear chronology or the logic of alteration, cannot be applied to any unconscious mental processes. Any and all references to time are exclusively bound up with the *work* of the system *Cs.*; its regulations, processes of representation, and outputs are inseparable from time. Since this system is developed as a founding part of the interiority of the psychic apparatus, any conceptualization of the atemporality of the unconscious can only be determined as a negative characteristic in comparison to conscious mental processes.[9] In the Freudian metapsychology, "acts of consciousness" and other symbolic activity are utterly unknown and unknowable to cerebral anatomy. Such activity belongs entirely to the province of mental life and is irreducible to the nervous system. Any relation that exists between the psyche and the anatomical activity of the nervous system can only be accounted for by a structure of representation that is autonomous to the psychic apparatus.

Let us also remember the process by which the drive emerges in order to help clarify an important point about the interiority of the psyche. Although Freud steadfastly upholds that psychic energy appears on the scene when nervous system energy fails to manage its own excitations, he was also very clear about two points. First and from the very beginning of the *Project* and onwards, Freud always maintained that the nervous system is not restricted to external excitations. As the organism's interiority becomes increasingly more complex, "the nervous system receives stimuli from the somatic element itself—endogenous stimuli—which have equally to be discharged."[10] The developing and evolving intricacy of this interiority, which corresponds to the appearance of the drive as a constant force that necessitates its own space into which it may direct and establish new pathways for the diminution and management of the surge of excitations, is coextensive with the second point. In "Drives and Their Vicissitudes," we see Freud's frequently cited claim that "an instinctual stimulus does not arise from the external world but from within the organism itself."[11] It is precisely because the drive "impinges not from without but from within the organism" that it operates according to different principles rather than by momentary physiological stimuli that are obviated in a single action by the nervous system. Psychic energy steps in at the precise moment when the nervous system fails to respond to and regulate its own stimuli. Since this energy is internal to the system itself, the force of the drive appears from within and impinges upon the interiority of the nervous system's own inside.

Certainly for Freud, the convolution of these two factors—excitations that are internal to the nervous system and the origination of the drive from within the organism—does not simply mean that there are two distinct types of energy (physiological and psychical) per se but rather a continuous transmission by which the second type (physical) differentiates itself from the first (physiological) while simultaneously rendering it a more composite type. This is part of the dynamics of the general economy of energetics.

In the opening lines of the *Project*, Freud states the primary aim of the work and its principal ideas. He writes: The intention is . . . to represent psychical processes as quantitatively determinate states of specifiable material particles. . . . Two principal ideas are involved: (1) What distinguishes activity from rest is to be regarded as *Q*, subject to the general laws of motion. (2) The neurons are to be taken as the material particles."[12]

As discussed earlier, Freud distinguishes between psi neurons, which function to discharge and eliminate endogenous excitations, and phi neurons, which control external stimuli. In the development of the theory of the contact barrier, which entails differentiation and conduction of stimuli between neurons, Freud establishes first and foremost that each single neuron contains within it the division of two classes of neurons—permeable (offering no resistance and retaining no trace of anything) and impermeable (offering resistance and retaining quantity)—and is therefore a model for the complete neuronal system. He goes on to rename the former class the phi neurons and the latter the psi neurons, which offer the distinct advantage of the possibility of representing memory. The drive appears as the force that threatens the contact barrier and thus the differential structure and functioning of the nervous system. The more nuanced and complex Freud's theory of neurons becomes, the more it becomes troubled by the obstinate problem of accounting for the problem of quality, which is given to us by consciousness as sensations whose differences are distinguished according to relations to the external world and to which the quantitative processes of the nervous system are presumed to be entirely foreign. Freud emphasizes: "it is to be expected from the structure of the nervous system that it consists of contrivances for transforming external *quantity* into quality."[13] Neither the permeability of the phi neurons nor the impermeability of the psi neurons can explain how and from where quality emerges as differential, conscious sensations.

To resolve this issue, Freud undertakes two coextensive revisions. First, he introduces a third system of neurons, which he calls the ω (perceptual) neurons in order to represent consciousness. Although psi and phi neurons work in tandem during the process of perception, the psychic process of reproducing or remembering presents the one exception to this rule because it does not bring about anything that has the peculiar character of perceptual quality. The states of excitation that occur within this third neuronal system remain separate from reproduction but give rise to conscious sensations. Second, he modifies his theory of the contact-barrier so as to add a new characteristic to the passage of $Q\eta$ (quantity of internal, cathected excitation). Rather than conceive of the movement of $Q\eta$ as the purely quantitative transference among neurons, Freud concedes that the makeup of the passage of $Q\eta$ must have an additional, nonquantifiable characteristic that is of a temporal nature. While these modifications amend the neuron and contact-barrier theories, they do so in support of the two principal ideas regarding the motion and materiality of neurons.[14] To describe the temporal nature as a necessary feature in the development of the nervous system, Freud employs the word *period*: "I speak of this as *period* for short."[15] Throughout his work, *period* will remain the shorthand term for his conception of time as it pertains to the relation between the structure and functioning of the psychic soma.

Temporality, for Freud, is derived from the general laws of motion that govern physical life. From the opening lines of the *Project*, it is perfectly clear that Freud follows the classical laws of motion to describe the relation between the nervous system and external forces and the particular motions (i.e., reflex arcs, muscular mechanisms) of the system in response to those forces. *Q*, as he states in the first of the two principal ideas at the core of the *Project*, is subject to these laws of motion. It is not until he comes to the problem of quality that he concedes the necessity that the same laws apply without contradiction to the psychical clarification of conscious sensations, which, according to him, owe nothing to cerebral anatomy but nevertheless have their basis in neuronal activity that is quantitatively material. With regard to the question of quality as arising from within the system, the laws of motion complicate the concept of permeability to the extent that it cannot be solely conceived on the basis of the resistances of the contact-barriers against the transference of pure external stimuli. Freud thus introduces the idea of the *period of neuronal motion.*

In Freud, neuronal motion involves the relation between time and the basic principle of inertia. To recall, the inertia principle states that the primary activity of neurons is the tendency to divest themselves of quantities of purely external stimuli while explaining the structural divergence of neurons into motor and sensory types as different means for neutralizing the reception of cathected stimuli ($Q\eta$). Inertia thereby expresses itself as the passing of a "wave-movement," like an electrical current, along pathways of conduction among cells.[16]

When Freud speaks of the period of neuronal motion, he is referring to the spatiality of the discreet temporal interval during which the amplification of energy moves from the zone of one neuron to another, causing *the state of becoming affected.* In Freud's account, the force of external *Q* does not merely result in endogenous excitation, that is, in internally cathected $Q\eta$. It is the formation of $Q\eta$ as the new form of Q. Immediately, the period of neuronal motion corresponds to the development of a new form, which, at this moment in the analysis, is the becoming of the outside of the inside proper to the system.

$Q\eta$ does not yet refer to psychic energy proper, which steps in when the nervous system becomes overwhelmed by the problem of resolving endogenous excitations that come from the force of the drive. For now, let us be perfectly clear that the occurrence of $Q\eta$ shows that the nervous system is endowed with an autonomous structure of representation. To be sure, Freud never contested the muscular and sensory liquidation of the external excitations produced by the nervous system as a type of representational activity. Instead he very clearly established that ultimately it is when the nervous system is confronted with the force of the drive and the foreignness of the inside from which the drive derives that it fails to represent itself. Even still, in the Freudian metapsychology, the structure of representation is coincident with the appearance of the drive. In one way or another, then, the inside of the system always plays with the forces of its own outside. Now, the distinction between external Q and internal $Q\eta$ takes place within the spatiality of the border zone between neurons, that is, within the nervous system. Accordingly, the distinction between inside and outside the nervous system corresponds to an internal partition of neurons. For Freud, then, the period of neuronal motion also comes to designate the apparatus of representation in which the emergence of $Q\eta$ is a starting point of the movement of expressions of the nervous system.

But neuronal motion does not yet fully account for the problem of quality since at this stage it only offers us a way of thinking the emergence of $Q\eta$ as endogenous nervous energy that, in a sense, detaches itself from the purely external energy in order to render itself as the cloven representation of the period as an interval of time. It does not completely describe $Q\eta$ as psychic energy. So far, it only answers the empirical question, which concerns understanding how the organicity of the nervous system appears in the body before consciousness.

Freud in fact offers a remarkable answer to this problem when he develops the perceptual neurons as the source for the coimplication of the period of neuronal motion as the elaboration of the passage of endogenous excitations through the spaces between neurons and the state of becoming structurally affected within the individual neuron and within the system more widely. Even when faced with the problem of accounting for the emergence of conscious sensations, Freud does not abandon the principle of inertia or the general principle that defines the structure of the nervous system as consisting in the contrivances of external quantity into endogenous quality. The nerve endings function as a "screen" that allows overwhelming quotients of exogenous stimuli to act upon the phi neurons, while at the same time these completely permeable neurons are assisted in managing the excessive quotient by the psi neurons, which protect against such higher orders of quantity.[17] Ultimately, however, smaller amounts of energy remain that must be liquidated. Consequently, the perceptual neurons enter into the schematic of neuronal development as necessarily cathected with $Q\eta$, which at this point has already been complexified into the inseparable intrication between, as Freud calls it, exogenous (external) and endogenous (internal) excitation. The tertiary class of neurons adheres to the principle of inertia and thereby necessitates a level of impermeability in their functioning in order to fulfill the primary aim of discharge. The perceptual neurons forestall the development of this particular feature. Instead, "the ω neurones behave like *organs of perception*," or "sense-organs."[18]

Freud submits that the differences of period emerge from the operation of the sense-organs as producing qualities that "seem to be *represented* precisely by different periods of neuronal motion."[19] In this capacity, the nerve endings at once work as screens—as simultaneously a partition and a shield that safeguards the internal realm of the individual neurons from increasingly complexified endogenous excitations—and as a sieve that screens in the sense of filtering "certain *processes* with a particular period."[20] The word *processes* is critical here. Straightforwardly, "certain processes" refers to perception and consciousness as psychical processes that give rise to sensations whose distinction and differences consist in being a relation with the external world. At the same time, and given the duality of the screen function of the nerve endings, "certain processes" includes the period of neuronal motion in which the perceptual neurons, otherwise incapable of receiving $Q\eta$, are grooved by and filled with the minimum amount of $Q\eta$ that constitutes the most fundamental basis of consciousness. This particular period establishes the coincidence between the phenomena of consciousness and processes of developing the perceptual neurons into the quantitative psychological structure. External stimuli pass through the phi neurons via the psi neurons into the perceptual neurons, where sensations are generated and represented by a specific instance of neuronal motion. Core consciousness thereby occurs as the movement of the generation and transformation of consciousness.

What does this mean? Insofar as the perceptual neurons enter the scene as already cathected with an expanded $Q\eta$, their appearance and particular operation transforms $Q\eta$ into psychic energy and thereby the psychic space, emptied of neuronal governance and freed for its own representation activity, on the basis of a quantum of neuronal activity. Thus the new originary form of $Q\eta$ is differential, yet articulated. Psychic energy is a form of exteriorization produced by the nervous system. Yet this form of exteriorization is an interiority that does not exceed the limits of its more primary or primitive interiority even though it remains differentiated from it. Granted, the process of representation at work in the nervous system is markedly different from the process of representing the drive. Unlike the drive, the nervous system does not send out an emissary on its behalf; rather it complexifies and develops itself through self-differentiation in its regimes of energy regulation and transmission, putting itself in tension with the drive. It is precisely that the mechanisms of the nervous system do not simply flow into the mold of the psyche without tension that the formation of the psychic apparatus takes hold.

The point to underscore is that the period of neuronal motion brings into view the crucial and irremediable connection between the nervous system's remarkable capacity to transform itself and the general structure and functioning of the psyche. The phylogenetic development of the nervous system is not just an answer to the empirical questions that consist in knowing, first, how organic bodies of any kind emerge within the physical world out of a state of inorganicity and, second, how an organic body emerges in that world prior to consciousness. Under the pressures of the external stimuli, the nervous system does not die; it does not sacrifice itself in the name of the advent of the psyche. It becomes more robust and increasingly more complex as it encounters and regulates itself. The psyche, in its turn, also grows in increasing complexity in its meetings with the nervous system. In its barest, this shows us that, through the interplay of self-differentiating movements, life develops and evolves itself in ways that not only act with the forces of the outside it produces, but also in ways that organize the relationship between the psyche and the nervous system differently at each stage. In other words, what Freud's period of neuronal motion invents—and this is no doubt what is so remarkable about his discovery—is a notion of temporality that can be thought as a process of temporalization that includes, without necessarily being more one than the other, the natural or empirical and the ontological. In fact, the period of neuronal motion renders the difference between the time of nature and the pure generation of horizon improbable to the extent that it dismisses the question of proper and of authenticity. And this, I would suggest, has the capacity to change the ontological meaning of the horizon of expectation.

For now, though, the period of neuronal motion also demonstrates that there is no expression for a pure psyche because it cannot exist as such. Insofar as the psyche is conceived as always already a subjectivity that depends for its possibility on belonging to a relation to what Lacan calls *das Ding*, the Thing—the "primordial function which is located at the level of the initial establishment of gravitation of the unconscious," the "prehistoric Other that is impossible to forget"[21]—the period of neuronal motion, I would further contend, allows us to see the different ways the configuration of the psyche develops, evolves, and transforms. The psyche forms and engenders itself after the prior state of things in constituting itself as a form of posterity for itself; it asserts the coincidence of the neuronal life of the nervous system and the symbolic fabric of psychic life. In short, the period of neuronal motion realizes the living being canceled within us; it is the time of the prehuman in which life and death equally include each other in their changes of states and movements. This time, the time within life, follows after the love/hate dyad as the structuring of its structure while extinguishing the burning difference between primordial or authentic temporality and vulgar, everyday lived time.

While Freud eventually goes on to abandon his discussion of neurons and neuronal motion, he will never let go of the word *period* as his shorthand term for the interactive dynamic of temporality in the system *Pcpt.-Cs.* (perception-consciousness) in particular and thus for the concept of time more generally. The core of the problem for Freud, more anterior than that of memory, though it necessarily belongs to it, is the formation of consciousness, since this supplies us with the possibility of conscious sensations and subsequently with the negative characteristics that enable us to begin understanding the dynamic work of the unconscious and thus of the psyche in its entirety.[22]

Let us recall Freud's famous statement from *Beyond the Pleasure Principle*: "We have learnt that unconscious mental processes are in themselves 'timeless'. Again, this means in the first place that they are not ordered temporally, that time does not change them in any way and that the idea of time cannot be applied to them. These are negative characteristics which can only be clearly understood if a comparison is made with conscious mental processes."[23] While these assertions stem from Freud's formulation of the unconscious as incapable of conceiving the concept of its own death, death is itself, of course, the signature of finitude. In order to furnish an eternal synchronic logic of the unconscious, he must first solve the problem of quality, which is the transient, diachronic logic of consciousness.[24] This leads to a fascinating analysis of the principal characteristics of the ego.

THE ANATOMY OF THE PSYCHE

"Cerebral anatomy," Freud decisively asserts in *Beyond the Pleasure Principle*, "has no need to consider why, speaking anatomically, consciousness should be lodged on the surface of the brain instead of being safely housed somewhere in its inmost interior."[25] Any union that exists between the psyche and the nervous system is inseparable from the way in which it is produced from the force of the drive that steps in at the moment the nervous system fails to master its own influx of external excitations. The inside—the interiority of mental life from which the drive originates—is a border zone, a spatialness of difference that is not of a proximity but of entangling manifolds, between the body and the psyche that establishes the exteriority of the nervous system within itself. Insofar as the force of the drive only manifests itself though representation, the particular relation between somatic organization and mental life is not of the psyche and the nervous system themselves but more precisely an indication of their phylogenetic synthesis that occurs entirely within this spatiality of interiority.

Developed within this intimate interiority, the Freudian "ego" is like a limb that mediates the relation between perceptions of the external world and perceptions of the inner world of the psyche. When Freud asserts in "The Ego and the Id," "The ego is first and foremost a bodily ego; it is not merely a surface entity, but is itself the *projection* of a surface," he is iterating a decisive point in his metapsychology: any relation between the mind and the body, between the symbolic and the natural, reveals itself as both mutable and structural, and consequently, the sovereign apparatus of representation with which psychic life is equipped is one way life literally makes sense.[26] In this description, the ego is a self-arranging form, a manifold interface, a meeting point between internal and external excitations that, for Freud, cannot be represented within the nervous system.[27]

The first part of "An Outline of Psychoanalysis," offers further clarification:

> Psychoanalysis makes a basic assumption, the discussion of which is reserved to philosophical thought but the justification for which lies in its results. We know two kinds of things about what we call our psyche (or mental life): firstly, its bodily organ and scene of action, the brain (or nervous system) and, on the other hand, our acts of consciousness. . . .
>
> We have arrived at our knowledge of this psychical apparatus by studying the individual development of human beings. To the oldest of these psychical provinces or agencies we give the name of *id*. It contains everything that is inherited, that is present at birth, that is laid down in its constitution—above all, the instincts, which originate from the somatic organization and which finds a first psychical expression here [in the id] in forms unknown to us. Under the influence of the real external world around us, one portion of the id has undergone a special development. From what was originally a cortical layer, equipped with the organs for receiving stimuli and with arrangements for acting as a protective shield against stimuli, a special organization has arisen which henceforward acts as an intermediary between the id and the external world. To this region of our mind we have given the name of *ego*. Here are the principal characteristics of the ego. In consequence of the pre-established connection between sense perception and muscular action, the ego has voluntary movement as its command. It has the task of self-preservation.[28]

There are two, coextensive levels of understanding in Freud's account of the ego. The first level concerns *the ego as it is derived from the cortical layer and formed into the hardened protective shield.* In this sense, the ego is the conjunction between the oldest, core self, within which the id is constituted and where the deep affection to life is reinforced, and the earlier somatic organization. The second level involves *the ego as it has finally arrived, through its gradual growth, in its own form, which gives form to the effects of the encounters with both the id as its inheritance and the inheritances the id acquires in its interactions with the external world.* It is no longer strictly a matter of the core self as corresponding to the inside of the psyche, on the one side, and the neuronal self as corresponding to the outside of the psyche, on the other side. From this point forward, the ego comes to designate a particular form of the relation between the unconscious and the neuronal that takes place within the internal manifolds of the psychic apparatus itself. The ego, in this sense, is a new starting point, the self-organizing, "special organization," of the psyche as part of the assemblies of life.

For Freud, the phylogenetic and ontogenetic heritage of the ego inheres in its psychical physiognomy that convokes a "pre-established connection between sense perception and muscular action," which enables its commanding, temporally ordering actions. The ego is born out of "*everything* that is inherited, that is present at birth, that is laid down in its constitution," including the indissoluble link between "sense perception and muscular action." While this suggests that the ego is wholly constituted in advance, pre-formed in the germ cell, it is important to remember the doubling play of the activity and the passivity of inheritance, which shows us that inheritance itself is always something to be engendered, regenerated, and constituted anew. The formation of the ego is a self-differentiating, developmental process that, in its increasing complexity of purposiveness, makes no distinction between the obscure, natural material and mechanisms of the living organism, on the one hand, and the typologies of psychic life that formulate the conscious self and its variegated elaborations of modes of being, on the other.

The ego, however, is not simply an anatomical analogy or figural representation of the border between motility and perception that reinforces the fundamental inability of the nervous system to produce its own autonomous expressions. One could certainly argue that the ego is itself the form of such an expression. Such an argument can be followed to the conclusion that expressions are reducible to a range of typological schemas. Yet Freud's discussion of the principal characteristics of the ego also reveals the conception of the ego as an interactive form of posterity that helps shape the psyche into something that gradually develops limbs and exercises within the general economy of life without causing life to fragment itself. It is through this process, which is both reflexive and nonreflective, that the ego makes for itself a constellation of selves that gather into a succession that involves the coexistence of states of consciousness in which the self exists only insofar as it lasts and produces itself from one moment to the next, orienting and determining itself in the matter of the protective shield that configures consciousness. In some sense, the ego is a subject with another subject.[29]

THE CONSCIOUS ORGAN EXISTS

In both *Beyond the Pleasure Principle* and "A Note upon the 'Mystic Writing-Pad,'" Freud maintains that the phenomena of becoming conscious and the leaving behind of permanent memory traces are absolutely incompatible processes. "*Consciousness*," Freud resolutely concludes in the earlier text, "*arises instead of a memory-trace*."[30] However, *the system Cs. regulates, organizes, and displays the coincidence between the expiration of excitatory processes and "the fact of becoming conscious*."[31] Accordingly, consciousness is produced instant after instant, as a succession of moments that involves the coexistence of *states* of consciousness. This is the output of the synthesis of perceptions between external and internal excitations as the process of becoming conscious. This method of working is, as Freud elaborates through the analogy of the Mystic Writing-Pad, specific to the unicity of the system *Pcpt.-Cs.*

> My theory was that cathected innervations are sent out and withdrawn in *rapid periodic impulses* from within into the completely pervious system *Pcpt.-Cs.* So long as that system [*Pcpt.-Cs.*] is cathected in this manner, it receives perceptions (which are accompanied by consciousness) and passes the excitation on to the unconscious mnemic systems; but as soon as the cathexis is withdrawn, consciousness is extinguished and the functioning of the system comes to a standstill. . . . Thus the interruptions, which in the case of the Mystic Pad have an external origin, were attributed by my hypothesis to the *discontinuity in the current of innervation*; and the actual breaking of contact which occurs in the Mystic Pad was replaced in my theory by the *periodic* non-excitability of the perceptual system. I further had suspicion that this *discontinuous method of functioning of the system Pcpt.-Cs. lies at the bottom of the origin of the concept of time*.[32]

Like the ego, the protective shield is itself an agent insofar as it is the subject of the system's organic history, which, for Freud, begins with an organism's most elemental, susceptible form of life—the vesicle.[33] In cellular biology, the vesicle is a small, porous, lithe structure within a cell consisting of fluid enclosed within a lipid bilayer membrane. The functions of vesicles vary depending on the type but range from transportation to secretion of molecules. In Freud, the primary activity of the vesicle consists in the unmediated reception of external stimuli. Without the accompaniment of other cells, Freud tells us, the surface of this fragile vesicle has no other possible spatial orientation except as facing towards the external world. By its very orientation, then, the surface is differentiated from its inner folds as "an organ for receiving stimuli."[34] As it experiences the ceaseless impact of excitations coming from the outside, "this little fragment of living substance" undergoes a transformation while it helps direct external excitations through the new and different courses it establishes, which involve those courses traveled in the process of the formation and gathering of germ cells into the central nervous system.[35]

Freud tells us that only a portion of the surface has completely altered—to its furthest extent—and that only one part can no longer be modified or altered in any way by the passage of excitations. This part of the surface, which is not a free-floating fragment, has become the veritable protective shield, the hardened piece of armor that works in the service of minimizing the effects of the external world upon the internal realm. As Freud carefully notes: "[The] outermost surface ceases to have the structure proper to living matter, [and the shield] becomes *to some degree* inorganic and thenceforward functions as a special envelope or membrane resistant to stimuli."[36] One part has accomplished the irreversible conversion of the organic into the inorganic; however, it maintains an autonomous supply of energy in order to ensure its present and future work against external effects that tend towards destruction. "By its death," Freud concludes, "the outer layer has saved all the deeper ones from a similar fate."[37] It achieves itself in actually erasing the limit between the living substance and the psychic subject. Similar to the development of the ego, the occurrence of the protective shield shows us once more that structure arrives in some sense after that which it structures. The protective shield, the element that remains of its own deconstruction of a proper structure, indicates itself after like an *a posteriori* transformation of living matter. The accomplishment of this irrevocable erasure comes to light in the perpetual activity of regulating and representing the system *Cs.*, without which the very concept of the unconscious cannot be thought, from within the anatomy of the psyche. Accordingly, the system *Cs.* is core consciousness that occurs as the movements of the little fragment's self-organization into the protective shield. It names the shifting relations between the irreversible and reversible effects of the interplay between the "structure proper to living matter" and the "membrane resistant to stimuli." In so naming, it paradoxically dissolves the very question of proper. This is the ego, core consciousness, the conscious organ that is the starting point of "our abstract idea of time" and which is "wholly derived from the method of working of the system *Pcpt.-Cs.* and to correspond to a perception on its own part of that method of working."[38] This method of working, which is both fleeting and organizing, is indispensable to the psychic elaboration of the event.

ANXIETY, THE FEAR OF DEATH, AND THE EGO

There is a very compelling change from the 1915 *Papers on Metapsychology* to the 1926 *Inhibitions, Symptoms, and Anxiety* that coincides with Freud's fundamental shift in the thinking of internal instinctual danger as the principal form of all danger to a thinking of the actual, external situation of danger. In the earlier text, Freud argues that anxiety is a reaction to an internal, instinctual danger and thereby the consequence of repression. In the later text, Freud inverts his thinking and describes anxiety as that which causes repression because it is a reaction to some materially real, external danger.[39] In the *New Introductory Lectures on Psychoanalysis*, Freud remarks on this inversion, noting, "We have learnt two new things: first, that anxiety makes repression and not, as we used to think, the other way round, and [secondly] that the instinctual situation which is feared goes back ultimately to an external situation of danger."[40] Whereas in the 1915 *Papers* Freud is concerned with showing how "neurotic anxiety" changes into "realistic anxiety" and corresponds to the transformation of an internal danger into an external one, in the later work he focuses on the precedence of realistic anxiety and its relation to external danger as a function of the ongoing development of the ego's dependent relation to the external world.

Having earlier established that the ego is the "sole seat of anxiety,"[41] Freud goes on to say, "In the course of development the old determinants of anxiety should be dropped, since the situations of danger corresponding to them have lost their importance owing to the strengthening of the ego. But this only occurs incompletely. . . . A few of the old situations of danger, too, succeed in surviving into later periods by making contemporary modifications in their determinants of anxiety."[42] There are two critical, coextensive thoughts expressed in this moment. The first pertains to the aforementioned—that instinctual danger is the internalization of an external danger. The second—the strengthening of the ego—expresses a phylogenetic development in the form of the ego in its three primary relations to the world, the id, and the superego as it adapts to the few old situations of danger that survive into the later periods of life.

The three situations of danger—birth, castration, and punishment—are the principal forms of the oldest, more primary danger that persists throughout life. Owing to the work of Otto Rank, who has "the merit of having expressly emphasized the significance of the act of birth and of separation from the mother," and the idea that "the experience of anxiety at birth is the model of all later situations of danger," Freud establishes that the danger of separation is the primary form of danger, which is more originary than instinctual peril.[43] Accordingly, external danger designates the radical exteriority of death and the immanent threat of destruction, which, for Freud, manifests itself within as the danger of separation. Although earlier, in *Inhibitions, Symptoms, and Anxiety*, Freud dismisses Rank's idea about "birth trauma" as "unfounded and extremely improbable," he nevertheless retains separation as the principal representation of the psyche's encounter with its own concept of death.[44]

Beginning with his investigation into the relation between anxiety and repression as it arises from the Oedipal complex, Freud explains the derivation of the chief forms of separation. Instead of affirming that, due to repression, the libidinal cathexis of the boy's mother as the object was changed into anxiety, which emerged as the symptomatic attachment to a substitute for the father, he realizes that the anxiety of being in love with his mother only appeared as an internal danger. It was only a neurotic anxiety. As a result of the anxiety the boy feels in the face of his libidinal demand, the danger of the "punishment of being castrated" appears as the "real danger" that "the child is afraid of as a result of being in love with his mother."[45] This does not mean, as Freud clarifies, that the danger is manifested as the threat of an actual castration. Rather, the fear produced by castration anxiety is an auxiliary fear, a rhetorical detour for the "fear of the loss of love."[46] The fear of the loss of love is itself a substitute for the fear of punishment by the mother, who threatens to retract her love, which in its turn is a rhetorical appearance of the more "original anxiety at birth" as the representation of the separation from the mother.[47] These other determinants of anxiety, which we can now put in their proper order as birth, punishment, castration, "repeat the situation" of real danger—the danger of leave-taking from the self—for which the trauma of birth is the first form of separation as a change in the form of a relation.

While distinguishing between the characteristics of traumatic neurosis and war neurosis in *Beyond the Pleasure Principle*, Freud offers an important clarification of the terms "anxiety," "fright," and "fear," which will come to have crucial methodological implications in his developing theory of anxiety:

> 'Fright', 'fear' and 'anxiety' are improperly used as synonymous expressions; they are in fact capable of clear distinction in their relation to danger. 'Anxiety' describes a particular state of expecting the danger or preparing for it, even though it may be an unknown one. 'Fear' requires a definite object of which to be afraid. 'Fright', however, is the name we give to the state a person gets into when he has run into danger without being prepared for it; it emphasizes the factor of surprise.[48]

In "The Ego and the Id," the incorrect assumption that fear and anxiety are synonymous terms in the thinking of danger pertains to the status of the psyche's own death as an entirely unrepresentable concept in the unconscious. He elaborates:

> The high-sounding phrase, 'every fear is ultimately the fear of death', has hardly any meaning, and at any rate cannot be justified. It seems to me, on the contrary, perfectly correct to distinguish the fear from dread of an object (realistic anxiety) and from neurotic libidinal anxiety. It presents a difficult problem to psycho-analysis, for death is an abstract concept with a negative content for which no unconscious correlative can be found. It would seem that the mechanism of the fear of death can only be that the ego relinquishes its narcissistic libidinal cathexis in a very large measure—that is, that it gives up itself, just as it gives up some external object in other cases in which it feels anxiety. *I believe that the fear of death is something that occurs between the ego and the super-ego.*[49]

Here Freud clearly suggests that the fear of death—the fear of separation from oneself—is itself an occurrence. Freud notes that the companion to the abstract concept of death is negative content, for which, to reiterate, there is no meaningful substance in the unconscious. The concept of destruction is not, accordingly, in itself the negative content. It is separation that retroactively gives death its figurative content. Freud immediately situates this content for which there is no unconscious correlative within the process of repression under the influence of anxiety as anticipation, which is indissolubly linked to the absolute suddenness of trauma and which gives rise to the dual construction and organization of the ego. In the face of the fear of death, the ego—the chief guardian that keeps watch over our vast psychic territory—protects precisely by surrendering itself in the meeting with the occurrence of something between the ego and the superego. What is *this something* that happens between the ego and the superego?

We already know of Freud's revised thinking of anxiety as creating repression in his analysis of the progression of birth-castration-loss as the love-punishment prohibition. In the occurrence of the depersonalization of the parental agency as the source of the fear of castration—the loss of the mother as an object to castration—the danger becomes slightly more vague and nebulous.[50] In the instant the ego recognizes the danger of castration, it sends out its feelers and innervates the psyche with the impulse of anxiety, which inhibits according to the agency of the pleasure-unpleasure principle. The ego knows very well that "the satisfaction of an emerging instinctual demand would conjure up one of the well-remembered situations of danger."[51] This instinctual danger is but the trace of a more prior, real danger—that of the psyche's own destruction—but nevertheless "suppressed, stopped, made powerless."[52]

In the case of repression, however, the instinctual impulse is still part of the id's cathectic process:

> What happens in the case of repression is that the instinctual impulse still belongs to the id and that the ego feels very weak. The ego thereupon helps itself by a technique which is at the bottom identical with normal thinking. Thinking is an experimental action carried out with small amounts of energy, in the same way as a general shifts small figures about on a map before setting his large bodies of troops in motion. Thus the ego anticipates the satisfaction of the questionable impulse and permits it to bring about the reproduction of unpleasurable feelings at the beginning of the feared situation of danger. With this the automatism of the pleasure-unpleasure principle is brought into operation and now carries out the repression of this dangerous instinctual impulse.[53]

At the same time, the ego, already marked by the radical exposure to the psyche's destruction and radically opened to whatever may come in the situation of danger, unexpectedly encounters itself, and then touches itself after, as it were, with its own feelers. In the process of this self-touching, the ego thinks, cognizes, and recognizes an emotion, the instinctive impulse of an instinctive knowledge it gathers from its own structural and functional relation to the vast territory of the psyche and from the other inhabitants of the soma it has been charged to protect. The ego complexifies itself from within the intricacy of its own frailty and the necessity of maintaining its primary rank at any cost. And thus the ego sends out its feelers, its cartographers, to survey the psychic topography before another developmental process starts putting a larger bodied troop into action. In the act of repression, the ego relinquishes a part of its essential organization.

The ego's thinking, which is not precisely the same as the awareness of the consciousness of laws, is engendering in three different, yet interrelated ways: it produces a constitutively new functional action, it is the result of having been produced, and it is the production of the relationship between that which is transmitted and that which is generated anew. This thinking appears as a doubling in which the ego's anticipation of death is its own surrendering of itself from itself. The doubling is the opening of a distance within division whereby the ego takes itself as an object, as a kind of reconfiguring of an essential separation from itself. It prefigures, in other words, death as an immanent mortal separation precisely by doubling itself and becoming, out of necessity for itself and for the other parts of the psyche, the double that takes leave of itself in the taking of itself as an object. Thus the self-separation of the ego opens the psyche to what Lacan calls the horizon of the encounter, the structure of anticipating death that also appears in all forms of anxiety and narcissism. The ego deploys itself as a transformable articulation point between different ways of apprehending death precisely by doubling itself and by relinquishing elements of its guardianship in the process of a self-differentiating and self-arranging movement that assembles a different, larger bodied troop and sends it on its way. The ego's separation, which again, operates from within the different systems of exchange and production, inheres in the emergence of the superego. The relinquishing of the ego thereby comes to designate the manifold organization of the ego's economy of protection as a triple movement involving development, evolution, and transformation in the complexification of the processes of self-sacrifice and self-preservation. This movement includes reactions to various environmental conditions that result in both irrevocable and reversible changes in form and in the subjects and objects of preservation. The ego's thinking is an indissoluble intimacy between its material and symbolic functions.

We see this clearly in Freud's very beautiful writing about the "phenomenon of the 'double'" in his essay "The Uncanny":

> For the 'double' was originally an insurance against the destruction of the ego, an 'energetic denial of the power of death', as Rank says; and probably the 'immortal' was the first 'double' of the body. This invention of doubling as a preservation against extinction has its counterpart in the language of dreams. . . . *This idea of the 'double' does not necessarily disappear with the passing of primary narcissism, for it can receive fresh meaning from the later stages of the ego's development. A special agency is slowly formed there, which is able to stand over and against the rest of the ego*, which has the function of observing and criticizing the self . . . and which we become aware of as our 'conscious'. . . . The fact that an agency of this kind exists, which is able to treat the rest of the ego like an object—the fact, that is, that man is capable of self-observation—renders it possible to invest the old idea of a 'double' with a new meaning.[54]

Doubling is what forms itself as a protective mechanism against the threat of destruction. Thus the originary separation of the ego from the subject is the very origin of the reflection whereby the ego takes itself as its own object. The double itself, however, is a transferable and mutable starting point for the entangling of the "idea of the double" and the ego's reflection in the face of its own destructive separation, which asserts the place where the superego begins its formation of its form according to its own determinations. The unexpected transformation of the superego shapes the effects of the encounter with the fear of death but only insofar as its sovereign development and functioning discovers the paradoxical absence of its determinate being. What is uncanny about the double is not its economy of excess in which it is but an empty place into and out of which meaning is emptied and filled according to capacities of self-observation. Rather, the uncanny lies in the "idea of a double" as the clearing away of the empty place where departing and arriving deviate and part ways. The uncanny of the double is precisely that it does not need to double itself because it already has something of a difference that deviates in it. The uncanny is therefore not primarily linked to the copy. It marks a kind of cohabitation between generation of concepts and the concept of heritage (which provide us with departure points), making it impossible to determine, with any certitude, the order in which generations succeed each other. In other words, the otherness of what appears before us does not primordially have to do with reflection and separation but rather with the troubling coincidence of another subject that asserts itself in the uncertainty of the encounter that occurs between chance as necessity and chance as accident.

TRAUMA, ANXIETY, AND THE EXPECTATION OF REAL DANGER

For Freud, the thinking of danger is firmly situated at the intersection between anxiety and anticipation. Real danger is characterized by anything that threatens to cut the ego from itself, since it is the self-separation of the ego that opens the structure of anticipation. Any happening that puts life in danger is thereby elaborated within the psyche according to the possibility of this threat and affects this structure. Consequently, any event, whether external and materially real or internal and psychically real, assumes and is disturbed by the anticipatory structure on the basis of the threat of separation. Insofar as the originary separation has taken place without actually occurring, the first trauma is, according to Freud, the real event—at once internal and external—without happening.

Given its seat in the ego, anxiety does not represent the loss of an object but more precisely the unknown, unwitnessable threat of separation. Any form of anxiety, whether internal or external, whether the amplification of a painful memory or a sudden upsurge of exterior excitation, is also necessarily characterized by an expectation that is its own condition of possibility since, as we see in both Freud's and Lacan's work, the very structure of anticipation is the originary, indestructible form of the unconscious. This peculiar temporality—in which the givenness of anticipation commands the law and action of all occurrence and elaboration—cannot always uphold the distinction between internal and external, between danger as a fright, in which the factor of surprise incites an instant of newness, and danger as fear, in which there is the reactivation and recurrence of an older memory.

In *Inhibitions, Symptoms, and Anxiety*, Freud offers one of his most moving portrayals of the difficult entanglement of the ego, trauma, danger, and anxiety as an expression of psychic helplessness, which, owing again to the work of Rank, he describes as a "danger" that connects the newborn's state of complete dependence upon the mother with the ego's stage of early immaturity.[55] He writes:

> The individual will have made an important advance in his capacity for self-preservation if he can foresee and expect a trauma situation of this kind which entails helplessness, instead of simply waiting for it to happen. Let us call a situation of this kind which contains the determinant for such an expectation a danger-situation. It is in this situation that the signal of anxiety is given. The signal announces:

> 'I am expecting a situation of helplessness to set in', or: 'The present situation reminds me of one of the traumatic experiences I have had before. Therefore I will anticipate the trauma and behave as though it had already come, while there is yet time to turn it aside.' Anxiety is therefore on the one hand an expectation of a trauma, and on the other a repetition of it in a mitigated form. Anxiety is the original reaction to helplessness in trauma and is reproduced later on in the danger-situation as a signal for help. . . . In relation to the traumatic situation, in which the subject is helpless, external and internal dangers, real and instinctual demands converge. Whether the ego is suffering from a pain which will not stop or be experienced as an accumulation of instinctual needs which cannot obtain satisfaction, the economic situation is the same, and the motor helplessness of the ego finds expression in psychic helplessness.[56]

Here, Freud plainly explains that when it comes to the danger situation, the subject is utterly helpless. The distinctions between external and internal danger, real and instinctual demands, and the danger situation and the traumatic situation become one and the same. Accordingly, the ego anticipates the necessity of rendering ineffectual the instinctual cathexis of remembered danger situations and immediately deploys "experimental action." It shifts its gears and tactics in a process that involves reactions to the environment, and begins protecting the psyche precisely by translating its motor helplessness into an *expression* of psychic helplessness, the "automatism of the pleasure-unpleasure principle," whereby it carries out repression as suppression. This expression is manifestly the ego's thinking, which generates the self-reflection of helplessness. Thus it does not matter whether the trauma is materially real or psychically real; it is always already triggered by and belongs to the structure of anticipation. It is thereby called an event without being precisely because it inheres in the experience of the mortiferous separation from the most fragile part of oneself at the site of its maximal fragilization. The fragmented and indestructible, as Lacan perfectly put it, horizon of anticipation.[57]

We know that this remarkable anticipatory structure, the inescapable citadel of annihilation, depends for its possibility on the originary difference between primordial temporality and subjective time, and thus on death as both its signatory and operator. It is precisely as Freud himself says: the traumatic situation "contains the determinant for such an expectation a danger-situation." The fear of death is the determinate object that constructs this most elegant structure, ensures its own immortality in the functioning of psychic life as the form of the unconscious, and puts into motion the regimes of events that constitute the psychic elaboration of trauma. Thus the traumatic situation only has triggering power within this fortress; but it forever remains imprisoned within the specter of death's ghostly silhouette. There is, as Freud urges us to consider, another scenario: the traumatic moment.

THE TRAUMATIC MOMENT

Having thus established, in his evolving theory of anxiety, that the double of the originary separation—the specter of separation—is an experimental action, an agency of transformation that plays with the imbricated composition of the external and the internal, Freud presses the question of what precisely constitutes the object of fear in the scenario of external danger: "What is it that is actually dangerous and actually feared in a situation of danger of this kind?"[58] He immediately points out that birth, as the primary model for the state of anxiety, "calls up in mental experience a state of highly tense excitation," which the pleasure principle cannot handle by its normal rules of operation. Freud deems this the traumatic moment.[59]

Accordingly, the logical correlative to the succession that characterizes the inversion in his thinking of anxiety from his *1915 Papers* to the 1926 *Inhibitions, Symptoms, and Anxiety* (neurotic anxiety is changed into realistic anxiety and the scenario of real danger) is the following: "what is feared, what is the object of anxiety, is invariably the *emergence* of a traumatic moment," before which the pleasure principle's usual mode of operation also begins to fail.[60] We are quickly and decidedly close to Freud's earlier discussion about traumatic flashbacks and nightmares, which awaken the patient into another fright, in *Beyond the Pleasure Principle*. But let us not hasten towards the familiar conclusion that banishes the fear of the emergence of a traumatic moment to the structure of anticipation. Here, the occurrence of trauma is the feared object of anxiety. In the traumatic situation that comes to affect anticipation, death is the feared object of the ego. A striking difference, with which we must contend, presents itself.

In the traumatic situation, trauma is a triggering influence that activates a specific regime of events—the ego complexifies itself, takes leave of itself, and puts into motion the automatism of the pleasure principle by sending out anxiety as a signal. In the traumatic moment, by contrast, trauma also possesses a shaping power whereby anxiety is not awakened by the ego's feelers as a signal of an earlier situation of danger but rather constructed by the original repressions that arise directly from the traumatic moment, in the moment of the ego's initial encounter with an excessive libidinal demand.[61] For the ego, there is a singularity in the invariability of the here and now of this first moment. It is true, Freud notes, that these first repressions form their anxieties on the model of birth, but they are nonetheless "generated anew for fresh reason."[62] *The occurrence of the traumatic moment is an event with being insofar as a new and different form of anxiety is born.*

Anxiety is thereby characterized by a twofold starting point—one that is the direct consequence of the singularity of the invariable initial traumatic moment and one that is the signal that anticipates and threatens the repetition of trauma. In the difference between the two resides the often overlooked matter of relative quantities. Freud reminds us of what we know from *Beyond the Pleasure Principle*, that it is only the magnitude of the sudden upsurge of excitation that translates the impressions caused by the violence of a breach that immobilizes the usual functioning of the pleasure principle and confers upon the situation of danger its significance. Certainly then, in both the scenario of the traumatic moment and the scenario of the traumatic situation, the primary operation of the pleasure principle as guarding against a particular injury to the psychical economies is derailed, causing the ego to relinquish its narcissistic libidinal cathexis in order to make use of an "experimental cathexis"—anxiety as a signal. There is, however, a period of amplification in between the two forms of anxiety, in which the impulses of self-preservation coincide with those of the pleasure principle.

We should be perfectly clear that the drives of self-preservation, which belong to the life drives, and thus the sexual drives, are "component instincts" that constitute the beginning of one's own death.[63] Generally speaking, to the sexual drives are distinct in their capacity to alter the aims of objects, to exchange one for the other, to replace one satisfaction for another, and so forth. Usually, then, the self-preservation instincts are rigid and admit no delay or alteration in the relation between aim and object. However, in the case of trauma, the duality of the ego imparts its own alterations upon the instinctual impulses, thereby dissolving the applicability of this distinction to the ego-instincts. While every instinct of self-preservation unquestionably remains, for Freud, a response to the possibility of mortal separation, it is not at all accurate to assume that the sexual instincts play no role whatsoever in the formation of traumatic neuroses, and that they are only formed on the basis of a threat to the drives of self-preservation alone. He states this very plainly in *Inhibitions, Symptoms, and Anxiety*:

> If anxiety is the reaction of the ego to danger, we shall be tempted to regard the traumatic neuroses, which so often follow upon a narrow escape from death, as a direct result of a fear of death (or a fear *for* life) and to dismiss from our minds the question of castration and the dependent relations of the ego. Most of those who observed the traumatic neuroses that occurred during the last war took this line, and triumphantly announced that proof was now forthcoming that a threat to the drive of self-preservation could by itself produce a neurosis without any admixture of sexual factors and without requiring any of the complicated hypotheses of psychoanalysis.[64]

In underscoring the link between the danger of death, the threat of castration, and the ego's dependent relations (of which the world outside is among these relations), Freud draws attention to the concept of narcissism as that which "emphasizes the libidinal character of the drive of self-preservation."[65] The point here is not the reiteration of what is well known—that the force of trauma, which throws the immanent movement toward the preservation of life and thus toward death, is the circuitous path that is itself a further detour. Rather, the point is that the two forms of anxiety offer us a way of thinking the coherence between object cathexes and the libidinal cathexis of the ego, whereby the diversions of the ego's libidinal cathexis towards object cathexes in traumatic neuroses are at once diverted expressions of the duality of chance and their figural correspondences.

Granted, even though Freud defines trauma as an effraction that unexpectedly breaches the psyche, he never abandons the concept of the first separation, that of the ego from itself, as the first trauma. Accordingly, the state of unpreparedness of the psyche merely supplies us with its own knowledge of the originary anticipatory structure of the psyche. Fundamentally, for Freud, every event, every accident is elaborated along the horizon of the anticipation of danger; the indelible is the structure of the effacement of the subject. This is why, for him, the immediacy of presence (the here and now) in the traumatic moment has both determining and triggering powers, and is at once an external event and a lived event without being more one than the other. It is also precisely why it becomes very difficult to uphold a distinction between the traumatic moment and the traumatic situation since if anything can be said to begin as the former, the latter is immanent within it. But there nevertheless remains the memory of this first time.

While anxiety is ultimately the abridged term for expectation, a state of readiness expectation, and a particular mode of defense, we cannot ignore the moment of amplification that belongs to trauma, that occurs as a distinct period of neuronal motion in which anxiety appears as two forms of an impulse that power up the automatism of the pleasure principle, the very heart of the ego's experimental action. In this sense, the traumatic moment is a piece that escapes the dimension of the traumatic scenario, the psyche's first encounter with the effraction that happens to it, but is nevertheless the gateway to it. The traumatic moment is a particular temporalized instant during which the ego engenders the very architecture and mechanisms of its protection. This is an accomplishment that includes a dimension of contingency and adventure, that is experience, because the ego acquires and readies its own material for itself.

Is it not possible to deduce that trauma is an event with a witness—the ego? Certainly the movement of the processes of psychic mechanisms involving the ego and anxiety would suggest this. Despite the confounding of the traumatic moment and the traumatic scenario, the psyche experiences the singularity of the immediate presence of the initial encounter, an experience that repeats and to which the awakening into another fright testifies.

THE EVENT REVISITED: THE PERIOD OF FANTASY

A rhetorical detour is necessary to address the pertinent objection that if in trauma any productive, organizing power is accorded to the *a posteriori*, then this owes to the primacy of the symbolic and thus to the power of the originality of metaphoricity, for which Lacan's famous concept of the unconscious as structured like a language provides a strong foundation. Also, Freud maintains that not only is any symbolic activity foreign to the nervous system, but the nervous system is not the author of any fictionalizing power. For Freud, what makes the psychic apparatus unique is its autonomous capacity for fiction, screens, scenes, and so forth; it is a completely sovereign apparatus of representation. I would suggest that taken together, the development of the psyche and the psychoanalytic concept of time that I have thus far been developing challenges the absolute irreducibility and exteriority of the missed encounter with death.

Freud's discovery of the latency period is a good place from which to begin the elaboration of an answer. In *Studies in Hysteria*, Freud observes a curious relationship in which sexually charged events occurring early in childhood are often activated only with another event. The first event is deemed traumatic "after the fact" only insofar as the second event, the mnemic elaboration of the first event, is just as determining a source as the actual occurrence of the original scene. Citing that "hysterics suffer mainly from reminiscences," Freud posits that the surge of overwhelming excitations is produced from the later scene, which in turn situates the pathological phenomenon of the first event within memory.

Earlier, in the first chapter, I established that in Freud's work the link between the external (exogenous) accident and internal (endogenous) events, between chance and necessity, relies on the transference from one signification of the event into the other. No event can be characterized as the external event coming from material reality or the lived event, which is meaningful for the psyche, without it being translated into the other as a symptom. In their "Preliminary Communication," Freud and Breuer establish "*an analogy between the pathogenesis of common hysteria and that of traumatic neuroses*" in order to develop "traumatic hysteria" as a particular concept and diagnosable condition.[66] According to their findings, "*each individual hysterical symptom immediately and permanently disappeared when we had succeeded in bringing clearly to light the memory of the event by which it was provoked and in arousing its accompanying affect* . . . . Recollection without affect almost invariably produces no results."[67] Thus the "precipitating" event or cause must coincide with an affect in order for there to be an effective traumatic impact.[68] Traumatic neurosis, however, presents a unique scenario in which the affect of fright is the operative cause and not the psychical injury per se. Furthermore, the precipitating causes of hysterical symptoms "can only be described as psychical traumas" and any experience that conjures "distressing affects—such as those of fright, anxiety, shame or psychical pain—may operate as a trauma of this kind."[69] There is clearly a correspondence between traumatic shock and hysteria. But what is the nature of this correspondence?

Freud's answer to this question, which is also his point of critical departure from Breuer, is clearly articulated in the prefaces to the two editions of *Studies in Hysteria*: the principal role of sexuality.[70] As Catherine Malabou rightly underscores, "Sexuality (in both of its senses, 'empirical' and 'transcendental,' as it were) thus appears to Freud as the privileged site of an encounter between the exogenous and the endogenous, or, more precisely, as the privileged site between an *incident* and *signification*."[71] Breuer, as evidenced in the case of Anna O., focuses on the accidental factor as the underlying cause of traumatic hysteria. Despite the fact that Breuer and Freud depart from one another on the nature of the equivalence between hysteria and traumatic shock, they nevertheless concur on the finding that in traumatic hysteria the precipitating event must be linked in particular with the affect of fright and thus with the overwhelming emotions of shock, paralysis, and psychical pain caused by the excessive influx of excitations. Trauma thereby asserts the *coincidence* between an unexpected, external accident and the surplus of endogenous excitations.

Drawing upon the phenomenon of conversion, Breuer goes on to distinguish between affect and an *affective idea*, in which the latter indicates the active, conscious presence of an affect that is discharged in an "abnormal reflex," and which subsequently provokes an emotional excess and yet another surge of excitations. An example that Breuer draws upon is the affect of fright that impedes the flow of thoughts while the affective idea of danger is active. The excessive incursion of excitations is converted into a symptom, which for Breuer is a somatic phenomenon that is described as a psychic trauma. In his assessment, psychic trauma is a "foreign body" that, in continuing to incite a surplus of excitations within the nervous system, "must continue to be regarded as an agent still at work."[72] So conversion involves the coincidence between affect and event as it inheres within the nervous system as a tripartite internal coincidence between an external shock, the insurgence of a surplus of excitations that the nervous system cannot properly diffuse, and the overwhelming emotions that eventually translate into a symptom.

Freud, in turn, does not omit the role of the nervous system but instead separates the accident from it in the sense that it is not formative of the relation between the pure chance of an external event and the pure chance for the lived event. As he indicates in *Studies in Hysteria* and reiterates in *Beyond the Pleasure Principle*, the accident cannot, irrespective of its force and on its own, cause an alteration in the general economy of energetics. It causes a large-scale disturbance "in the functioning of the organism's energy."[73] In both the structure and the economy of the accident, Freud exchanges what is for Breuer the causal power and value of the alteration in the energetics of the nervous system with a symbolic dimension that is irreducible to neural functioning. Throughout his writings, Freud maintains that this symbolic dimension is formative of the synthesis between the external, material event and the internal, lived event and assigns the energetic economy of sexuality and its vicissitudes causal authority.

Two aspects are thus evident from the beginning of his formulation of the relation between the eventual forces, which evolves in its increasingly nuanced interpretation of the role of the external event in trauma. First, Freud maintains the supremacy of the external event over the internal, lived event. Second, he situates a particular element in all of its radicality at the forefront: fantasy. Without fantasy, there would be no intimate exteriority, as Lacan calls it; there would be no internalization of shock and, subsequently, no conversion into affect or symptom.

The shift in Freud's thinking of the nature of the synthesis between the internal event and the external event is most noticeable in the transition from the seduction theory to the concept of a psychic reality. In the 1896 "Heredity and the Aetiology of the Neuroses," Freud cites the following as the three main causes of neuroses: "conditions" (namely hereditary); "concurrent causes" (emotions and traumatic accidents); and "specific causes" that are linked to "important events," which occur in early childhood and are acts of sexual assault.[74] The gravity of these incidences ranges from the most "severe traumas" like rape and incest to the "astonishingly trivial."[75] Freud asserts that one or multiple external events that relate to an actual, factual reality of a premature sexual experience lie within every case of hysteria. In other words, neurotic symptoms arise from instances of actual childhood seduction scenarios that are based in the patient's historical reality. Freud soon comes to question, however, the widespread prevalence of sexual abuse among children in families and admits that he "over-estimated the frequency of" sexual seduction scenarios.[76] He revises his assertion by suggesting instead that many memories were fantasies retroactively constructed like screen memories.[77] If patients suffering from hysteria trace their symptoms to traumas that did not have a material source, then such scenarios, Freud posits, were necessarily created in fantasy.

Fantasy is thus a "psychical reality" that should be considered alongside the historical reality, or "practical reality" as Freud also calls it, but not confused with it.[78] Insofar as external events derive their efficacy from the activation of certain fantasies and the excitations that these fantasies incite, fantasy itself becomes constitutive of a duality between external and lived events rather than of what arises in between them. Here Freud upholds the role of fantasy in the formation of the relation between the outside event and the internal event, but he maintains a distinction between psychical and material reality. "We should still do well to remember," he concludes in *The Interpretation of Dreams*, "that *psychical reality* is a particular form of existence not to be confused with *material reality*."[79] Yet in the seventh and final chapter of the work, which opens with his narrative of the "Dream of the Burning Child," Freud offers a more nuanced and primary understanding of psychical reality as a manifold and of fantasy as the mode in which the event occurs in the psyche.

I will return to this dream and look at Lacan's reading of Freud's interpretation in a moment. For now, let us turn briefly to the famous case of the Wolf Man, which corroborates the idea that, in designating a primordial unity between chance and necessity, between the external accident and the internal elaboration of the psychic event, fantasy itself is an initiatory occurrence of the doubling of chance that convokes and inheres in the manifold of psychical reality. Published in the 1918 "From the History of an Infantile Neurosis," Freud's distinctive narrative begins with the Wolf Man's account of a terrifying dream in which he discovers a group of white wolves sitting in a tree in front of a window. In terror, he screams, awakening himself from the dream.[80] In the course of the analysis, Freud eventually comes to ascertain that the core of the dream concerns an unconscious scenario in which, at the age of one and a half years, the Wolf Man, in his parents' bedroom because of an illness, witnesses his parents' copulating. Unlike in the slightly earlier text, "General Theory of the Neuroses," Freud does not emphasize a distinction between repressed traces of a material reality and the retroactive comprehension or significance of mnemic traces after its registration.[81] In fact, Freud goes a step further to say that the question of whether the primal scene in the Wolf Man's case "is phantasy or a real experience . . . is not in fact a matter of very great importance." "These scenes," he continues, "of observing parental intercourse, of being seduced in childhood, and of being threatened with castration are unquestionably *an inherited endowment, a phylogenetic heritage*, but they may just as easily be acquired by personal experience."[82] What is germane to the Wolf Man case is precisely the primal scene as fantasy—not as a phantasmatic construction—and the inseparability of fantasy from the very structure of psychic reality.

There are two domains of fantasy implicit in this conclusion. The first, which is the one directly referenced in the exclusion of the irrelevant, concerns the *fantasy of* alternate scenarios, the stories and fictions patients tell themselves as a leave taking from everyday, practical reality. This is the level Freud and Breuer discuss as hypnoid states in *Studies in Hysteria*. The other, the one that is elaborated in the "Dream of the Burning Child," involves *fantasy as* the unexpected encounter and the link between the internal accident and its metaphoric and metonymic figurations. The threefold aspect of fantasy—fantasy of different scenarios, fantasy as the surprise occurrence, and fantasy as the linking between the accident and its rhetorical detours—comes to form an unstable primary imbrication within which the unconscious scenario unfolds. Freud's reference to the threat of castration extends "inherited endowment" and "phylogenetic history" beyond simply meaning the transmission or reservoir of collective experience. Here, then, Freud invokes not only the phylogenetic inheritance of fantasy as constitutive of the unity of the external event and the internal event but also, at the same time, the phylogenetic inheritance of the unconscious as the mutable form of the relation between the structure of the psyche and the concept of its essential self-separation.

As the occurrence of the unconscious event, fantasy dissolves the clear distinction between psychical reality and the intimate inside of the psyche and the material, historical reality to the outside, giving rise instead to psychic reality as a manifold, within which the surprise happening of a chance event is coincident with its mimetic figurations in the internal elaboration of the event. Thus the pure chance of an event occurs as much from within the psyche as it does from the outside, since an irruption from the outside triggers a more primary source, which becomes the precipitating cause of the constellation of symptoms. Accordingly, psychical reality thereby assembles itself into a new form that plays with the activity and passivity of the uncanny double of chance, which is the double of necessity. In other words, at play in our encounters with what is really traumatic is the doubling of chance as accident and chance as necessity and the double of necessity as both mechanistic and teleological.

THE CHANCE FOR THE THING

In the case of trauma, the chance occurrence of an accident opens the possibility for the necessity of the repetition compulsion whereby the necessity for the compulsion to repeat is meaningful and, by the same token, the meaning of this compulsion is necessary. In this, the duality of chance there is an immediate tautology between meaning and necessity, for we cannot know for certain which value, the necessity of compulsion as meaningful or the meaning of compulsion as necessary, is greater and lesser. It is thus equally the necessity of compulsion (telos) and necessary compulsion (mechanism); the determining causal value of the difference between these two types of necessities is improbable. Thus trauma also involves the doubling of the category of necessity. As the protective functioning of the ego also demonstrates, chance itself is a heterology in which chance as accident and chance as necessity are always confounded by each other, including the other in its own processes.

The distinction between the traumatic moment and the traumatic scenario dissolves, and as we know, the compulsion to repeat takes over. However, as already discussed, the repetition compulsion ultimately adheres to the pleasure principle. Accordingly, it is impossible to think the general movement of being within the anticipatory structure without convoking a being-towards-existent. By the same logic, the imperishable character of psychic life signifies the other of its own signification as being-towards-death.[83]

In a sense, Lacan accounts for this in his thinking of the Real. For Lacan, the inaugural separation of the ego by *das Ding*—the Thing at the core of the unconscious—is the mark of an ontological lack, the absolute other within the ego. This division, which is necessarily the inscription of finitude, is the architecture of the horizon of expectation. This is the fundamental structure by which the Thing, by virtue of its own structure, is opened to being represented. The Thing is situated in the relation that puts the subject in the "mediating function between the real and the signifier," but it can only ever be represented by emptiness, precisely because it *cannot* be represented by anything else.[84] The Thing, which is "at the center only in the sense that it is excluded," "the prehistoric Other that it is impossible to forget," can only be posited by the unconscious, whereby the unconscious represents by articulation (in the form of a sign) "representation as a function of apprehending" as exterior.[85] The horizon of expectation that the Thing comes to affect can "only be posited as a final structure, as a vanishing point of any reality."[86] Consequently, the very architecture of the structure of anticipation inheres in its own structural negation. This negation inscribes itself therein by opening the structure of the event as the conjugated possibility between a chance occurrence and an event that is wholly unanticipated, unthinkable, impossible, and thus cannot occur.

The strange meeting place where the horizon touches its own vanishing point constitutes the phenomenon of accidental chance and where, then, the concept and subject of the unconscious come to be. For Lacan, the events that cannot happen belong to the Real and thereby exceed any horizon of anticipation. It is in this sense that the Real is exterior to the Symbolic and is not inscribed by lack. It cannot, properly speaking, correspond to any symbol, which requires a structure unified in its fissures in order for the unconscious to represent, as an articulation point in the form of a symbol, representation as a function of apprehending. This is what is properly traumatic in trauma—the utterly inassimilable and unapprehendable that is beyond occurring. For Lacan, the Thing is that which is immanent within the Real, "the primordial real" that dwells within the very constitution of the psyche in its own suffering "from the signifier."[87]

This suffering, this strange self-touching of the Thing in pain, is the doubling of the Thing, the instant in which its own deep interiority emerges from within its own intimacy and prefigures its own destruction as an avowal that an aspect of itself has already taken leave into nothingness. The signifier from which the Thing suffers is precisely its own spectral double that represents itself in the presentation of signification as the existence of a hole, an emptiness, as *a nothing.* Insofar as the ghostly double of the Thing is the "something strange to me, . . . at the heart of me," that opens the psyche to its constituting of the anticipatory horizon of its own annihilation, the Thing is the occurrence of the Real, the persistent occurring of the unthinkable event to me.[88] The operations of the Thing function to enable the unconscious to anticipate its emergence as the relation to its own destruction, to become, in a sense, its own subject. Starting from itself, the Thing takes a form and develops by self-differentiating itself. We might thus say that in this regard, the Thing, as the missed encounter, is acquired and prepared as the material for the very architecture of the psyche.

Lacan himself hints at this in his discussion of the construction of the vase:

> Now if you consider the vase from the point of view I first proposed, as an object made to represent the existence of the emptiness at the center of the real that is called the Thing, this emptiness as represented in the representation presents itself as a *nihil*, as nothing. And that is why the potter . . . creates the vase with his hand around this emptiness, creates it, just like the mythical creator, *ex nihilo*, starting with a hole.[89]

At once the potter and the hole, the Thing inheres within itself as a form of the immanent alteration of the ontological lack of an encounter with the missed encounter since the structure of the unconscious depends for its possibility on the givenness of the lacunary functioning of the Thing. Its function is thereby holomorphic, and on the basis of this operation produces itself as a figure of isomorphic difference. The Thing presents itself as a *non-thing*, a *nothing* that is an ontological porosity, a structural spacing that rather curiously involves the destruction of the impossibility of the Real.

While Lacan suggests a notion of materiality in the narrative of the vase, everything is eventually consigned to his well-known Real-Symbolic-Imaginary triad.[90] However, the appearance of the Thing as the absolute gap occurs on the basis of the necessity of the Symbolic in the psyche. The Symbolic is the accident that befalls the Thing, forever consigning this other Thing to suffer in the symbolic fabric of the psyche, trapped within the heterology of chance and the tautology between necessity and meaning. Thanks to the Symbolic, the Real is separated from itself. The Real, then, is impure, for there is always the inclusion of symbolic function in it. We recall that for Lacan, the essential question raised by symbolic function is the introduction of a gap. The functioning of the primordially real Thing is the pure space through which the meaning of the other, suffering, symbolic Thing is shaped, methodically, as though with the routine habit of a potter's hands, as the structural spacing of the unconscious. Born somewhere between chance and necessity, the death of the real Thing is at once the occurring of the symbolic vitality of the psyche and the appearance of itself as an otherness within, as a form that suffers in being an ontological nothing in its symbolic excesses. In its shifting between the Real and the Symbolic, the Thing shapes its own meaning. Its hands form to the effects of encounter between the Real and the Symbolic, while this encounter takes hold in the different stages of gathering itself. The referential function of the other, symbolic Thing is present only as an absence functioning to form the spacing in which meaning is contoured into the molding of the urn as psychic life, the originarily anticipatory structure of the horizon of expectation from which and within which the Lacanian triad of the Real-Symbolic-Imaginary promulgates itself. Both the referential function and the material object, the symbolic and the material coincide in the point of the leaving behind and letting go of the place of void. The very symbolic fabric of psychic life finds itself in the contact point between material and symbolic function. The Thing names the real element that survives its own destruction and that can arrive to hold together the triad. The vase, this figural structure of structural spacing, follows after as its form of posterity and as the apprehension of a new object—a pure novelty which does not pertain to *creation ex nihilo* but rather concerns the irrevocable change in the form of an intimate relationship.

AUTOMATON BURNING

In his famous reading of Freud's reading of the "Dream of the Burning Child" in "Tuché and Automaton," Lacan elaborates on the duality of chance in the concept of the Real, which lies "at the heart of experience."[91] His discussion is guided by a question simply expressed: "Where do we meet this real?"[92]

For Lacan, the central question apropos the dream, which he reads as a dream of the accident, is, "Where is the reality in this accident?"[93] Is the accident that which awakens the father; is it the falling candle that sets the child's arm alight; or does it lie within the dream itself, that is, in the actual appearance of the child, standing before his father's bed, grabbing his arm, speaking to him? What is authentically burning?

In Lacan's assessment, the *tuché*, which he translates as "the encounter with the real," designates the occurrence of the Real by chance and without any contrivance or mechanism. By contrast, the *automaton*, which he allocates as "the return, the coming-back, the insistence of the signs, designate the modes by which we see ourselves governed by the pleasure principle."[94] It describes the mechanized insistence of the network of signifiers by which the pleasure principle primarily operates to minimize stimuli within the psychic economy of energy. They are the automatism of the "*subjectifying* homeostasis that orients the whole functioning defined by the pleasure principle"; they are the events that can be assimilated by the psyche.[95]

Lacan begins his analysis by recalling that in the prior week's lecture he identified the necessity of revising the relation between Aristotle's use of the terms *tuché* and *automaton*, which he notes as having long suffered from incorrect translations in the function of cause. In that vein, Lacan notes that the *tuché* in Aristotle means "fortune," which denotes something that occurs purely by chance. Lacan authorizes his final translation of the term as the encounter with the Real on the basis of his interpretation and translation of *tuché* as chance (*hasard*). *Tuché* in Lacan's ultimate meaning operates according to the Real as the essentially missed encounter. Insofar as its first presentation in the origin of analytic experience is in the form of trauma, *tuché* designates the real as the unanticipatable, undetermined, and inassimilable manner in which trauma occurs, strictly by chance, as the impossible encounter with the Impossible Real.

The *automaton*, by contrast, denotes functional instruments and moving devices with a concealed mechanism so that it appears to operate spontaneously and autonomously, or has already intrinsic within it this particular character of operation. For Lacan, then, the automaton first designates something that works entirely by its own self-sufficient and self-sustaining mechanism that repeats by and as a mechanical necessity. This is the basis on which his use of *automaton* expands on Aristotle's notion of the concept and the network of signifiers inherited from modern mathematics to name the particular mode in which the unconscious immediately quilts the effects of the Real into the psychic fabric of the Symbolic.[96] This Impossible Real, then, "is that which always lies behind the automaton."[97] In "Tuché and Automaton" Lacan plainly maintains that "Freud's true preoccupation," as the case of the Wolf Man reveals the role of fantasy to him, is precisely the "the question—what is the first encounter, the real, that lies behind the phantasy?"[98] His preoccupation with this question "can almost be described as an anguish," and "this real brings with it the subject, almost by force so directing the research, that, after all, we can today ask ourselves whether this fever, *this presence*, might have conditioned the belated accident of his psychosis."[99] From the outset, then, he challenges the necessity and meaning of Freud's proclamation that the dream confirms the theory of dreams of wish-fulfillment.[100]

Lacan is perfectly aware that trauma is of "apparently accidental origin" and that the function of the real in repetition and the insistence of signs is itself the occurrence of *tuché* "*as if by chance*."[101] At the same time, and in answer to the question of how the dream can impel the subject to produce the mechanism that enables the repetition of trauma, he contends that an essential part of the real remains the prisoner of the toils of the pleasure principle. And let us not forget that, for Lacan, the Thing actually suffers from the signifier. This is precisely why, for Lacan, the reality of the automaton, the son's words, "Father, can't you see that I'm burning?," "the firebrand—of itself it brings fire where it falls," is more real than the material reality of the falling candle and the burning that ensues.[102] The "terrible vision of the dead son taking the father by the arm" is the beyond the reality of the *tuché*, the flame; the "something actually more fatal," the essential real imprisoned in the laboring unconscious, within its labored firebrands, occurs "*by means*" of the *tuché*.[103] The "forever missed" encounter thereby occurs "between the dream and awakening," between the sleeping father and the not yet awakened father, between the father and his son.

"The awakening," Lacan tells us, "shows us the waking state of the subject's consciousness in representation of what has happened," which is the irrefutable materiality of the death of a child. But Lacan asks again, "In this entirely sleeping world," "what, then, is the accident?"[104] Lacan will go on to elaborate the awakening itself as its own accident, its own trauma that "works in two directions—and that the awakening that resituates us in a constituted and represented reality carries out" the task of unveiling and liberating the prisoner, the piece of the real that is the Real, for which there is only one *delegate*, that governs the symbolic activity of psychic life.[105] To answer and conclude his essay, he revisits the *fort/da* game in *Beyond the Pleasure Principle*, ultimately arguing that "the reel is not the mother reduced to a little ball by some magical game[,] . . . it is a small part of the subject that detaches itself from him while still remaining his, still retained."[106] Regardless of whether or not events may happen as lived events that can be assimilated into the psyche, they still occur within the horizon of expectation that is, for both Freud and Lacan, the originary structure of separation, which can never be effaced since by its very nature separation signifies its own destruction. Thus in both Freud and Lacan, separation retroactively gives death its figurative content. For Freud, castration is the phenomenal form of the threat of death because it means separation, and for Lacan, it is the presence of the Thing that is the threat of death. In any case, the real causal power lies in the structure of separation as an *a priori* structure of effacement. For them, every external trauma is internalized into the adventure of separated symptoms. No matter what actually happens, trauma is a destruction that always already occurs; and thus it is a kind of transcendental structure insofar as the anticipation of danger is the horizon that opens toward every event. Consequently, erasure is always a structure, the repetition of a more originary trauma. The determining character of this structure, reinforced by the indestructible primacy of the symbolic, is what remains resolutely problematic in both the Freudian and the Lacanian thought of trauma.

Now, for Lacan, what is authentically burning in the dream are the words of the child, the child's address to the father, "Father can't you see I'm burning," and not the actual arm of the child. The contingent encounter of reality—the candle falls onto the cloth covering the dead child and sets it alight—triggers the true Real, which is the unbearable apparition of the child reproaching his father. Thus the reality of the automaton, the reality of something more fatal, is more real than the *tuché*. The *tuché* is only a means by which the automaton or the Real happens because, as Lacan says, "What is repeated, in fact, is always . . . something that occurs *as if by chance*."[107] Chance is only an "as if," a motif. Thus the proper finality of fortune, of contingency lies in the symbolic. What finally happens in the missed encounter with the Real is the Symbolic. Accordingly, there is only one mode of occurrence and it is the automaton. Thanks to the Symbolic, the Real, the automaton, the necessity of the repetition of a more originary trauma occurs only as if by chance. Trauma thereby encounters the Symbolic and is held prisoner by it.

Yet the paradoxical, proximal space of sleep that is also the space of dreaming is, for Lacan, the moment between perception and consciousness. Having recounted an episode in which he is awakened by a knock on the door before he actually awakens, Lacan questions the nature of who he is at the precise moment that he knows he is waking up, that he is "*knocked up*":[108]

> But here I must question myself as to what I am at that moment—at the moment, so immediately before and so separate, which is that in which I began to dream under the effect of the knocking which is, to all appearance, what woke me. Observe what I am directing you towards—towards the symmetry of that structure that makes me, after the awakening knock, able to sustain myself, apparently, makes of me only consciousness.[109]

Somewhere in that pregnant moment between perception and consciousness, the "symmetry of that structure that makes me," is born the strange yet familiar figure of the boy—at once, without necessarily being one more than the other, "gone" and "there." This boy reaches out and grabs his father's arm. But the father he touches is also actually a subject; for he is the fundamentally altered father qua father whose own alteration occurs in the shaping of a knowing of the death of a child. In the gap of separated forms, the place not able to be properly assigned to consciousness or the unconscious, occurs, actually by chance, the intimate meeting between a subject and another subject. In that instant, the formation of a form of grasping death arranges and displays itself, making different effects of the missed encounter. Here, now in Lacan's text, we discover again an opening of the order of succession to its chance—another instance in which the father follows after the son. This time, the mute cry of the dead son finally arrives to interrupt the sequence of filiation so as to let the father go, leaving him the chance to appear after.

In this moment of real anguish, the boy's words, "Father, can't you see that I'm burning?," are, as Lacan says, more real; there is "more reality in this message than in the noise by which the father also identifies the strange reality of what is happening in the room next door."[110] The sentence is the "firebrand—of itself it brings fire where it falls," the *automaton* that is more real than the *tuché* of the actual fire and the noise in the next room. These radically disembodied words, separated from their body, come to affect the repetition of rite, the careful molding of an urn. The automatism of repetition accomplishes the *subjectifying* homeostasis of the definiteness to the horrible fortune of the burning child by its own inventive work of signifying commemoration, "a rite, an endlessly repeated act" for the "not very memorable encounter."[111]

For Lacan, the finality of the *tuché*, of that which happens, lies in the automatism of separated words. So indeed the dream is an encounter with the Real as a missed encounter. But does not Lacan's analysis miss the form of something else? In this "knocked up" moment of fantasy, in the place of the unconscious scenario where father and son touch, separation realizes itself, inuring the symbolic in the grasp of the missed encounter. Somewhere between the before and the after, the burning words are thrown into the adventure of the play of repetition's return. As a result, there is the altering form of a relation that takes hold, dodges the place of void between departure and arrival, and deviates the usual order of things. In that pregnant meeting, a starting point for another path without an originary determination emerges. Such is the place where the energies of the dynamic interactions of the psyche's separation from itself occurs as a process of transformation that forces the otherness of the real to change itself. It is here that, by chance, the necessities of trauma involve the encounter with the missed encountered; it is here, in this unstable place that trauma includes the experience, the adventure, and the surprise of the intimate meeting with the nonanticipatable form of the son who paradoxically detaches his father in leaving him the chance to awaken.

Far from only affecting the structure of anticipation and expressing the imperishability of the relation between the psyche and its own destruction, might we not deduce that trauma starts a process of transformation by opening a difference in causality and an exchange in necessity itself? It is true that every trauma is a trace, but every trace, as Freud describes in "A Note upon the 'Mystic Writing-Pad,'" "grooves" itself into the deep waxen layer of the unconscious and is "visible as dark writing upon the otherwise smooth whitish-grey surface of the celluloid."[112] Even the trace itself has the shape of a furrow; something of it arrives to come before the "dark writing" that confers visibility upon the borderlines of its absence. Even though it is after, this element arrives before the before to organize a new path between things. In this sense, trauma is not only an indissociable contact point between the material and symbolic. It is also the interface where the border between the two is impossible to define.

CHAPTER 3

Whither Partition?

"His name," we are told, "was Bishan Singh but people now called him Toba Tek Singh."[1] When news that, a few years after the Partition, the governments of India and Pakistan had ordered the transfer of inmates in lunatic asylums finally reaches Bishan, he inquires, "Where is Toba Tek Singh?"[2] No one can answer his question. When Bishan's turn to cross the border finally arrives, he asks the official the same question. He is told that Toba Tek Singh is in Pakistan. The news sends Bishan back towards the line of his fellow inmates. Refusing to be transferred, he exclaims, "Toba Tek Singh is here!"[3]

In a moment occupied by ambiguity, the guards attempt to assuage Bishan, explaining, "Look, Toba Tek Singh is in Hindustan now—and if he's not there yet, we'll send him there immediately."[4] He installs himself in protest in "a place between the borders and stood there as if no power in the world could move him."[5] At the approach of dawn, a loud scream pierces the silence, and "in the middle, on a stretch of land that had no name, lay Toba Tek Singh," prostrate.[6]

Where is Toba Tek Singh? The ambiguity of this question will never be deprived, for hithermost are the currents of the other questions: Where is Toba Tek Singh going, where did Toba Tek Singh actually arrive, is Toba Tek Singh expiring? Whither the unassigned, nameless place between borders and without a proper destination?[7]

Whether seen as irreducibly outside or as recuperable into the historiographical project, scholars of the 1947 Partition of British India have consistently taken up the uncertainty at work in the story's central query, "Where is Toba Tek Singh?," and in Bishan's tragic end for the primacy of its symbolic dimension. How and what the ambiguity signifies about the relations between the creation and institution of new, independent nations, the profound quandary of national belonging, social suffering, and individual pain is taken to be a surplus—understood as something that exceeds or escapes discourses of trauma, modernity, nationalism, imperialism, colonialism, and so forth—that gathers and gives meaning to the experience of Partition as an inassimilable event.[8] The studies share attention to the ambiguity as disclosing a repressed ambivalence at the origin of traditional discourses of colonialism and modernity that produces a form of sovereignty that haunts, disturbs, resists, and subverts their presumed hegemony. As Bhabha puts it, "The ambivalence at the source of traditional discourses on authority enables a form of subversion, founded on the undecidability that turns the discursive conditions of dominance into the grounds of intervention."[9] In other words, "Where is Toba Tek Singh?" is a question of the form of nation. What are the politics of the truth and meaning of the formations of its forms: forms of identity; forms of subjects and subjectivities; forms of political organization; forms of culture; forms of society; forms of discourse; forms of citizenship; forms of difference, forms of thought; forms of sovereignty; forms of agency; forms of life?

Laying prostrate, the matter and meaning of Toba Tek Singh's resistance ultimately lies in the eventality of the fortune of the place "in between borders," the place with "no name," where "no power" can "move him." This place, which is at once within, between, and after the Partition, cannot be designated in any sense. It is without a proper name, and it does not belong to either nation. It is an unassigned place empty of legacies, of discourses, of predeterminations, of telos. At the same time, however, it is the interface where the different Toba Tek Singhs confront each other in the intersections of memory and inheritances, congealing, as it were, into an unprecedented form of resistance that has no proper object or subject. Insofar as he does not properly belong to either nation and because he fallen on a ground that does not have a stable objective reference point, precisely what is Toba Tek Singh resisting? The quick reply is that he is resisting transfer itself: the troubling transfer of his home to a new place without actually moving to a different geographical location and the troubling transfer of himself to a new geographical location without actually changing the place of his identity. Put otherwise, he is playing with the unstable relationships between things. The problem the question "Where is Toba Tek Singh?" projects is the unsettling of an unstable partition as a surface after-effect that is foundational to the regimes of division, separation, allocation, and differentiation that come before it. Such then is the central question that this present chapter seeks to address: whither partition?

AT THE BORDER

According to its own concept that designates a process of division, differentiation, allocation, and separation, partition inheres in and convokes itself in the ambiguity of the border as ordering the organization, orientation, and development of the formations of forms. The border is a limit between what has been divided and a limit in itself. The semantic and rhetorical spaciousness of the word *border* expresses its symbolic and material powers, bearing witness to the discursive aspects of spatiality and its signifying structures of representation, as well as to itself as a differentiated zone within which organizations of forms of society, culture, and politics emerge in producing their own conditions of possibility. John Welchman, whose work draws upon the work of Derrida, Foucault, Laclau, Bhabha, and others, captures this conceptualization when he writes, "No longer a mere threshold or instrument of demarcation, the border is a crucial zone through which contemporary (political, social, cultural) formations negotiate with received knowledge and reconstitute the 'horizon' of discursive identity."[10] This idea of the border, however, is preoccupied by its own space within the horizon of possibility. It establishes a cartography (and diagnosis) of regimes of identity and difference that puts us in the heart of the question of posterity and in the movements to produce posterity.[11]

The involution of materialism and idealism that has come to designate the concept of the border is strikingly, though disturbingly, captured by Deleuze and Guattari's development of the construction, selection, and metamorphoses of *bodies without organs* along "lines of flight" in *A Thousand Plateaus*.[12] At and within the border there is a difference of intensity in being that disrupts the consistency of active instances from passivities. This disruption is a process of selection that sorts the differences in identities that are most apt to maintain a tradition while producing the criteria as it operates. Accordingly, whatever form of body, of posterity may escape and cross the barrier in its metamorphoses is always and only "a question of a becoming that includes the maximum of differences as a difference of intensity."[13] Thus the eventality of thinking the border as a space through which the horizon of identity is reconstituted is the accomplishment of the intensified body without organs according to its own principle of selection. Any dialectical output of materialism will lead one back to the finality of the border as a figural improvisation of a deconstructed body without organs. As such, the border remains a transcendental operation that works upon all forms of identity that turn upon it as bodies without organs in order to ensure the accomplishment of its subjects as such. Does this mean that even if the structure of the living being is a crisscrossing between self-invention and given, the living being cannot avoid the certain fate of becoming a more incorporeal body? Are we always, in a sense, at the border, accomplishing an essential erasure of the subject in the formation of new forms of identity?

This concept of the border brings to light the border as a cloven structure, an originarily contradictory unity that yields form to partition as ordering formation according to the order of succession. In both its materialisms and symbolizations, the border is at once a repeating act and an act of repetition that confers value to the organization of geopolitical formations in the order, creating standards, hierarchies, and types of identity in the process. The border marks itself twice according to the law of reversal that turns upon the essential division between the symbolic and the material. The border may therefore be understood as a moving limit, but it circulates only between repetitions of the same that are different and repetitions of difference that are the same. Relative to itself, this idea of the border cannot be a fundamentally shifting terrain. It also cannot by itself produce posterity because it proceeds from the tendency of partition to organize the very idea of proper—of what is authentic to a place, a people, a society, a nation, a community, a culture, and so forth. Such a conceptualization of the border conceives of the ideas of inheritance and heritage according to the double aporia of genealogical inversion as the initiatory reversal. Even if the border is thought of as a materialism, it is nonetheless constituted by a teleological horizon that regulates and orients the gestures of the self-organization through which new identities and subjects acquire their content. In other words, any formative process is subordinated to the finality of the border as the necessary mode of occurring of difference and identity; like a postcard, such a concept of the border only produces a strange stereotype from within a closed loop.

THE TIME OF (FOR) NATION

In *Dissemination*, Derrida very clearly establishes the structure of the "double mark" as ordering the order of all appearances and the process of appearing in general; and thus as the law according to which all philosophical concepts are necessarily marked twice, first by their metaphysical meaning and then by their ultrametaphysical significance.[14] It "sketches out the closure of metaphysics: not as a border enclosing some homogenous space but according to a noncircular, entirely other, figure."[15] Even more explicitly, he writes:

> This structure of the *double mark* . . . is worked in turn: the rule according to which every concept necessarily receives two similar marks—a repetition without identity—one mark inside and the other outside the deconstructed system. . . . No concept, no name, no signifier can escape this structure.[16]

Deconstruction is not, properly speaking, a method, an analysis, or a critique; it is a tendency that supersedes the dialectical process.[17] More precisely, as the movement that destabilizes the apparent unity of all tradition, deconstruction inscribes and articulates what occurs—not what is or is not. This is its own operation of rupture, of originary reversal working through the philosophical tradition to reveal how the concept of tradition or else heritage is originarily structured by the irreducibility of the plurality of language.[18] Accordingly, deconstruction does not have and cannot have any author or translator. Even though the double mark "escapes the pertinence or authority of truth," the redoubling of the mark, as an economy of excess and supplementarity, accomplishes in advance the dislocating force of deconstruction.[19]

Deconstruction is thereby always at work. The self-deconstructive tendency, the spacing and temporization that predestines presence to differ irreducibly from itself and consigns it to the irreducible play of noncoincidence with itself, corresponds to a form of writing and the movement of the trace. As it follows, the trace does not derive from any sort of presence but always comes before presence and that which it traces. The deconstruction of presence, then, does not emerge from any sort of presence outside but rather destroys the very concept of presence before it has the chance to establish its own autonomy precisely by exposing its own originary break, its own initiatory catastrophe.

In his famous play with the double inscription in "DissemiNation," Bhabha presents the most sustained confrontation between the dialectic and deconstruction in his thinking of the narrative of modernity and "the finitude of the nation."[20] In this text, Bhabha develops a concept of the modern nation as a "ubiquitous form of *living* the locality of culture" that always unveils and resists "the mark of the ambivalence of the nation as a narrative strategy" in "the chronotrope of the local."[21] The value of the indeterminacy of modernity is precisely its own repressed ambivalence. Drawing upon Benjamin's concepts of empty time and the time of the now, Bhabha brings to light the encounter between the "continuist, accumulative temporality" of "the pedagogies of life and will" and the time of the present in which "the repetitious, recursive strategy of the performative" enunciates itself.[22] This confrontation occurs in the "living principle of the people . . . as that continual process by which . . . [t]he scraps, patches, and rags of daily life must be repeatedly turned into the signs of a national culture, while the very act of the narrative performance interpellates a growing circle of national subjects."[23] It works to uncover the ambivalences of the productions of modernity that become "the site of *writing the nation*." [24] As Bhabha develops it, these sites are the productions of forms of cultural difference that seize hold of the effects of the encounter between the time of the now and the empty time of modernity in order to engender new traditions that become the necessary modality of disrupting the homogeneity of history as that which establishes a seriality of causal connections.[25]

For Bhabha, the time of the now is the time of writing that throws "into relief the temporal, social differences that interrupt our collusive sense of cultural contemporaneity," opening the Heideggerian "boundary, the place from which something begins its presencing in a movement not dissimilar to the ambulant, ambivalent articulation of the beyond."[26] It is the borderline on which we live, the place from which forms of life begin their self-developments. In Bhabha, the finitude of the nation consists in the "liminality of the people—their double inscription as pedagogical objects and performative subjects."[27] This, according to him, necessitates the time of writing since it is only the dissemination of the irreducible plurality of the singular that accomplishes the disavowal and subversion of teleologies of development and horizontal continuities of community in the organization of new forms of life.[28]

Any new, unexpected formation of a form of cultural difference, such as the figure of hybridity or any other marginalized or preemptively excluded people and community, born of a dialectic of historical materialism is given in advance by the character of the finality of contingency as the necessary mode of the occurring of subversion and agency. This telos of finality guides, arranges, and determines in advance the structure within which any self-formative process begins and develops.[29] Any form of nation therefore corresponds directly to the determining causal value of contingency. In other words, the borderline, which is another name for the source in Bhabha, understands the difference between modern time and local time as the primordial difference between ontological horizon and objective time of appearances. The finitude of the nation names the temporality of the question of the intelligibility of the nation and its diverse modes of being. Thus the production of forms of cultural difference is regulated by a prior orientation towards an object, which is the before or original contingency, that is nothing other than the writing of difference. The dynamic immanent to Bhabha's dialectic is deconstruction. There is, then, no production or apprehension of a pure novelty but only instead the production of the stereotyped character of pure production or development.

In Bhabha, this is because the symbolic, defined as the doubling and double—the excess over the real, the supplement—is the critical strategy for any form of resistance, subversion, agency, and sovereignty. The concept of colonial mimicry, which acts out the ambivalence of colonial power through a series of parodic and permanent rituals that evoke cultural difference and other new forms of identity, is precisely such a strategy. Although Bhabha opposes mimesis to the symbolic, the gap or the time lag produced by the play of the difference between the immediate temporality and modern temporality, and thus by the symbolic process within, is its condition of possibility. In "The Postcolonial and the Postmodern: The Question of Agency," he puts it this way:

> The contingency of the subject as agent is articulated in a double dimension, a dramatic action. The signified is distanced; the resulting time lag opens up the space between the lexical and the grammatical, between enunciation and enounced. . . . Then, suddenly, this in-between spatial dimension, this distancing, converts itself into the temporality of the 'throw' that iteratively (re)turns the subject as a moment of conclusion and control: a historically or contextually specific subject."[30]

Whatever new forms of identity are born of such a strategy, such subjectivated identities are nonetheless the presentation that formalizes the effects and consequences in accordance with the logic of structural spacing. They ultimately serve to confirm the classical divide between the material and the symbolic and sustain the primacy of the symbolic in general. So this deconstructive inspired idea of mimicry cannot by itself produce a form of posterity that overcomes the structures of power it seeks to subvert because it does transform the character of the relation between the before and beyond and the after. In her materialist critique of Bhabha's deconstructions of the hegemonies of colonial power and modernity, Benita Parry goes so far as to call it a "self-righteous rhetoric of resistance."[31]

Insofar as Bhabha's development of forms of postcolonial and postmodern agency in *The Location of Culture* seeks itself in the enunciations that give form to the effects of the colonial encounter and of modernity, it recalls what Althusser designates as the "transformed, disguised form of idealism," the materialism that is constituted and entirely governed by particular teleological horizons. Bhabha's materiality bears the mark of the primacy of the trace, and thus of the symbolic over matter.[32] Althusser carries this materialism to its utmost, posing "it may be a mere trace, the materiality of the gesture which leaves a trace and is indiscernable from the trace that it leaves on the wall of a cave or a sheet of paper."[33] Further, "Derrida has shown that the primacy of trace (of writing) is to be found even in the phoneme produced by the speaking voice. The primacy of materiality is universal. This does not mean that the primacy of the infrastructure (mistakenly conceived as the sum of the material productive forces plus raw materials) is determinant in the last instant." Rather, everything depends on the aleatory, on the "thinking of contingency as a modality of necessity," which is resolutely nondialectical because both the origins and the effects of the encounter proceed from the dice throw.[34] In other words, such materialism is a specific form of causality that operates as a regulative structure formulated to organize and order the phenomenal distributions of the relations to events implied in identity and differentiation.

It would seem, then, that we are irrevocably placed, as Bhabha puts it, beyond "the border of our times," on the borderlines of the living being, situated firmly in the empty space of excess that is over, above, and exterior to us.[35] Like Toba Tek Singh, we are seized at the border against our will, assigned and directed in advance towards territories of differentiation. How, then, do we release partition from its own symbolic hold?

AT THE PARTITION

In bringing together the two logics of contradiction in the dialectic and in deconstruction, Bhabha presents us with a synthesis that confirms postcolonial agency as an expression of the radical human historicity by grounding the temporality of the nation and the plurality of its modes of being in the pure production of the horizon of authentic possibility and thereby in the achievement of its borders. The time of the postcolonial and the question of agency it brings about is the effect of man's truth as a history of being, which is the also the history of the metaphysical tradition. Man proceeds according to the classical distinction of life as given by an irremediable divide between the natural, and hence the material, and the spiritual or symbolic. The latter is that which assigns and gives meaning to the material aspects of life and to living in general. The symbolic is indissolubly linked to the spiritual domain insofar as it consists in convoking the activities and passivities of living as the very fashioning of being into a work of art. We are always in the mold of affection for the self. As it has been widely shown in the notable work of Said, Spivak, Chakrabarty, Fukuyama, and Sen, for example, the historicity of this most human partition unequivocally belongs to the tradition of continental philosophy and the narrative of European enlightenment and consciousness.[36] The very thinking of the transition from Being to being as the appropriating event, of the *a priori* synthesis as the originary relation between self and object, or the phenomenal givenness of the other, formalizes the effects of this partition as a kind of transcendental structure in positing these relations as pre-existing forms of knowledge and thinking about the subject. Such relations synthesize and demonstrate the subject as a constitutively European man, the human norm who describes and prescribes the naming of the name of man as the body who thinks, knows, judges, and cognizes, and who is thereby the work of art.

An unequivocal effect of what has been termed the postmodern has been the delocalization and destabilization of the ontological and epistemological singularity of the Enlightenment. By unveiling the tendencies of the presumed superiority of modernity in narratives of cultural and intellectual self-reflection as modes for the production of knowledge, the phylogenetic inheritances and ontogenetic transferences of the term "postcolonial" bear witness to this.[37] At the same time, then, the term "postcolonial" bears the double mark of the sovereignty of the symbolic as that which necessarily surpasses the material. Let us think of the following themes in which this is the case in the analytic strategies of postcolonial critique: irreducibility and crossing out as the literary expression of a new messianism; confrontations with forms of epistemic violence that produce in advance of the subject the nondialectilizable (im)possible silence; dialectical sublations within negative economies of value; the inassimilable presence of a global or globalized forms of despondencies that describe the capitalist economies of our contemporary lives.[38] As it presently stands, the postcolonial, whether it speaks of the border as that which separates territories, nations, and cultures or mutely gestures towards the outline of the border that separates terms and concepts, produces a subject who constantly emerges as the repeating character of what repeats itself out of its destruction.

Whether these modes of postcolonial critique proceed from the materialist vantage, from the symbolic, or from other critical gestures that unveil what the philosophical tradition reveals of its own acts of epistemic violence, there is the shared idea of the postcolonial as playing a double role. Insofar as it asserts a coincidence with the inauguration of new political organizations, it necessarily challenges its own structure and conditions of possibility. In itself, the postcolonial is already a tool for the deconstruction of hegemony and its direct and indirect structures of power. The self-reflexivity of its doubling economy is that which enables the ideological and materialist critiques of the term itself and of those that it deploys by producing the excesses that cannot be taken up by the political discourses that are themselves constricted by their own borders. Whether a strategy of postcolonial critique pertains to the doubling economy of negativity of deconstruction or the dialectic, or to the nondialectizable moments in between the two, it is in the thinking of the production of the supplementarity of indeterminacy—understood here as that which, by necessity, supersedes, exceeds, or is outside the structures and systems that produces its conditions of possibility or impossibility—as the critical tool for the formation of resistances and sovereignties that the essential partition of life remains. What assigns meaning to the materially real or describes the development, evolution, and transformation of diverse forms of life is the designation of life as essentially and irremediably divided within itself, and as necessarily starting out with the need to overcome itself, to transgress itself, to separate from itself in order to be a sovereign subject who exists in the world. The very structure within which the dynamism between liberty and determinisms and between materialisms and typological schemas originates is the symbolic domain of being. Inasmuch as the postcolonial proceeds according to a doubling economy of surplus, the irreducible plurality of possibilities and potentialities of life will always cut back through itself, and cancel itself out in the dissemination of difference. In spite of its precise analytics of the deduction of the plurality of subjects, the postcolonial turns upon the irreducible promise of the plural and the necessity of dissemination as the most effective deconstructive answer to sovereignty. This idea of the work of pluralization is indebted to the old distinction of life as given by the ineluctable need of life to fragment itself in order to resist and be sovereign. What the postcolonial approach misses is, as Althusser would say, "a materialism of the encounter" that "gives form", in its processes, to the effects of the duality between contingency as necessity and necessity as contingency without singularly turning upon the reversibility of difference and the order of succession.[39] As it stands, what the postcolonial lacks is the inclusion of the unstable character of the causal necessity of partition in its movement of self-differentiating development and evolution.

The unique history of the 1947 Partition of India offers us another way.

THE TWILIGHT OF PARTITION: THE 1947 PARTITION OF BRITISH INDIA

It was famously at the stroke of the midnight hour between August 14 and 15, 1947, that British imperial rule formally ended and independence in India and Pakistan was inaugurated.[40] This auspicious moment has come to be encapsulated by Jawaharlal Nehru's iconic speech, "Tryst with Destiny," which he delivered to the Constituent Assembly of India on the eve of August 14, 1947, in New Delhi. "Long years ago," Nehru begins, "we made a tryst with destiny, and now the time comes when we shall redeem our pledge, not wholly or in full measure, but very substantially." "At the stroke of the midnight hour," he continues, "when the world sleeps, India will awake to life and freedom."[41] In his nationwide address after taking the oath as the first governor-general of Pakistan on August 15, Muhammad Ali Jinnah echoes the sentiments of the fulfillment of will and freedom: "August 15 is the birthday of the independent and sovereign State of

Pakistan. It marks the fulfillment of the destiny of the Muslim nation which made great sacrifices in the past few years to have its homeland."[42] In both speeches, the emphasis on destiny brings to the fore an interplay of determinisms (self-determinations and predeterminations) and liberty from within the framework of partition. Destiny in both speeches appears as that which enables this interplay inasmuch as it proceeds from the unstable determinisms of the legacies of colonialism. The fulfillment of destiny is expressed as a particular freeing of partition itself as a place of dispossession, one that relinquishes the accumulations of the past in beginning the formative processes of India and Pakistan as new, independent nations. Such is the shared expression of freedom and the awakening of the nations into life. But in what ways does the assertion of this new form of life organize and indicate itself?

Although partition and independence imply other, they are not one and the same. Within partition itself, there are multiple conceptions of the Partition of 1947 that are invoked in the elaboration of the thinking of the event of Partition.[43] The roles determinisms and sovereignty play in the making of the 1947 Partition and continue to play in the ongoing development of India and Pakistan as modern nation-states have been extensively discussed.[44] In addition, and in the wake of more public acknowledgments of the conspicuous silence in Partition historiography regarding, for example, the experiential dimensions of communal violence, mass migration, and the abduction of women, the event of Partition became an explicit thinking of the trauma of Partition.[45]

What concerns us here, however, is not any kind of genealogical or historical critique of the Partition that entails an elaboration of the different references and meanings signaled in the term. Notwithstanding that such critiques are not within the scope of this project, they will elide the question of what, in their own structures, the concepts of history and genealogy, both of which take human history to be the other of natural history or nature, owe to the classical concept of life as partitioned and pertaining to existence. What is germane to my focus on the 1947 Partition is a particular relation between the subject and repetition that is gathered in the establishing of new geographic borders. More precisely, I aim to think the border as an event that makes the material and the symbolic meet and fuse together rather than as an appropriating event or figural improvisation that repeats itself from its own erasures. To that end, my reading is not interested in demonstrating how repetition itself produces something nonidentical—breaches and singularities that necessarily interrupt and break the law of its mechanisms. In other words, my attention to the ambiguity of the return of repetition is not in the vein of the Deleuzian production of discontinuities that unfold their capacity for their return in order to beget new traditions under the sign of difference, which is echoed in Bhabha's concept of hybridity.[46] To the contrary, I seek to undertake a reading of the borders that turns upon the elaboration of the traumatic event that I developed in the previous chapters in order to question the ideological, regulative tendencies of the structure of partition. To do so, I will traverse the ways cleared by the geographic formation of the borders between Pakistan and India and thus by their forms of posterity.

IN THE NAME OF THE LINGUISTIC-GRAPHIC BORDER?

It goes without saying that there are numerous factors without which the 1947 Partition cannot be thought. Among them are of course the name and the border. Quite simply, partition cannot be thought without attention to the drawing of entirely new geographic borders where they had not previously existed or without India and Pakistan as the proper names of nations. Let us focus on the etymology of the word *Pakistan*, which will bring to light how, even in the order of the linguistic act, there is an interplay that paradoxically dissolves the question of being named as the origin authorizing any formative process of individuation.

Although there are several accounts of who first conceptualized the word *Pakistan*, its spoken and written announcements are largely attributed to Sir Muhammad Iqbal, a Muslim poet, philosopher, and politician, and Rahmat Ali, a Cambridge University student at the time. In his presidential address to the twenty-fifth session of the All-India Muslim League on December 29, 1930, Iqbal pronounced a territorial vision for the possibility of an independent Muslim nation by naming the Muslim-majority provinces in the northwestern region of the subcontinent.[47] Three years later, Ali self-published a pamphlet titled "Now or Never: Are We to Live or Perish Forever" in response to Iqbal's call for a Muslim-majority state in the northwestern region of British India. In that pamphlet, he outlined "PAKSTAN" as an acronym representing the different Muslim-majority provinces: "P" for Punjab, "A" for Afghania (the Northwest frontier province), "K" for Kashmir, "S" for Sindh, and "stan" for Baluchistan.[48] Ali also drew attention to the Urdu and Persian translations of the prefix *pak-* and the suffix *-stan*. The Persian word *pak* translates as "pure" and "clean." In both Urdu and Persian, the suffix *-stan* translates as "land of," "place of," or "country." *Stan* is itself a cognate of the Sanskrit word *-sthǎna*, which also refers to place. On the matter of the inclusion of the "I," some accounts note that the letter was inserted to help with the pronunciation of "PAKSTAN," while others suggest that the "I" stands for the Indus region or for Iran.[49]

Itself a form of nation comprising borders between territories and letters, ideas and territories, letters and words, and so forth, Pakistan organizes itself into a name in the process of forming the localization of a place. In this moment in which there is no precedent for the actual name itself, the geographic and symbolic dimensions of the word are equally intricated, without being more one than the other. The form of a word acquires and assembles its geographic material for its own use and symbolizations, producing a form of a proper name that follows after. The name Pakistan was its own invention—a novel name named for itself. What is very interesting is that even in the idea of Pakistan, which arranges its different territories into an acronym and then a name, we see three levels of formation occurring in the very constitution of Pakistan as a subject and subjectivity of an independent Muslim nation: on the level of the formation of thought about the ideal nation, in the institution of the will to start its new political life, and in the linguistic shaping of its topography. In each level, there is something of the schematization of scheme that comes into view—a particular style of the formation and transformation of a thought into a proper name. What we see is a gradual differentiation and complexification in letters, which means that, in each of its historical occurrences, the path of the interplay between the geographic and the symbolic is assembled and manifested in different ways.

Any demonstration of Pakistan as a proper name and of its performative functions as a speech act will quickly lead us to the necessity of the sign as the very condition of possibility for the idea of the proper name. The idea of a proper name, as Derrida has shown, requires the invention of a sign of a singular entity and no one or nothing else. At the same time, it cannot be absolutely unique since to be a name necessitates being a signifier, which means it must be at once repeatable and significant. The proper name is a mode of address in which we must be able to call it and call it again even in the absence of its referent. A proper name is an attempt to utter something repeatable about the unrepeatable. Accordingly, a proper name cannot be simultaneously proper and name.[50]

The name "Pakistan" thereby seems to adhere to the law and action of the double inscription, and accordingly, to the general movement of the trace. Further, any subsequent configuration of Pakistan—political, geographic, social, cultural—would thereby be the irreducible graphic element of the structure of writing. This writing is taken as arche-writing, the spacing and temporization that, from the very beginning, ensures that presence can never be coincident with itself as presence. In other words, it is not a writing in the everyday sense of producing a written form; rather, the name always and irremediably corresponds to a form of writing. Hence the name itself appears to undermine the intimate intricacy between the material and the symbolic by returning the name only to its figural and sculptural principle of meaning. However, and far from suggesting that discussions of any form of Pakistan originarily obliges us towards a theorizing of writing as the paradigmatic apparatus that explains and programs all formative processes and meanings by way of a hermeneutics of the discursive differences that track the ambivalent, contradictory movements of the symbolic, the process of establishing a new cartography for the subcontinent undermines the grammatological moment.

THE MANY-MAPPED SUBCONTINENT

The Lahore Resolution of 1940 played a key role in the Partition. Though the notion of a Muslim-majority homeland was not a new concept, it was the first time that the Muslim League adopted Pakistan as a policy. Jinnah's demand for a Muslim state consisted of two major elements. First, the Muslim-majority provinces in northeastern and northwestern India would be established as separate areas with no adjustment to the existing boundaries unless it was absolutely necessary and minimal. No population transfers or disturbances of ties to homeland and location were envisioned in this part of the plan. Second, a balance of power must be established between Pakistan as a Muslim-majority state in relation to the Hindu-dominated "Hindustan."[51] On August 16, 1946, a three-day riot in Calcutta erupted on the streets in response to mounting tensions regarding different proposals that would meet the substance of the demands from both the Indian National Congress and the Muslim League. These riots, which came to be known as the Great Calcutta Killing, ignited a wave of communal riots that transformed the Indian subcontinent.[52]

Cyril Radcliffe arrived in India on July 8, 1947, only six weeks before the August 15 deadline for Britain's exit from the subcontinent.[53] His task, as chairman of the Boundary Commission, was to divide the Bengal and Punjab provinces in a manner that would help resolve the conflicts and communal riots. He was accompanied in this assignment by eight High Court judges, four from both provinces, each of whom was elected by the Indian National Congress and the Muslim League. Two separate commissions, one for each region, were created with four commissioners heading their respective regional focus. Although equal representation was granted to both parties, disagreements over the precise location of the new borders ultimately resulted in failed negotiations.[54]

Four maps eventually emerged: two maps presented by the Indian National Congress, one map presented by the Muslim League, and one map presented by the Sikh representatives on the Boundary Commission. The borders in each of these maps were drawn according to certain criteria, such as concerns for existing administrative boundaries, census figures on population distribution, and infrastructure elements such as power lines and waterways. Each of the maps emphasized population distribution, reiterating the value and hierarchy of identifying the territorial demarcations of Hindu, Muslim, and Sikh areas as key criteria for the cartography of the two nations. Each map had the goal of trying to produce order while reproducing ideologies of sovereignty pertaining to communalism, religious identity and questions of citizenship, and the process of decolonization. In the end, there was no consensus among the members of the Boundary Commission as to which map should prevail. One map was criticized for representing areas as bearing a non-Muslim majority when, according to the Muslim League, the area was believed to be populated by a Muslim majority. The Sikh map claimed more of the Punjab region than the maps proposed by the commissioners for the Indian National Congress. The map created by the Muslim League featured Amritsar, a city in northwestern Punjab, not far from Lahore (now a major city in Pakistan), as a small piece of Sikh land completely surrounded by Muslim territories.

Instead, Radcliffe himself drew out his final decisions on different maps before the August 15 deadline, ending the commission's cartography of the Indian subcontinent.[55] The mapping of new geographic borders where they had never before existed resulted in the separation of contiguous majority areas, as indicated in the commission's maps, and it specifically divided Lahore and Amritsar, two large urban areas in the Punjab region that are approximately twenty-five miles apart. His different maps, the ones he used for drawing his lines and the ones he attached to his award, revealed his preference—and some would argue need—for maintaining already exiting administrative boundaries over natural boundaries such as rivers. As Lucy Chester puts it, "Radcliffe's use of administrative boundaries reinforced the impact of imperial rule. . . . Radcliffe's award retained for the postcolonial states of India and Pakistan (whether they wanted it or not) a central element of the legacy of imperial rule."[56]

Although independence in the newly anointed nation-states of India and Pakistan was announced at midnight between August 14 and 15, the precise locations of the newly established borders were not revealed. In the days immediately following the declaration of independence, the geographic reality of the borders was unknown to the people. No one knew where Pakistan and India actually began and ended. The Radcliffe Award was announced on August 17 when Mountbatten publicly released the map, despite strong opposition from Pakistani and Indian leaders who had seen the award on the previous day. The final map featured a two-winged Pakistan separated by about one thousand miles of Indian territory. It was, as Jinnah famously remarked, "a moth eaten Pakistan."[57]

In her very interesting article, "The Fashioning of a Frontier: The Radcliffe Line and Bengal's Borders Landscape 1947–52," Joya Chatterji argues against the often deployed surgical analogies to describe the Partition, and in particular the drawing of new borders as a "purely technical affair" meant to repair the ailing subcontinent.[58] She writes:

> So partition was in no sense like an operation that was concluded in August 1947. The border is far from being the trace of an event long over, like a healed and fading incision scar. It is still in the process of being formed. Its creation was not merely a matter of drawing a line through a map by a qualified technocrat: it was created again and again, by a number of different agencies, on the ground through which it ran. Its shape (both literally and metaphorically) has varied, and continues to vary, through time.[59]

Although Chatterji ultimately offers for scrutiny an argument about the remainders of the border, her analogy of the trace of an event to a healed and diminishing organic wound in fact recalls the term "trauma" to its familiar Greek definition, which means "wound" and derives from the verb *titrosko*, 'to pierce'. Crucial here is that the Greek definition upholds the ambiguity between an organic and symbolic injury. Trauma indicates a wound that results from either a psychical or physical intrusion—without necessarily being more one than the other. Thus in her emphasis on the ongoing, open formative process of the borders as a persisting series of changing shapes, Chatterji presents an idea of the border as a suture that engenders, in its process of stitching together the opens ends of the wound, a form of a partition that encounters the Partition, something like what Freud calls "a State within a State."[60] While she aims to dispel the surgical metaphors used to describe the end of the Partition, Chatterji nonetheless formulates the border as that which, from one assemblage to the next, operates over the same material. Insofar as the border, like trauma, is conceived as an articulation point between different regimes of transmission, it is at once synchronic and diachronic, at once structural and mutable.

Still, Chatterji's discussion of the ongoing alterations of the border recalls Freud's affirmation that "alterations of the ego," which are caused by disturbances, pertain to changes in character.[61] While "alterations of the ego" exhibit agency, they are either "comparable to scars, . . . left behind," or, if they are the effect of trauma, they end "often enough in a complete devastation or fragmentation of the ego" that void the appearance of a new character.[62] While this does not suggest that the creation of form through illness is solely responsible for the formation of new identities, we can begin to see that every act of the border recreating, reshaping, and engendering itself is a return of the organic wound and thus a return of repetition that makes the form and functioning of the border mutable and transformable. Like a scar, the border, suturing the skin of the territory and text, makes and distributes its meaning differently, revealing within it new organizations that render different effects of truth.

In a one sense, the Radcliffe Award was also like an Althusserian crystallization, a fortuitous encounter that gave form to the effects of the confrontations with the cohabitations between necessity and chance.[63] That is, it was a moment when the double of necessity—expressed as the need to adhere to a time line, the need to resolve a conflict with the Boundary Commission, the need to quell communal violence, the need to transfer power from one regime to another, the need for the geographic demarcations of the new nations—responded to internal demands in its confrontation with different contingencies by opening difference in causality. There was both a teleological and mechanistic necessity at work in the autonomous processes of self-differentiation that constituted and developed the nations as independent forms of posterity. In this regard, the Indian and Pakistani nations do not merely come after imperial rule, they are the following generations that are producing an essential transformability in the border. Thus even the crystallization of the border, of the giving and taking of its form as a materialism of the encounter, is challenged by the ambiguity of the relation to the activity and passivity of award that renders the border an unstable place, shifting between the directions of identity and difference.

On the one hand, the Radcliffe Award was adjudicating and differentiating. It conferred value and meaning upon forms of nation and forms of identity in subordinating them to criteria, and thus to a sorting of difference in the political order. On the other hand, it was unallocating and self-renewing in the sense that it unbinded itself from its own rule. It disengaged and dispossessed itself from the sovereignty of colonial legacies by opening the field of the subcontinent to developmental processes of increasing complexity involved in nation building. The ambiguity of the Award loosened the frame of colonial and imperial determinism, allowing for the interplay between freedom and determinisms from within the structure and mutability of the border. It forced the borders to write a preface, as it were, to India and Pakistan's independence, but it could not determine what followed. In a particular way, then, the borders are always engendering the conditions for a contingent form of an encounter that are not dictated by a hierarchical anteriority of meaning. Their own legitimacies are constantly being made possible by the confrontations with the developing, evolving, and transforming self-inventions of the Indian and Pakistani nations.

The point here to underscore is that the Radcliffe Award inhered in not just the profound ambiguity between what was and was not assigned, but more precisely in the unstable ground upon which it attempted to settle the violent divisions. In its own interactions with the identities and subjects that it creates, the border challenges, by loosening its own frame, the priority of the link between the category of difference and the idea of the interminable return of the same and copy. The eventality of the border involves processes of releasing difference within necessity, contingency, and causality and not in determining the outcomes of their relation by reproducing the elements in order to engender and constitute itself. Less like an ailing wound and more like the movements of transformations in the wound, the border dissolves the law of reversibility in order to make possible ways of apprehending novel forms of nation, of posterity that can no longer be termed the postcolonial.

In this, the geographic border shares something of the indeterminacy of authorization occurring in the emergence of the name "Pakistan" in the 1930s. These different forms of nation are always shifting the directions of difference and identity, playing with both the reversibility and irreversibility of difference, and thereby unblocking from within the structures of knowledge about the subject, a deeper place in which there is no concept of what is proper to itself. What the many-mapped subcontinent helps brings into view is the power of the subject to unsettle the places of the partitions that have been handed down by the heritage, tradition, and history of a past that already passed away.

WITHOUT DESTINATION

There is a rather moving, brief moment in Amitav Ghosh's novel *The Shadow Lines* in which Tridib, the narrator's cousin, discusses the entwining nature of the experiences of love and justice. "Between that state and its metaphor," he says, "there is no more connection than there is between a word, such as mat, and the thing itself: they are utterly indifferent to each other, so that we may heap the metaphors . . . till the end of our abilities, and yet find no trace at all of the state itself."[64] A similar expression is echoed a bit later, in the grandmother's pronouncement that her upcoming visit to Dhaka, her childhood home, was not one in which she could "come home to Dhaka."[65] During the time of her childhood, Dhaka was part of British India. The 1947 Partition shifted the place of Dhaka to Pakistan, and then, following the 1971 Liberation War of Bangladesh, Dhaka became the capital location of Bangladesh. Her home was a shifting place without changing location, a place without a proper destination. At the heart of the grandmother's turmoil is a quandary about the altering and unstable character of contact with her home. In response to her dilemma, the narrator proclaims: "How could you . . . 'come' home to Dhaka? You don't know the difference between coming and going!"[66]

In these two moments, there is a shared expression of disconnection, dispossession, and uncertainty. For Tridib, the primary concern lies not in the arbitrariness of the sign and the power of the empty value of the floating signifier or in its capacity to erase the line to the state. Rather, it pertains to an indifference of the conditions of materially real experience to the conditions of the figural, and visa versa, that is internal to their dynamic. This indifference disrupts any pregiven synthetic power of one over the other. An estranged, disaffected couple, the state and the metaphor discover themselves intimately entangled without knowing the difference. That we establish connections and that we insist on the symbolic to its ends, accumulating it in the process, is just, according to Tridib, a matter of happy chance. For such an activity is but the persistent becoming of contingency in the manner and style of an assumed necessity. In themselves, the symbol and the material thing are an indifferent, yet imbricated couple, not contained in the other for their freedoms and givens, but nevertheless belonging to and interacting with the other. They are always forming and transforming the matter and meaning of themselves, without going outside the interactive economies they make possible. As such, there is always a resistance to the primacy of the graphic element from within its own frame, a certain dialectical clearing the way for expressions of the intermediary state of things that cannot be absorbed by the program of trace.

For what we see in the grandmother is her status as a foreigner without a proper destination. Between her and her home, she cannot identify difference in advance; there are no set criteria that will determine the direction of her identity. Between the grandmother and place, there is a strange indifference that reveals the unstable relation between coming and going, between arriving and deriving, and the shifting between the immovability of what has actually changed and the reversibility of change. In the final instance, there is also a trauma that cannot anticipate the posterior form of separation, for it is one that occurs in the formation of a border that engenders an identity without a proper name.

THE BORDERLINES OF TRAUMA

Discussions about the trauma of the Partition tend to emphasize the singularity of inassimilable explosions, which are constitutively involuted and solicited in each other: the eruption of an unprecedented level of communal violence; mass migration; forms of gendered violence; intensities of conflations between religious identities and their politicizations; the loss of home and family; scissions to communities where those with different identities once lived peaceably as neighbors; and crises of belonging, for example.[67] Moreover, such discussions, which emphasize the singularity of trauma as a discourse that produced differentials asserting experiential coincidences between the personal and the collective that cannot be accounted for in the discourses of nationalism, tend to dominate Partition historiography. Like any such experience, the traumas of the Partition inhere in the intersections of the external, materially real event and the internal, psychically lived event, between legacies of colonialism and unprecedented occurrences, and thus in the encounters with missed encounters.

A remarkable aspect of the border illuminated by the process of mapping the Indian subcontinent is precisely its own power to engender and regenerate retroactively the conditions for contingency from within its own doubling economy. Again here, doubling is understood not as the production of excess that proceeds from a tendency towards pure negation but as an internal, interactive dynamic that dismisses the commanding play of the prearranged terms of its own framework by including experience.

Months before the official announcement of the Radcliffe Award, communities and individuals were embroiled in experiences of violent effractions to the psyche in, around, and across the regions that were to become the actual geographic demarcations. The exchange of populations and the communal violence throughout the different regions, cities, and villages came to affect ideas of where the borders between India and Pakistan would be and needed to settle. The trauma turned upon the confrontations between the different types of contingencies of the necessity of borders and the different types of necessities of the contingency of the borders. In a sense, there were two starting points of events that reveal a split in causal character. On the one hand, the border is an unallocatable, unstable shifting ground between things; it has no direction proper to itself. On the other hand, the border is structural to the extent that it governs the differentiated movements of self-development pertaining to both sides. This is not to say that it is doubled by its negative, which then operates to cancel itself. Rather, the border, as one of the subjects of trauma, transformed and instituted itself in its own continuous disconnection from itself through the gradual shaping of the gaps between that which came before and that which followed after the wound. Inseparable from its interactions of external environmental factors, the border was fundamentally moving, at once yielding forms to the effects of the traumatic encounters with the duality of chance and renewing the conditions for the surprising encounters with the contingencies of violence and migration. The border was something like the changing shape of its own indifference to the touching of the wounded, which is an expression of its own state of being wounded. Into the landscape of the subcontinent, the borders, formed by the traumas of violence and migration, carved the wounded territory of otherness. The traumas of the border consisted in releasing a void between the state of things and its metaphors that forced otherness to transform itself. The paradox of the border is precisely that it is a nonsensical place that cannot order forms of knowledge as the similitude of identity and its series of differences. It is the place of coimplication which allows us to think complexity from both sides, coincidentally between the two, without rendering a difference between what is more or less authentically promising.

This opening of the border as the void promising democracy, justice, home, refuge, and legitimacies was itself made possible in part by the expectation of geographic boundaries. At the same time, however, the territories of trauma were subsequently made available for a kind of analysis by the members of the Boundary Commission. Their maps were similar to acts of reading in which each turn produced different maps. In this sense, their borders were themselves linguistic, psychic, political, social, cultural, and geographic acts of reshaping, regenerating, and engendering the changing forms of nation, revealing from within partition new organizations of it. Owing to the mutual, free interactions between the subject and its repetitions, the borders were also surprising returns of repetition.

Partition history, then, seems to share something of the ego's history of self-differentiation and transformation as it occurs from within the energetic economies of psychic life. In one regard, it involves the expressions of its own ontogenetic and phylogenetic heritages and developments in being a particular mode of transmitting political, social, and cultural specificities of the colonial and imperial histories, which issues forth the precolonial and preimperial histories from one region to another. Partition history also refers to the manners and styles of passing these inheritable specificities from one generation to the next in the development of independent nations and the ongoing formations of forms of the nation. In another regard, partition history concerns the ways in which the interplay among the geographic, the linguistic, the social, the cultural, and the psychic is indicated differently in each of its instances. Finally, it relates to the different ways borders are relinquishing themselves through the organizing of memory, alteration, and transformation that take surface after-effects into account. Partition history, we can say, is the unrecorded history of the instances of transformability in the relation between the material (or else, the natural) and the symbolic internal to the lives that produce them. Partition history thus no longer takes the historic to be only the result of their difference, or the other of the progressive time of modernity.

Insofar as the unique development of borders during the 1947 Partition reveals partition to be something like a mutable dialectic between the geographic elements and the symbolic exchanges, is it not possible to suggest that partition history is also both trauma's history and history's trauma, which is to say, the process of the real change in and the relinquishing of their own prior concepts? What would this idea of the relation between trauma and history, which does not consist in rendering meaning as the result of the split between the symbolic and the material, come to look like? It would not evoke the visage of a new form that in its dissemination of difference or parodic miming becomes ungraspable to mimesis itself. Thus it would dismiss the opposition between the performative and the symbolic as the source of postcolonial agency. Without being able to anticipate a complete answer, I will at least say that the growth and development of this idea would involve the experience of its own deconstruction. Perhaps then it would look something like Toba Tek Singh.

Let us ask anew: Where is Toba Tek Singh? The question will never be deprived of its unstable place. When, upon learning that his home village had been assigned to Pakistan, Bishan proclaims "Toba Tek Singh is here!," he refuses to move from his place in between borders. It is in the story's final image of man and land as a double interface between regimes of transference that we begin to see the form of his resistance against the assignation of his identity, of the place of his home, and of his selfhood. It occurs on three levels in the constitution of his subjectivity: in the formation of a thought about the relation between his identity and home, in the institution of his willfulness of will (as Nietzsche would have it, the most radical form of will, the will to will itself) to remain "here," and in the self-contouring of his body and land into the transforming form of a gap between his being and his life. The movement of Bishan's resistance does not bring into view an accumulative process of presencing, an unfolding of becoming. The movement by which the formation and self-differentiation of the thought of the "here" organizes itself, reveals something of its own will. It is a clearing away of the excesses—of the tides of appropriation and possession—that display, by the work of its own energetic economies from within his structure of being, the utterly unnamed, unnameable place without jurisdiction or destination. The resistance and sovereignty of Toba Tek Singh appears as the releasing of the repressed political status of a starting place of dispossession, which is emptied of any kind of determinate being, and thus free of any power that "moves him" towards a certain telos. In a moment when it seems as though absolutely every person and place has been awarded to Pakistan and India, a nonanticipatable, unexpected form of resistance emerges in Toba Tek Singh through the default of the identification of the source. Such is a form of resistance that arrives like a burst of laughter in making a name for itself with all of the resources life contains.

WRITING'S ANGUISH

Writing is "dangerous and anguishing," Derrida asserts in "Force and Signification," because the inscription alone creates meaning precisely by entrusting it to the "groove," to a "relief."[68] The mark takes as its fatal risk the objective of the emancipation of meaning. The mark is itself the mark of its own finitude, for "writing as the origin of pure historicity, pure traditionality, is only the *telos* of a history of writing whose philosophy is always to come."[69] Writing, and by accord any concept of the subject that comes to affect its structure and movements, repeats itself out of its own deconstruction. This is its truth, which is always already inscribed therein. In this regard, the finality of borders, even their mobility, never comes from the outside like a pure accident. If we take Toba Tek Singh to be in the form of writing, he will always arrive from his own deconstruction and back into the loop of catastrophic inversion, and so live in it in the sense that his telos is the fulfillment of borders, the accomplishment of his limits.

However, and we recall from our earlier discussion of the memory-trace, the inscription is first and foremost a *form*. The groove has a depth and shape to it. This form, as Derrida himself acknowledges, at once reveals what is other than the same (deconstruction) *and* that which is other than the other than the metaphysical tradition, and thus other than deconstruction. The inscription suffers from what he calls the "overflow," the excess of form that is the yield of the self-deconstructive movement that negotiates tradition by supplanting it.[70] The overflow is "the moment of the attempt-to-write": it involves the surplus of both the will and the attempt to write.[71]

For Derrida, the will to write pertains to both freedom and responsibility. Inseparable from its relation to Being, the surplus of will discloses itself within the very structure of sovereignty as the movement of originary trace (ultrametaphysical appearance of being) and the visibility of image (metaphysical appearance in general) that, in its own appearing, reveals how visibility is conferred upon being in the first place.

> In its relationship to Being, the attempt-to-write poses itself as the only way out of affectivity. . . . To be affected is to be finite: to write could still be to deceive finitude, and to reach Being—a kind of Being which could neither be, nor affect me by *itself*—from without existence. To write would be an attempt to forget difference: to forget writing in the presence of the so-called living and pure speech.[72]

In its relationship to Being, the attempt-to-write here is the overflow of the very willfulness of will, the originary opening of will to itself.

In his very interesting piece, "Admiration of Nelson Mandela, or the Laws of Reflection," Derrida discusses Descartes's notion of wonder and admiration as that which opens us up to the world. According to Descartes, wonder is the first of the six passions because it orients the subject both to the world and to itself. It is thereby the minimal definition of a human subject, of a being who is able to open itself to the surprising things. In this regard, wonder means admiration and the capacity to be astonished, which is an affective opening that simultaneously marks the origin of all affects. Descartes assigns wonder the first position of the six passions—it comes before love, hate, desire, joy, and sadness—because it has no opposable term.[73]

However, the wonder we see in deconstruction, as Derrida elaborates it in the idea of admiration as that which at once astonishes and questions, is the structure of auto-affection and therefore of hetero-affection, since the latter is said to inhabit the former. In other words, it is difference as pure negation that opens the possibility of reflection without ever closing itself upon itself, the capacity to be perennially affected as always already affected by the affecting of time.[74]

The attempt-to-write, which presents itself as the only exit from affectivity, is the will's own wonder—difference without opposition that is deprived of affective attachment. The willfulness of will is thus the attempt to forget ontological difference itself and to forget the link between that which unites the loop of the eternal return of the same with a proper name and the movement of difference. It is an attempt to overcome the finitude of the subject as its imperishable structure of knowledge. This is indissolubly tied to the idea that time is the first trauma for the human—the originary wound and persistent wounding that the human is attempting to defeat. According to its own concept, the human is a contradictory unity—a cloven structure marked by the regime of the two ends of man. The "end" of man is, as Derrida elucidates in "The Ends of Man," at once two ends: the death and the completion of man. The idea that man must overcome his own finitude—as a unity between the infinite and the finite, the mortal and the immortal—is already inscribed in the very notion of the human. The truth of man is its destruction and the destruction is the fulfillment of its truth.[75] Forgetting would thus be an instant of repeating the human according to its own governing structure of knowledge. To forget writing is to accomplish a certain writing of human reality—that the human is always in the shadow of itself, a living memory that repeats itself from its own spectral returns of time, eternally sculpting itself into forms of itself.

Inasmuch as forgetting is writing in the flesh of living, which is to say a forgetting of a certain ontological difference (the change from Being to being), forgetting forgets itself. It is a return of repetition that brings relief to the need to attempt-to-write. Forgetting is twofold without the possibility of accumulating surplus because it is always voiding the synthetic value of the law of the double inscription in which difference operates and makes itself known. In other words, forgetting is a process of releasing of the unstable partition of being, and an unveiling of an indifference between the conditions of material and the conditions of the symbolic and thus to the finality of the finitude of existence (so an indifference to the indifference of the symbolic) in the structure of the living being. Forgetting is a particular causal value of the wound. There is, as Althusser writes, no law that "presides over the encounter in which things take hold."[76] In a sense, forgetting is the astonishing power of life to transform its own relationship to otherness precisely by keeping the relation open and forcing otherness to change itself, without subordinating things to the finality of the symbolic.

At the heart of the necessity of the law of the attempt-to-write is a foundational power that is both derived from experience and a birthright to transform one's own relationship to otherness. The law itself bears witness to this in the necessity of the finality of contingency as the necessary mode for occurring. The activity of our relations to repetition, it would seem, cannot avoid relinquishing partition and thus the codes and criteria for determining how being must maintain and elaborate its relationship to otherness and the other. What then of responsibility? The forgetting that I propose cannot avoid challenging the structure and meaning of demand and response, and thus questioning the juridico-political domains. It no doubt questions ideas of amnesty, restitution, reparation, and forgiveness and runs the risk of becoming the mechanism that repeats foundational violence.

In his discussion of the "*universal urgency* of memory" in the example of histories of colonialism in "On Forgiveness," Derrida warns of the dangers of forgetting. "*All* Nation-States are born and found themselves in violence. . . . Before the modern forms of what is called, in the strict sense, 'colonialism,' all States . . . have their origin in an aggression of the *colonial* type. This foundational violence is not only forgotten. This foundation is made *in order* to hide it; by its essence it tends to organise amnesia, sometimes under the celebration and sublimation of the new grand beginning."[77] In both their concept and their method, memory, repetition, and forgiveness must exceed the juridico-political domains of the sovereignty of the state because in so transgressing, "what is most sacred in the living" is protected, maintained, and asserted in the emergence of notions such as human rights and crimes against humanity.[78] If responsibility remains in the waves of amnesia, in what tasks would it consist? Perhaps it would be a relief and mourning of writing—a kind of assembling of the other's pain without taking their place, and a carrying together of the self and the other without opposition.

Whither partition? The instability of this question will always maintain itself precisely because it asserts the philosophical and political status of that which is deeper than, yet above ambivalence: the places deprived of expectation and dispossessed of the need to make a promise, the places of forgetting where forms of nation start to engender and constitute themselves. Can we risk the dangers of divulging such fragile, trembling places so youthful in their processes of autonomous development?

CHAPTER 4

Rwanda Transforming

Bisesero, a lush, mountainous farmland region located in the Karongi District of western Rwanda, derives its name from Abasesero, the name of the region's Tutsis, the historical majority population of the area. During the 1994 genocide, the hills of Bisesero—most notably the hill named Muriya—offered a moment's protection from the brutal attacks. In May, thousands of Tutsis began to take refuge on top of Muriya. Approximately fifty thousand Tutsis organized what was the strongest and longest-lasting opposition to the Hutu militia. For nearly three months, they resisted attacks until coordinated efforts from the fleeing government of *génocidaires* eventually defeated their efforts. Between May 13 and 14, the Tutsis in the Bisesero region, including the thousands that sought refuge atop the Muyira hill, were attacked with heavy artillery. More than forty thousand were killed during that attack. One month later, the French army arrived in Bisesero with the intent of stopping the genocidal violence but discovered that only about twelve hundred survived the most recent campaign of violence. A few days later the French army left, claiming that they would return in three days' time. Just as soon as the French departed, the Hutu militia returned. By the time the French returned, nearly all of the remaining survivors had been killed.[1] Carved into the Muriya hill, which has come to be known as the Hill of Resistance, stands the Bisesero Genocide Memorial. The Bisesero Memorial, one of Rwanda's state-regulated memorial sites, is named the National Resistance Memorial. It houses the remains of the nearly fifty thousand genocide victims who were killed during those attacks.

In "Faith and Knowledge: The Two Sources of 'Religion' at the Limits of Reason Alone" Derrida discusses the messianic in a slightly different way from the one we see in, for example, *Spectres of Marx*. In this text he interrogates the self-sacrificial tendency of life to invert itself into its contrary. The very movement of living is the continuous exposure of one's own life to its own destruction. If life is doomed to die, then what is death? Such is the difficult question at the heart of "Faith and Knowledge."

Derrida elaborates an answer according to the problem of the source, which is another name for life, in the context of the return of the religious during the 1990s. He discusses how religion and rationality, including their most extreme forms, "develop in tandem, drawing from this common resource."[2] The source persistently doubles and redoubles itself, and by accord the horizon of expectation doubles itself. This doubling economy that is immanent to the flesh of the living is the opening of a more originary promise than the promise. Life at once anticipates its own destruction, yet does not and cannot know what is coming. For Derrida, the advent of life is a pure opening in the sense that it is simultaneously the opening of an expectation and the opening of something to come, of an engagement with the other (the relationship to messianism, to respond before the other). This promise, the messianic, is what he later calls faith. Such a concept of faith consists in the very fragilization of fragility. It is a persistence in one's own being, in which life has faith in its own vitality that is at the same time an address to the other, an asking of the other to have faith in oneself. This economy of faith cannot be separated from the promise since this is what maintains even the materiality of living. Life itself is the "first name: *the* messianic, *or messianicity without messianism*," since it is "the opening to the future or to the coming of the other as the advent of justice, but without horizon of expectation and without prophetic prefiguration."[3] The messianic is also, then, a particular mode of happening in which what is yet to come is always a betrayal to the horizon of expectation.

The "*universal urgency* of memory," of which Derrida speaks in "On Forgiveness," the necessity of turning towards the past and taking "this act of memory, of self-accusation," is also a particular modality of the necessity to "respect the secret," the fragilization of fragility, the promise without promise.[4] Derrida asserts this as a "trans-political principle," "a political rule or position taking."[5] Acts of memory give particular form—forms of thought, forms of politics, forms of justice—to our confrontations with the betrayals to our horizons of expectation. At the same time, acts of memory seize hold in order to last and ensure the necessity for political responsibility and negotiation. The secret is the originary link that bonds substitution and mimicry to transformation.[6]

We see this echoed in Pierre Nora's concept of *lieux de mémoire*, the places of memory. According to Nora, these places are created by the interactions in the "play of memory and history," which produces a double excess, the excess of fluxibility and reification, according to the necessity of the "will to remember" as the necessary condition for the circularity of the play of the symbolic.[7] The will to remember, for Nora, is the opening of acts of memory to their own will to imagine. "*Lieux de mémoire* only exist because of their capacity for metamorphosis," which is bonded to the will of the imagination to invest even an "apparently purely material site, like an archive," "with a symbolic aura."[8] "The *lieux* . . . are mixed, hybrid, mutant, bound intimately with life and death, with time and eternity enveloped in a Möbius strip of the collective and the individual, the sacred and the profane, the immutable and the mobile." Their "fundamental purpose" is "to block the work of forgetting."[9] The labor of forgetting, we recall, involves the assertion of a starting place of dispossession through the processes of transformation. Indebted to the priority of symbolic function for their existence and persistence, Nora's places of memory consist only in the giving of a place to and for the messianic, and remain, therefore, an aesthetic or poetic expression of a new messianic time. What, other than figural improvisations of the historic, actually happen here, in these places of memory?

Critical fields have taken up the idea that sites of memory, such as memorials and monuments, and other practices of memorialization are acts of memory that, by their very nature, are political discourses that politicize and legitimize social orders and institute juridical concepts of justice and are therefore always reiterating the primacy of our collective, human duty to remember so that the atrocities of the past will not be repeated. We see these themes explored in work ranging from that of James Young and Marita Sturken, who share attention to sites of memory like memorial museums and public modes of commemorative practices, to that of Michael Rothberg and Marianne Hirsch, who pay attention to diverse cultural formations of memory as scenes of writing.[10] To be sure, the public sphere of acts of memory brings to the fore questions of human rights as they pertain to genocide and other crimes against humanity. Yet, whatever their aim or guiding principle, these critiques of and addresses to the work of memory constantly emerge and appear according to an analytics of performative power that opposes processes of symbolization by proceeding from the (re)introduction of a gap. The structure of the symbolic inscribed therein is thus the very condition of possibility for the performative, ensuring that its effects faithfully follow from its displacements. Across the different fields, the secret of the promise of a new messianism has long been upheld as what the work of memory must maintain and confirm.

Discourses, concepts, codes, orders, and so forth are resolutely concerned with what has been profoundly injured, what truths must be acknowledged, what needs to be repaired, what requires reconstitution, what calls for healing, what demands punishment, and so forth—that is, with what needs to be thought, judged, and determined in the law. The resulting reifications of places of memory indeed contain an acuteness of repetition to the extent that there seems to be the shared thought of the work of repetition as opening up the possibility of or effecting transformations by safeguarding what is most sacred to human life and living.

That something entirely metamorphosed and new, which has been produced by repetition itself, can be extracted out of repetition by contracted activity has been extensively developed by Deleuze in his remarkable text, *Difference and Repetition*.[11] Even if we submit that not all formations and practices of memory can be perceived as mimicking the general structure and movement of writing in processes of the developments and evolutions of social, cultural, and political orders, the ethical bases for the injunction against forgetting are clear enough. To forget would amount to acts of repeating foundational violence.

It is in the shifting places of memory that this chapter discovers itself in proposing (and perhaps arranging) a dangerous confrontation between repetition and forgetting that brings relief to writing by dismissing the absolute necessity of the motif of promise as that which effectively brings about change and transformation. It is unquestionably an extremely difficult and delicate task to break through the primacy of the symbolic and, by accord, the ethical necessity of scenic removals in scenes of haunted memories. In this attention to the memorialization of the genocide in Rwanda, I aim to relinquish the eventality of the return of repetition, to negotiate letting it go so that whatever returns may follow along with its own life. So I aim also, in a way, to forget. Yet the forgetting that I am trying to develop includes the relation between repetition and the processes of life as a dynamic, interactive space that unbinds repetition from that which it repeats. In so elaborating, I am not here aligning my reading of repetition and forgetting with the accomplishment of memorialization as the production of a creative act that occurs in the process of bearing witness to the other's trauma through a mortiferous separation that cannot return.[12] Rather, I uphold my contention that trauma includes the experience of death in its processes of transforming forms of separation—that is, the wound—all the while arranging and indicating the coincidence between the material and the symbolic in different ways at each time.

Recall from the earlier discussions on the Freudian pleasure principle and the fear of death in the ego that there is no idea of proper when it comes to the event. It is at once materially real and psychically real without being more one than the other. Trauma triggers the commencement of the binding of repetition as a chronological stage, but the elaboration of what follows cannot be determined by it. Trauma, as we see in the famous "Dream of the Burning Child," releases from within psychic life an essential transformability in the wound by surprising itself with an intimate meeting that grabs hold of the encounter with otherness and forces it to alter itself. The law of repetition bears witness to this power in its own necessity. To memorialize would thereby consist in restoring the other's capacity to experience and acquire the material of trauma and so exchange the distributions of meaning and prior effects of truth in new ways. Such a process of memorialization would involve forgetting and bring reprieve to the other's need to attempt-to-write by restoring back to them their loss without assuming their place.

THE POLITICS OF MEMORIALIZATION IN RWANDA

Generally speaking, the Rwandan government's practices of commemoration and national mourning, such as public burial ceremonies, have been widely criticized for producing master narratives about Rwanda's colonial history and the 1994 genocide.[13] In the aftermath of the genocide, the Rwandan government adopted the ideology and rhetoric of a unified national identity in its state policy of reconciliation that replaced any reference to Hutu and Tutsi ethnic identities in bureaucratic processes. Nevertheless, state practices of memory maintain the distinction by defining Tutsis as genocide victims and Hutus as genocide perpetrators, and have sought to regulate public acts of memorialization. A profound example of this is the government's reference to the genocide as the 1994 Genocide against the Tutsi in Rwanda, which is sometimes abbreviated as the Tutsi Genocide or the Genocide Against Tutsi in its bureaucratic life.[14] Another example can be seen in the government's attempt to centralize collective memory through a series of exhumations at smaller local and family memorials and consolidate them into the national and district memorials.[15] This has led to tensions between individual and collective commemorative practices and those endorsed by the government. Organizations such as Ibuka (Remember), a survivors' association, for example, were required to negotiate with the government on the ways in which the remains of victims would be displayed.[16] Discourses of a new, unified Rwanda have been criticized for echoing the "mythico-historical" narratives of the precolonial period in which Hutu, Tutsi, and Twa were far more flexible categories that were contingent on local contexts and on clan and lineage affiliations for social distinctions in daily life.[17] The insistence on categories of identity in local and national politics traces to Rwanda's long history with centralized state power.[18] The relation among recovery, reconciliation, and coexistence or cohabitation (the terms are often used interchangeably in sociological studies of postgenocide Rwanda) that has often been taken to formulate the structure of life after the genocide has resulted in what some argue is a chosen form of collective amnesia.[19]

The Kigali Genocide Memorial, which opened its doors on April 7, 2004, in commemoration of the tenth anniversary of the 1994 Rwandan genocide is a locus for these and other politics.[20] Originally developed through a partnership between the Kigali City Council and the Aegis Trust, a British anti-genocide organization, the Kigali City Council currently operates in coordination between the Rwandan government's National Commission for the Fight Against Genocide (CNLG), a federal commission housed in the Ministry for Sports and Culture, and the Aegis Trust.[21] Inspired by the U.K. Beth Shalom Holocaust Centre, the Kigali Genocide Memorial was designed as a memorial museum, a type of museum specifically designed with the intent to balance commemoration and education.[22] Since its inception in 2010, the CNLG has been regulating all aspects of national genocide commemoration ranging from commemorative practices to offering advocacy for survivors to acquiring, managing, and now digitizing the storage of archival materials such as the *gacaca* files.[23]

The Kigali Genocide Memorial is composed of a series of memorial gardens, a library and documentation center, ten mass exterior graves that contain the remains of approximately 250,000 victims, and three permanents exhibitions.[24] One of the permanent exhibits, titled "Wasted Lives," seeks to situate the Rwandan genocide in the context of genocidal violence in the twentieth century. It features the histories of the Holocaust, the Armenian genocide, the Cambodian genocide, the Herero genocide, and the Balkans. Another permanent exhibit is devoted to the children. It commemorates a number of children who were killed with photos and narratives about them, which were donated and written by surviving family members, including, if possible, the parents. The most extensive of the three permanent exhibitions is "Jenoside," which is devoted to the history of the genocide and is divided into three sections titled "Before," "During," and "After."[25]

The "Before" section begins with Rwanda before it was colonized by the Germans in the 1890s and progresses through Rwanda's colonial history, with an emphasis on how the introduction of the classification system during Belgian colonial rule in the 1920s essentialized racial and ethnic differences and forever altered Hutu and Tutsi relations.[26] The "Before" section continues through Rwanda's civil war in 1990 and ends on April 6, 1994, the day the plane carrying Juvénal Habyarimana, third president of the Republic of Rwanda and a Hutu, and the president of Burundi, Cyprien Ntaryamira, was shot down near the Kigali International Airport.

The "During" section focuses on the one hundred days of genocide during which approximately one million Tutsis were killed, which commenced the day after Habyarimana's plane was shot down.[27] The "After" section highlights the refugee crisis immediately following the genocide, and it features information about the International Criminal Tribunal for Rwanda, which was established by the United Nations Security Council in November 1994. It ends with statements regarding the international community's failure to intervene and prevent the explosion of genocidal violence.[28]

BISESERO

Bisesero is distinct among other nationally sponsored memorials, like the Ntarama and Nyamata churches, which were converted into memorial sites by preserving their original edifices, because it was purposefully constructed. In this, it shares with the Kigali Genocide Memorial an intention of structural design. Bisesero has not received sustained critical attention, save for mention of it belonging to what has been coined as "thanatourism," or dark tourism, which, as Mona Friedricha and Tony Johnston consolidate and define the term's critical expansions, denotes "travel to sites motivated by a desire to encounter death or disaster" or hermeneutic lenses "to interrogate and position the interaction between tourist and death specifically, and society and death more generally."[29]

Unlike the Kigali Genocide Memorial, Bisesero does not offer its visitors an explicit narrative of the history of the genocide. It is the only memorial designated as the "National Resistance Memorial." From its architectural and spatial design to its organized display of bones, the basic performative dimensions of the commemorative strategy are clear enough: to act out the incommensurability of experiences of genocide and the duty of memory through a series of imitative acts and permanent rituals of display. These imitative acts and rituals of display produce the singularity of the Tutsi experience as a form of resistance on the Muriya hill and its locality on the level of experiences from within the Tutsi community, on the level of the relation between the specificity of the genocide and communities exterior to Rwanda, and on the level of comparison among the nation's memorial sites. Certain of the necessity of its ethical urgency but nevertheless calling into question the other traditional forms underpinning the nation's memorialization in its very design, Bisesero, it would seem, is an example of what James Young has called the countermonument: "painfully self-conscious memorial spaces conceived to challenge the very premises of their being," a form of memorialization that negates its own form.[30]

The main memorial complex is composed of nine buildings organized into repeating clusters of three adjoining buildings, which are themselves repeating structures. A stone pathway, designed as a series of switchbacks, directs one through each building and connects the buildings. Located at the base of the hill are a memorial sculpture consisting of a large rock surrounded by nine spears and a small wooden makeshift building with a corrugated metal roof that houses skeletal remains of victims. The skeletons housed in the wooden building at the foot of the memorial complex lie next to and on top of each other on wooden bunks and inside coffins.[31] The nine communes (or sectors) that formerly made up the Kibuye province are represented by the number of buildings and spears; the spears retain the additional signification of indicating a primary weapon used during the resistance. The nine buildings, which collectively house the remains of approximately fifty thousand victims, are sculpted into a side of the hill that was cleared of its natural density of trees. The buildings and stone pathway ascend up the hill in a zigzagging manner.

The steep, winding architectural plan of the buildings and the pathway demand a physicality of the visitor experience that evokes the harrowing duality between organized opposition against and desperate attempts to flee from the imminent death of the Tutsi experience on the Muriya hill. The journey up the hill progresses through the buildings and through the passages among the heaps of the skeletal remains of those who were killed on the hill and in the surrounding villages, resurrecting the locality of violence at each step. Immediately, the specificities of the past that are conjured appear as mimetic forms of presence, as rememorations that evict the past from itself and operate as hermetic encodings of discursive differentials within the indissoluble regimes of transference, exchange, and production.

Inside, the visitor is confronted with the calcified disembodiment of bodies, which demand the necessity of turning towards what has happened while safeguarding the apprehension of their particular experiences of the other. The other's trauma, the bones articulate, can never be apprehended, replaced, or overcome by another's experiences or acts of memory that occur as witnessing. Thus the finitude of memory seems to persist in the doubling excess of the vitality of its universal urgency and necessity while urging the necessity of the visitor to respond. At every instant, the visitor's encounter is compelled by the design's interplay among the pathway, the clusters of buildings, and the display of bones inside, all of which can easily be taken to mime the necessity of the universal urgency of memory that presides over its changing expressions.

Any materialism of memorialization thereby seems obliged to articulate only the program of the law of the reversal of before and after between arche-writing and structure before processes of life have the chance to start up. The direction and modality of any act of memory at Bisesero seem to be entirely mobilized in advance by the anticipatory strategies effected by the structure of writing, which always exposes the necessity of the attempt-to-write as presiding over the contingency of writing. At Bisesero, one can indeed make a case for the unexpected appearances of the efficacy of symbolic excesses resident in forms of resistance that stage themselves and archive the historicity of the genocide. Whether calling into question the underpinnings of the nation's memorializations or recalling the Tutsi resistance, the teleology of death, trauma, memory, genocide, and responsibility is the way any act of resistance in the Bisesero Memorial is said to conceptually and practically transgress the figure of the law. In the very formation and rememoration of the living being, the question of posterity is put to us by the exigencies of survival that come before us. This is the hermeneutic horizon of meaning carved out by the seminal adventure of the trace.

This teleological principle brings to light the ambiguity intrinsic to the designation of the Bisesero Memorial as the "National Resistance Memorial." The different ways of reading *national* (as part of the proper name, as a resistance to the "national," as a "national" resistance to something, or as the nation's resistance) at least begs the simple question: what is resisting what? Further, what precisely is legitimizing what? What does this resistance actually look like? The answer to these questions are infinitely confounded by the fact that the social, political, cultural reproduction of memory tend to be founded, in advance, by criteria that define particular programs that correspond to sets of values of ethical urgency and that, in turn, fix the criteria for political and ethical legitimacy. The dominant ideological tendencies—whether of the ontological order or in the practical social, cultural, and political domains—preestablish criteria, since the necessity of the reproduction of memory is taken to be an act that confers meaning upon the production and dissemination of difference, which, by accord, creates and begets new traditions and systems of order and rule. Yet to insist on either a dialectical teleology of materialism or the symbolic order of self-negation leads one to the same end: the structure of resistance is accomplished entirely in advance as a reproduction of those dominant ideologies and of ideological tendencies. Any transforming process, which would include the development of forms of resistance to the nation's politics of memorialization and impressed-upon ideologies about makeups of a national identity, that may pertain to Bisesero as a place of memory is preemptively canceled by the insistence on symbolic overflow as the resource from which the self-development and appearance of any materiality draws and orients itself.

However much the ambiguity intrinsic to Bisesero as the "National Resistance Memorial" may be maintained in acts of preservation, the instability of memory's place nevertheless reminds us that the ways we relate to *a priori* schemas of otherness can die and be invented and engendered after.

THE AMBIGUITY OF THE VIVACITY OF MEMORY AND THE ECOLOGY OF THE MIND

In his discussion about "the general problem of preservation in the sphere of the mind" in *Civilization and Its Discontents*, Freud develops his famous analogy between Rome, "the Eternal City," and the imperishable character of the psyche. He is perfectly aware that the analogy is an imperfect one, owing to the fact that the past in the psyche is always capable of being "revivified," whereas it is only the ancient ruins that remain of Rome's past: "in mental life nothing which has once been formed can perish—that everything is somehow preserved and that in suitable circumstances . . . it can once more be brought to light."[32] Not unlike the city, however, psychic life, in its "normal course of things or as an exception," bears witness to its growth and evolutions.[33]

For Freud, the problem of preservation in psychic life indicates an ambiguity intrinsic to the vivacity of memory and its imperishable character. This is clearly presented in his analogy of the phylogenesis of highly developed species in the animal kingdom. The survival of a species is necessarily the preservation of a lower order species in which the very permanence of a form of survival is preserved by the shaping of the passing away of what is underneath. The phenomenon of the preservation of the past is precisely that it is a tight imbrication of a lived past and the memories of an older, primitive form—a delicate, entwining interaction between extinction and persistence. What distinguishes this phenomenon in psychic life, however, is the unstable nature of the memory of primitive forms. For Freud, this is the memory of the past of an ancient state of inert matter. "In the realm of the mind, on the other hand, what is primitive is commonly preserved alongside of the transformed version which has arisen from it."[34] On the one hand, the advent of the drive bears witness to this transformation from inert matter into organic life. From within their energetic economies, the drives thereby involve formative processes that modify the necessity of an originary determinate being. We remember that drives can change their aim and object. That chance plays a role in mechanical necessities means that no event or phenomenon can be subordinated to the finality of the symbolic. On the other hand, the fundamental shifting of memory's place reveals the ways in which the form of the psyche—that is, of the unconscious—is coincidentally structural and mutable. The ambiguity indicates the unstable ground between the reversibility and irreversibility of exchange and difference, for the uncertainty is a result of the transformability in the structure of the psyche. It is, in other words, an arrangement of the insupposability of the difference between the time of nature and a pure messianic temporality.

Psychic life and the vivacity of memory thus realize the memory of the prehuman erased within us. Memory has no proper place, no proper direction. We can thus say that memory involves a return to nature and thus to a time before the drives and the pleasure principle, to primitive potentialities that loosen the structure of life and the living being. Owing to its own dynamic syntheses, every act of memory, and thus every act of repetition, asserts the instability between the reversibility and irreversibility of time and change. To clarify, the primitive here is understood as a starting point for an early stage of growth and transformation, and not as the problematic figuration of the savage, uncivilized man upon which colonialist and imperialist ideologies turned.[35] Insofar as this place is an unstable, mutable meeting point between the contingency of necessities and the necessity of contingencies, it renders the primacy of the symbolic that which is most suitable to respond to efficient, external causes improbable. By its own processes of increasing complexity of use, purpose, organization, and reorganization, life makes the ambiguity of memory's vivacity. In its capacity to engender anew the conditions of possibility for contingent encounters, that is, in its inclusion of surprise, adventure and journey, life itself changes psychic life by forcing the imperishable character of memory to forget and let go of itself.

"Here too," Freud tells us, in "the body of an animal or a human being, we find the same thing." More particularly, it is in the theme of childhood, which recalls the earlier discussion of the uncanny as that which does not double itself as an excess but instead as that which arranges and displays the uncertainty in the duality of chance in different ways, that we see the prehuman or primitivity as the transformability of forms of survival to be the mutable character of the relation between the particular manners in which a form constitutes what has survived and the general form of survival. This idea of survival is not primarily related to the copy, to the loop of the interminable returns of the same different or the different same in the schema of difference and identity:

> The earlier phases of development are in no sense still preserved; they have been absorbed into the later phases for which they have supplied the material. The embryo cannot be discovered in the adult. The thymus gland of childhood is replaced after puberty by connective tissue, but is no longer present in itself; in the marrow-bones of the grown man I can, it is true, trace the outline of the child's bone, but it itself has disappeared, having lengthened and thickened until it has attained its definitive form. The fact remains that only in the mind is such a preservation of all the earlier stages alongside of the final form possible, and that we are not in a position to represent this phenomenon in pictorial terms.[36]

Far from negatively revealing the phenomenon of the indestructibility of the imperishable character of psychic life, Freud's presumably inadequate examples of Rome and the development of the body—and to this I would add the mystic writing-pad—in fact reveal preservation in the sphere of the mind as an ecology of the mind.[37] For all of his insistence on the unconscious as the psyche's originary incapacity to conceptualize its own destruction, Freud's persistent returns to nature in his writings in fact disclose the idea of the gradual growth and evolution of the psyche. He presents us with something like an ecology of the mind in which the living being experiences the changes in the relation to what comes before—to inheritance, heritage, lineage, family, and so forth—in constituting and engendering the form of posterity. In the end, it would seem that something of the form of the psyche can and does actually die. Psychic life is always interacting with external and internal environmental systems, factors, and operations. Preservation owes itself to the power of life's transforming processes, which are neither purely mechanistic nor completely presupposed. The ecology of the mind is, we can say, both the dying of certain or originary difference and the living of transforming difference. In other words, the anatomy of the psyche is such that its form and functioning never really consists in its own vivisections from its own biological body; it isn't actually body without organs that knows how to draw its borders in order to live on beyond the inevitable. The psyche also grows and transforms itself. It is itself, like an embryo, an exchanging form of the movements of self-differentiation that are increasingly complexified in their interactions with nature and other empirical things. As he says, "we are not in a position to represent this phenomenon in pictorial terms." This is perhaps Freud's own response to posterity—to the main question put to him by his own critical posterity: a concept of the unconscious for which there is no scene. Indeed, one cannot even picture it. Such a concept would perhaps be the following offspring changing the form of the psyche.

THE CHILDHOOD OF TRANSFORMATION

Postcolonial and psychoanalytic narratives of pain and suffering privilege the resistance of the indestructible past in the formation of new identities. Despite their divergent paths between and within the discourses, there is the shared conception that whatever disruptions and changes trauma may solicit are owed to a certain flexibility of identity that is already inscribed in the living being. That trauma transforms its subject to the extent that what is called the surviving identity changes the essential relation to the more ancient past in dissolving the determining causal value of that past as the heritage of a past always already passed away is not at all considered. The hermeneutics of the subject in these narratives ultimately serve to confirm that the exigencies of survival constitute a certain truth with regard to an ancient history that cannot be possessed. In short, what is unilaterally missed is the consideration of the possibility that trauma forces itself to transform in acquiring material from the experience of the interactions between contingency and necessity for its own use. To think about trauma as changing and modifying *the trauma* does not pertain to or result in the repudiation of past events, histories, and experiences. Rather, it involves the destruction of the indestructibility of the past or the persistence of an anterior condition or state as the governing telos for self-formation. What is unilaterally missed in the thinking of trauma that appears in the range of psychoanalytic and postcolonial approaches to the event is the return to nature, or else the return of repetition in psychic life that restores the conditions of possibility of the encounter of chance after the encounter has already occurred.

In his very rich study of the Rwandan genocide, *When Victims Become Killers*, Mahmood Mamdani focuses on the preservation of the colonial past in the development and differentiation of all forms of political identities (cultural, economic, social) in Rwanda as the consequences of state formation. In particular, he elaborates a thinking of the genocide from "within the logic of colonialism," in which the politicization of "*indigeneity in the first place*," transformed indigenous life in the region into a political world "organized around a binary preoccupation" between the settler and the native.[38] In this world, Mamdani further argues, the Tutsi were constructed "as a privileged alien settler presence."[39] Thus Mamdani develops it as "a native's genocide. It was a genocide by those who saw themselves as sons—and daughters—of the soil, and their mission was one of clearing the soil of a threatening *alien* presence."[40] There is a distinct return to the primitive in relation to the other that echoes Freud's discussion of childhood and preservation. Though Mamdani does not put it this way, his emphasis on daughters, sons, and soils articulates the Rwandan genocide as an event of childhood, as a return to and of primitive potentialities that troubles the concepts of family and heritage. To the extent that the Hutu and Tutsi were forced into the politicized world of the dialectic between the settler and the native, which continued after Rwanda gained independence in 1962, the violence convoked itself in the "clearing away of the soil," as he nicely puts it, of "the very legitimacy of a presence as alien."[41] In this way, the violence exposed a void within what was proper to otherness, forcing otherness to transform itself.

This echoes what Althusser identifies as Rousseau's "vision of any possible theory of history" in *The Social Contract*: "The social contract then no longer appears as a utopia, but as the inner law of necessity, in its legitimate or illegitimate form, and the real problem becomes: *how does it happen that one never rectifies an illegitimate (prevailing) form, transforming it into a legitimate form?*"[42] Although Mamdani elaborates the forms of Tutsi and Hutu identities created by the colonial encounter and the ongoing encounters with colonialism, he does not posit the genocide as a transcendental condition for history in general, or situate it within symbolic excess. Rather, the generations after colonialism recreated the conditions of the unexpected form of an encounter while arranging and manifesting the ways interactions occur differently in each of their historic instances—after the colonial encounter occurred. For him, the genocide was an attempt to force a transformation in the *a priori* character of colonialism in contemporary Rwanda. It would seem that Mamdani's thinking of genocide presents itself as an answer to Althusser's question. According to him, the idea of the clearing away of otherness from Rwanda's soil was the loosening of preestablished structures and the opening of the undesignated land to the encounter without a presiding law.

For all that Mamdani offers in the thinking of this specific genocide as an instance of transformation, his critique steadfastly emerges according to the observation of the legacies of colonialism as the originary trauma. That the genocide also consisted in the morphological perpetuation of criteria and social norms implemented in advance and which reproduced the order of the dominant ideology of the Hutu, such as the policy of "ethnic equilibrium" that used a quota system to allocate positions to Tutsis in educational institutions and state apparatuses, maintains the presiding order of a more ancient history.[43] There is no way for the genocide to avoid the fact that it followed from a program that operated to identify difference in advance according to a principle of selection that determined what deserved to return or did not. To be sure programs of selection were established by colonial rule and continued to unfold themselves throughout the course of Rwanda's evolving political life.

This does not escape Mamdani. In his concluding thoughts regarding the possibilities of political and democratic futures in postgenocide Rwanda, he suggests the idea of childhood as a new concept of custom:

> When a particular version of history (custom) is found wanting, in this case because it builds on the authoritarian strand as if it were the entire past, this surely cannot be the reason to junk the very notion of history. From a reified language fortifying a despotic authority, custom needs to be rethought as a thread of life, not only one that makes us but also one that we make. To smash one version of the past as a prison dressed in the language of custom, one needs to turn that very past . . . into a plural resource for more open futures.[44]

To think custom anew as a thread of life is to think of it as childhood, as passing through the ends of anteriority and of posterity—as the outline of a form not yet fully formed and which is in need of its own determination. Childhood is a play between liberty and determination, between growth and given, between inheritance and inheritor.[45] Such a reconceptualization of the concept of custom, for Mamdani, is the very destruction of the custom of assuming the indestructibility of the past as that which structures the horizon of expectation and the anticipatory view upon the future of difference. But we must ask:

does this thread of life, this offspring really arrive to break the order of the sequence of filiation and thus "the past as a prison dressed in the language of custom"? We are forced to say no. Like chance, childhood remains a motif, an appearance that comes about by means of the thread that passes between the ends of the past that come before it, ever more tightly weaving it into the source from which different futures may issue forth.

Identifying the link between childhood and savagery in the Victorian rhetoric of empire, Bill Ashcroft argues that the "child embodies the crisis of colonial subjectivity" and the ambivalent "connection between filiation and authority in colonial rhetoric and practice."[46] The metaphor of childhood, he contends, is itself "designed to resolve" this "ambivalence of subjectivity"; though the child always slips between "abjection and subjectivity" the child is formulated at the limits of knowledge about subjectivity.[47] Whatever possible additional futures may seem to be opened by the primitive time of childhood is canceled in advance by the "allegory of the child" as "'written into existence by empire.'"[48] Although the child emerges according to the plural, unpredictable, and unstable potentialities of an alternative "post-colonial future," the child cannot avoid being a mere "evocative sign of transformation."[49] By accord, the postcolonial subject becomes "the mimicking other, the transformed and transforming subject."[50] Although in Ashcroft's assessment, childhood ultimately comes to subvert the hegemonic structures of colonial power in its transformations, he does not posit it as transforming the determining causal value of the symbolic. It persistently tracks the ambivalent movements of writing.[51] Thus his notion of childhood flows from and into the excesses of the symbolic. It is precisely as Deleuze beautifully elaborates the idea of pluralized futures in his discussion of the Freudian concept of fantasy: the "childhood event" is a third future, lying in wait, "the dark precursor." Such an event, for him, is the metamorphosed identity born of exhaustion in the "theater of all metamorphosis, or difference in itself" and that smashes and supersedes its prior forms while figuring itself a form of a complete novelty.[52] Childhood, then, does not escape the primacy of the symbolic because, as Deleuze also insists, identity must be understood as beginning from difference. In this thinking of childhood, which crosses the philosophical tradition and the analytics of postcolonial critique, there is no production of novelty; there is only the repetition of a scenic, stereotyped character of lineage.

Yet there is still something in Mamdani's reformulation of the concept of custom, for it also plays with the double meaning of habit as referring to both a general and an acquired way of being. Indeed, we have seen something similar in the naming of Pakistan, in the development of borders during the Partition, and in Bishan Singh's resistance. To destroy the customs of assuming that all formations of identity owe to the indestructibility of the past and are reducible to typological schemas requires another way, one that involves the contracting of a new habit. It is in the starting of the formation of an idea of habit, which occurs on three levels: on the level of the generation of a new thought, on the level of the instituting of the willfulness of the will to make something of one's life, and on the level of the self-formations of new forms of identity, culture, politics, and society.

BISESERO FORGETTING

From the now barren, memorial side of the Muriya hill to the zigzagging concretization of the buildings and pathway to the organized heaps of bones that repeat the idea of order to the architectural and sculptural assertions of countability, the Bisesero Memorial gathers and indicates the unstable places of memory and the wounds of genocide in different ways at each instant of its design. It questions the relation between the pure elements, rules, or structure of trauma and its objects of knowledge and experience by revealing the unstable place of the transformability of the transformation of the Rwandan nation and the novel concepts of life its movements produce. Here it is not that the trauma of the genocide is presented as an object at the same time as that which it signifies. Rather, the different aspects of the Bisesero Memorial display this relation through a complexification and differentiation in the ways memorialization develops by itself in processes of reshaping, regenerating, engendering, and repairing the wounds of genocide. Between rememoration and commemoration, Bisesero presents the correspondences between the categories of trauma and memory and their objects in a twofold, uncanny way. In one way, the development of practices of memorialization conforms to the outlines of trauma offered in advance of the specific type to which it defers. In the other, it concerns an autonomous development of memory and the wound. To be sure, the totality of the memorial and its individual components bear witness to and memorialize the childhood of Rwanda's transformation. The violence of the pluralization of the colonial past and the dissemination of differences in the Hutu and Tutsi identities is commemorated and memorized. But the synthesis of memory in Bisesero's architectures is also productive and generative in the strong sense insofar as it is a self-differentiating movement to produce posterity that engenders and constitutes itself as such.

What is the reality of the produced—of the forms of identities, thoughts, society, culture, nation, memory, survival, and so forth that we see occurring in the structures of theoretical (pure formal, logical procedures) and practical experience (empirical, material information) at Bisesero? There is, of course, no single answer except to say that, as it pertains to the central aim of this chapter to think the eventality of memory, it counters at once any idea of pure empirical derivation and any idea of a preformed or predetermined entity. Playing with the unstable ground between the irreversibility and reversibility of difference, Bisesero emerges as an ecological form of memorialization and resistance. This means that the writing of the state's different political discourses onto its memorial bodies is always incomplete.

In its barest, the structure and movements of writing bear witness to the attempt-to-write, and thus to the problem of the legitimacy of the primacy of ontological difference by forgetting the irreversible change into a being given in its affective attachments that keep one irremediably open. Between arche-writing and structure, there is the problem of the question of the meaning of the nature of anteriority, of what comes before, contained in the term writing. This response, that is, writing's attempt to prove the authority and legitimacy of the always already is put to it by its own critical posterity. Any interpretation of memorialization at Bisesero as archiving the ambivalent tracks of writing includes the process of forgetting that devalues the authority of stemming from certain difference as the way to describe the manner in which things happen and create meaning. Even the persistent care for the messianic in peeling away the secret of experience from its presence in order to keep it intact, inaccessible, and irreducible somehow manages to display its own unstable ground.

However, the insistence on the finality of the irreducibility of the radical exteriority of violence, which renders the subject incapable of responding to trauma in any way other than to confirm its inaccessibility, accumulates on the sovereignty of the past as always already gone, which in its turn programs the activities of living into elaborations of flexible identities that never actually break from custom. "To smash one version of the past as a prison dressed in the language of custom," as Mamdani says, requires the formation of a new thought about life and the will to power itself into making something of this new idea of life. Perhaps, then, it is now time we admit the idea that life contains the power to transform itself without transgressing itself. Indeed we must now restore back to life the capacity (at once a self-structuring capacity and the capacity for movement) to invent and produce logical structures and relations to *a priori* schemas. For the Rwandan genocide is a profound demonstration of the return of the repetition of *indigeneity*.

Far from being the repeating character of the constitutive double bind between settler and native, the violence of the genocide was an instant in which the dynamic interactions among the different regimes of inheritance and orders of generation revealed the paradoxical gap within the limit of knowledge about subjectivity—the fundamental instability and mutability of the difference between pure messianic time and the time of nature. All assurance about the time in which generations succeed each other was rendered impossible by the genocide. To be sure, the radicality of the violence certified the emergence of an astonishing sovereignty of Hutu power that aimed at being the most effective deconstruction of the sovereignty of prior codes, laws, and programs. The effects of this violence, this cruel form of sovereignty, marked itself in the flesh of its own subjects as new types of colonizations that are never completely repressed though they are continuously displaced. Indeed this is the dangerous difficulty of any autonomous constituting process. It cannot completely protect itself from inventing new forms of cruelty.

To answer this conceptual and empirical risk, one may insist that survival in the aftermath of the genocide, thought and elaborated as a critical repetition of accumulations of past structures or as figures who, in their form of the psyche, are held henceforth in abeyance of their death that has already come to pass. However, such interpretations emerge according to the assumption that trauma and the compulsion to repeat automatically sorts, decides upon, and differentiates among what returns, what does not return, or what is designated to return. What must not or cannot come into presence always affirms alongside it what can, does, or should come into presence. This is the very logic of negative possibility. The determinist character of the compulsion to repeat, which relies on the hierarchical value of binding at all stages, is thus a principle of selection.

Survival borrows from the experience of the encounter with death that is disclosed in the dynamic syntheses of psychic life and life in general. What is very difficult from the perspective of the universal urgency of memory, inasmuch as the Rwandan genocide illustrates how otherness itself is forced to change itself and that prior accumulations are destroyed, is that we are required to elaborate a new relationship to the other's pain and suffering without the assumed transmissibility of the otherness of trauma and by accord, without the absolute need for transference. For the structure of transference has heretofore constituted the very urgency and demand of response.[53] What is needed instead is a new conception of affects that does not solely pertain to the specular resuscitation of the subject.

To an extent, Bisesero challenges its visitors to will what Nietzsche refers to as an "active forgetting" of self so that we may gather the other's losses, pains, and suffering without proceeding from the regard for one's self and without assuming their place—a forgetting that forgets the need to attempt-to-write.[54] The activity of this forgetting thereby involves a relationship between self and other as at once a mutable and structural synthesis. It helps show us that the ground between the reversibility and irreversibility of difference is shifting and unstable. It shows that life produces things that cannot necessarily be recuperated into a structure of reflexivity or into discourse. At the same time, the activities of forgetting are a carrying of the growing, evolving, and transforming relationship between self and other, between the two together, from two sides. It is, we may also say, a restoring of chance back to chance and thus to the processes of engendering posterity itself. The challenge is to learn ways of apprehending and welcoming pure novelties after the event and without the promise of expectation.

RWANDA TRANSFORMED

On July 18, 1994, after having launched an attack in Kigali that defeated the Hutu militia, the Rwanda Patriotic Front (RPF) established a coalition government with Pasteur Bizimungu (a Hutu) as president and Paul Kagame (a Tutsi) as vice president and defense minister. The government was officially sworn in the next day. Immediately thereafter, Rwanda experienced an influx of many of the Tutsis who had fled to Uganda and Burundi. At the same time, there was a mass exodus of approximately two million Hutus, mostly into

Congo and Tanzania. To understand the full measure of the impact of the refugee crisis upon the region is an immense task that cannot be sufficiently undertaken here. However, it cannot go without mention that it created a triangulated assemblage among the political identities in Congo, Uganda, and Rwanda that, in all of its dimensions, is simultaneously interpreting and experiencing the inheritances of the genocide and of the precolonial and colonial eras in ways that are provoking a shift in the ability of heritage to be exchanged between the before and the after in any fundamental manner.[55] Without going further into the politics of this matter, which continues to display itself in different ways in its systems of production and processes of education, it will suffice to say that it too is an event that is forcing the symbolic order to transform itself. To determine how the State regulates, controls, and perpetuates types of regimes of exchanges with the past is one challenge.[56] To examine whether the event, change, and difference are both empirically and conceptually entering a novel era, devaluing the persistent primacy of symbolic in the ways life makes sense of its wounds, is a different challenge.

It would be easy enough to expand further on the political, social, cultural, and economic makeup of contemporary forms of identity in Rwanda, showing how they are constituting the forms of posterity in modifying and changing the character of the relation to what comes before. This means that such forms do not even owe solely to the psychic etiology of the ecology of the mind I have been attempting to develop. However, I wish to underscore that throughout this study, I have also been trying to challenge the idea that the causal value of the relation between trauma and life in the structure of the living being must be thought without a subordination to the finality of the symbolic and thus without any kind of psychic predestination. I have been insisting on this because trauma demonstrates that the concept of cause signifies something very different from that which finally happens, and that cause is not contained within what finally happens though it necessarily belongs to it. It also presents us with an idea of the transformability of difference that does not simply root itself in the energetic economy of the libido. As we see in *Beyond the Pleasure Principle*, trauma forces binding through repetition only as a phase so pleasure can regain control over the psyche. Trauma itself can never determine what follows or in what ways following generations go along with their own lives. This is an exceptionally important factor. Freud certainly insisted that the aim of the life drives is the tendency to bind, form, and combine into greater unities, that the aim of the death drive is to decompose and destroy, and that these drives are fused. From the tendency of cells to combine to construct more complex organisms to that of the enjoining movement of unity at the origin of civilization, Freud always maintained the necessity that the libido form attachments and enable detachments in its own processes of self-differentiating development and evolution.

However, and as I have also been attempting to develop, what might be taken to be a new globalized form of trauma, such as the Rwandan genocide or the 1947 Partition of India, also presents us with a novel concept of life that dismisses the priority of an irreducible difference between the material (or else, the natural) and the symbolic.[57] However, we are faced with the difficulty that the very activity of apprehension runs the risk of making novelty an extension of what comes before it. It seems as though the answer involves a return to nature that reminds us that the structure of the living being is not constituted by an irremediable partition between the symbolic and the material, but rather includes and borrows from the experience of their different coincidences in its formations. The coincidence between the two makes it impossible to know what is more or less symbolic or what is more or less material since the causal character of their relationship is both transformable and structural.

The famous problem at the heart of Freud's theory of trauma is precisely the question of whether or not there is a beyond of the pleasure principle. Ultimately, as I argued earlier, Freud contends that there is nothing beyond the pleasure principle; the pleasure principle always recovers its authority over the psychic apparatus. That Freud responds in the negative to this most perplexing question is also very important since logic shows that this necessarily affirms the possibility of the opposite. The difficulty here is that Freud himself was never able to illustrate a thoroughly other form of the psyche that is formed as a result of its encounter with death, and which would confirm the existence of a beyond of the pleasure principle. In other words, he would have needed to admit that the structure of the unconscious is both mutable and structural, and that it can and does transform itself.

This is as it seems, but it is not precisely the case. What has been blocking our view and guiding our gaze is the idea of "beyond," which in the psychoanalytic and philosophical traditions alike, is customarily taken to mean what is over and above, or at a greater distance on the basis of an accumulating surplus. In fact, this completely different form of the psyche in which the unconscious changes its structure is evident throughout Freud's work. It appears to us in what I have called the anatomy of the psyche, the period of neuronal motion, the conscious organ, and the ecology of the mind—each of which shows that transformations in the very concepts of the event, trauma, and wound really do happen. The horizon of expectation, and thus its typological schemas, involves material from the adventure and surprise of separation. We catch a glimpse of this in Lacan's reading of the "Dream of the Burning Child." Nothing in psychic life is immutable or invulnerable.

With these thoughts in mind, I return to the widow, who I introduced in the prologue and who I would suggest urges us to conceptualize transformation anew on both the theoretical and practical levels. As I mentioned, that the widow continues to live as neighbors with the Hutu man who committed the cruelties about which she spoke is not unique. In the years following "the events of 1994," as she and many other survivors refer to the genocide, Hutus and Tutsis have continued to live and work as neighbors, as they did in the years prior to the genocide. Rural subsistence farmers, like the other widows I met that day, had no choice but to establish some kind of truce in order to facilitate the cooperative based work and exchange that is necessary for daily living. Cohabitation was and continues to be a necessity in the sustainability of everyday life for many rural farmers throughout Rwanda.[58] But let us ask the question: what is produced by the complicitous cohabitation of necessity and chance in daily life after the genocide and in what ways is it transforming the determining causal value of the past? Again, though, to determine whether exchange and production are themselves at once empirically and conceptually in a new era is not the same as determining how current systems of exchange and forms of production are regulated by preexisting structures of circulation.

The possibility of opening this difference in determination, I would say, is what was striking in the widow's emphasis on the fact that things in Rwanda are now all together *transformed*—even when they may resemble prior contexts. She spoke about the politics of identity in postgenocide Rwanda but never once did she refer to herself as Tutsi or as Rwandan. In reference to herself as she is now, she only ever used the word *transformed*, while remarking about the absence of any other suitable word. "The events of 1994 transformed me, I am transformed." This is what she repeated throughout our conversation. There are no words for this meeting, for this assembly—for this thing.

Here I will not offer any hermeneutic analysis of the widow's subjectivization. If I follow current theoretical partitions that insist upon the finality of the symbolic as the primary order of things and the finitude of existences as the indestructible structure of knowledge about the subject, I will not deviate from the path that serves to confirm her capacity to live on and to subjectivize her change. This would lead us back to the affirmation of the exigencies of survival as stemming from being a finite, vulnerable being that unfolds itself within the mold of an already flexible and resilient identity. What else can a hermeneutic view reveal except how texts are made and how their texture is woven according to the catastrophe of the before and the after that tears life asunder? Would I not, in my critique, merely mime what I read, which would once more remind us that we are irremediably partitioned and traumatized by the originality of the temporality of time. Such an activity amounts to a process of selection in which the criteria for what form of difference deserves to return is assumed in advance. Insofar as the very category of difference is only primarily related to the eternal return of the same and copy, and thus to the law of reversal, our theoretical apparatuses constantly participate in the selection and affirmation of what, between life and death, has already been sorted.

The challenge is to free the problem of the subject from the partitions that repress and regulate it and its relations according to the binding economies of the extension of modes of being. To welcome and adopt the self-differentiating growth of novel forms of life—like those that we see asserting themselves in different ways and places throughout Rwanda—without resorting to the poeticization of messianic structures as towering over them—such is the other task that now makes it extremely difficult, if not unacceptable to give absolute priority to the symbolic order of life.

After Word

In February 1981 in Paris, Derrida delivered an opening address to a Franco–Latin American meeting of the International Psychoanalytic Association (IPA) titled "Geopsychoanalysis . . . 'and the Rest of the World.'" In this talk, Derrida offers a very interesting polemical critique of the IPA's parenthetical statement that named its primary geographic areas that defined the divisions of the psychoanalytic world. It lists "America north of the United States–Mexican border; all America south of that border; and the rest of the world."[1] He plays with the IPA's gesture of naming the "rest of the world" in "its ongoing worldifications" and Freud's discussion of the symptom as a body foreign to the ego that is an absolutely irreducible "foreign body."[2] He demonstrates that this "rest," which "lies beyond the boundaries of psychoanalysis," is a name and location shared by the roots of psychoanalysis as well as that which names the conditions of the future of psychoanalysis. The central question of this lecture is the question of the "geo," the *form* of the original relation in psychoanalysis; "for psychoanalysis has an earth, sole and singular," that must be distinguished from its world.[3] This question asks about the *soul* of psychoanalysis, about the secret alliance between the loop of the eternal return of the irreducible exteriority of foreignness and of the singular life of psychoanalysis *who* has revelations about it. As we recall from my earlier discussion about naming, there can be no eternal return without a proper name. To circumscribe this question, Derrida announces himself as the body who is foreign to the IPA's worldification: "I constitute a symptom, I am the symptom, I play that role."[4] I ask: whither the disease of (this) foreign body? Whither the unstable, shifting "geo" of psychoanalysis?

Without getting into the details of his argument, he shows that the originality of the idea of the foreign body in Freud's concept of the symptom is that the transcendent economy of foreignness is reliant upon the "body" that it leaves in itself of the "body of the ego" that encounters it.[5] Two forms within a form. The very thought of the eternal return of the otherness of the other is inseparable from the proper name (ego, psyche, subject, psychoanalysis) of the one who *thinks* it. The "geo" of psychoanalysis is the movement of this continuous formation of form. It is thus hard not to notice Derrida's thematization and symptomatic play of the "beyond" of psychoanalysis as the form of a foreign body, at once a natural body that has a history and a historical body that has a natural subject. How can we ignore that Derrida's own analysis of the very form and functioning of the psyche blurs the boundary between nature and history?

Here we should remember that Freud develops the symptomatic dimension comprising the domain of lived events and thus as inhering in the duality of chance. If the form of psychoanalysis is taken as a symptom that programs its own symptomatic acts, as Derrida's demonstration would urge to consider, then we must inquire about from what psychoanalysis is actually suffering.

In the summer of 2000 at the Sorbonne, Derrida delivered the keynote address to the States General of Psychoanalysis, called "Psychoanalysis Searches the States of Its Soul." This talk renewed the question of symptom; indeed it suffered from the problem of the question. The heart of the lecture is an inquiry into the question of cruelty and the unique capacity of psychoanalysis to respond to contemporary forms of evil that seem to be annulled of any sense. He proceeds according to the pointed claim that "psychoanalysis has not yet undertaken and thus still less succeeded in thinking, penetrating, and changing the axioms of the ethical, the juridical, and the political where the theological phantasm of sovereignty quakes and where the most traumatic, let us say in a still confused manner the most cruel events of our day are being produced."[6] What precisely are these "most cruel events"?[7] What is the geopsychoanalytic concept of this form of trauma?

Derrida presents geopolitical changes in cruelty as variations of the form of sovereignty that appeared in the emergence of modernity. According to him, psychoanalysis has not yet accounted for the "state and the beyond of the state;" that is, it has not considered the veritable "mutation on the subject of the subject and of the citizen subject" effected by the state's sovereignty over the "life and death of the citizen."[8] In short, it has not elaborated the question of cruelty.

Let's put aside the problem that Derrida's thinking of sovereignty, which appears here as very close to Foucault's concept of biopolitics, proceeds from the classical idea that the living being is irremediably divided between its natural, material aspect and its spiritual or symbolic domain. This partitioned notion of life and living hinges on the concept of finitude as the proper name for the being of a living being and for the experience of consciousness as the veiled consciousness of laws. Needless to say, that Derrida assumes the modern form of sovereignty, and therefore the concept of cruelty to be adaptable to all forms of life and death, including, then, its most radically evil, globalized form is now, to my mind, increasingly difficult to justify. Is it really the case that cruelty entered the scene once and for all in the eighteenth century?

For all that he elucidates by way of contemporary geopolitical mutations in the structure of juridico-political acts, and for as much as he condemns psychoanalysis for not yet accounting for that which has been occurring since the Second World War, it is rather curious that Derrida never once considers the possibility that the form of the psyche has actually changed in its encounters with the contemporary "quaking of the human earth" that has cracked open "a new scene" of "unprecedented juridical performatives."[9] In his account of the failure of psychoanalysis, he indicates that the fundamental operations of the drives have not been immune to the contemporary global phenomenon of cruelty that has appeared in the ongoing "process of worldwide-ization of the world."[10] "All the 'mythologies' that Freud speaks of, in particular the psychoanalytic mythology of the drives, are tied to conventional fictions, that is, to the authorized authority of performative acts."[11] How can we ignore this moment in which Derrida suggests that the modern form of cruelty has marked a fundamental damage in the form and functioning of the psyche to the extent that its core subject—the unconscious—is now vulnerable to its own deconstruction? How can we deny that the epicenter—the surface, focal point of an earthquakes' hypocenter, or the place of the greatest destruction—of this worldly, (geo)quaking is localized in the very immutability of the structure of the psyche?

The question that comes before us, though, is, what is psychoanalysis properly suffering from? At bottom, is the cruelty of which

Derrida speaks the violence at the heart of psychic suffering in general that makes the way for its own scenic revivals? What is proper to cruelty, and does cruelty come to affect "one of those horizons most proper to psychoanalysis"?[12]

Derrida opens his talk with a beautiful exposition of the finality of cruelty in the condition of suffering, showing that cruelty will always invent and determine its subject. Nonetheless, it seems as though the subject of the psyche has been transformed into an ontological stranger, deprived and dispossessed of citizenship in its own state by globalized forms of cruelty. A foreign body within its own body, "a State within a State," has pierced the elaborations of it own fabric, and psychoanalysis is commanded to respond to this contemporary challenge so that it does not remain "rooted in conditions of its birth" and can instead "interpret with renewed expense" its importance in the contemporary geopolitical scene.[13] And yet, and despite Derrida's own observation that there is a want of perspective in psychoanalysis's resistance to what remains primitive in these unprecedented cruelties, he nevertheless calls upon its old mythologies to respond.

Derrida argues that psychoanalysis must return to the profound thinking of the irreducibility of the death drive, since it is only this which *a priori* makes possible the messianic structures that allow for negotiation with new forms of globalized cruelty. Derrida retains Freud's thinking of sadism or masochism as figures of the death drive, and thus maintains the determinist character of the death drive. At the same time, it cannot be elided that psychoanalysis has experienced the contemporary destruction caused by the "quaking of the human earth." The phenomenon of this new, emerging form of violence is precisely that it asserts the unstable psychoanalytic status of its *geo*, that is, of the character of the psyche's relation to the earth and to nature. In imposing plural assemblies and versions of traumas, which render impossible any kind of distinction between interiorization/internalization and exteriorization/externalization, this new form of violence has provoked an irreversible shift within the symbolic texture of the very identity of psychoanalysis. For if this were not the case, then what need would there be constitute the death drive anew, what need would there be for psychoanalysis to "transform itself at this rhythm," what need would there be for psychoanalysis to prove the legitimacy, the value, of its regimes as most suited to respond to violence, to suffering, to disease, to illness, to wounds?[14] Isn't it possible that this renewal is actually the emergence of a new form of the psyche that forces absolute otherness to transform itself by inventing a new concept of finitude and a new relation to death?

I would suggest that in Derrida's lecture, we in fact encounter the emergence of what was only in its childhood twenty years prior in the lecture on "geopsychoanalysis": the growth of a concept of life that asserts, in its increasing complexification of the problem of suffering, the coincidence between the earth and the world, between the natural and historicity, between the material and the symbolic. The difficulty is that we cannot apprehend it with our familiar ways, for this concept of life plays with the forces of its own beyond. Perhaps we can call this geopolitical moment historic. However, it would be so only insofar as we admit that it is impossible for the old concept of history, which formulates meaning from within the field of historical becoming and as the difference between natural phenomena and pure contingent facts on the one hand and events and human agents on the other, to hold its ground.

A profound political lesson of the Rwandan genocide is that violent disturbances to the psyche involve the return of repetition, or else the return of nature. The period of neuronal motion dismisses the question of origin and proper, and thus the difference between primordial temporality and lived time. It is a time that carries life and death together without sublation or turning upon itself to reveal the absolute fragility or sacredness of life. What we see in Rwanda's processes of education are the different ways the period of neuronal motion restores back to temporality its lost object: the question of time. Perhaps then one piece of the genocide's unrecorded history is the actual accomplishment of the end of the difference between pure messianic time and actual lived time, or else the temporality of time as the origin of any formative power.

The transformation of the drive, which bears witness to the primitive and constitutes our susceptibility, is also always threatened from within by the return to nature that can destroy not only the subject and what is taken as the object, but also the character of the relation between the two. By the work of its own dynamic interactions with the environment, memory forgets the fields of becoming and the horizon of authentic possibility in the living being, and leaves us the chance for a time that is before the drives and the authority of the pleasure principle.

Whether or not these ideas hold ground, I will nevertheless admit that I can no longer accept that trauma, the completely surprising, responds to the utterance and that identity opens itself only according to what the automatism chooses for return and nonreturn. To put it differently, the ontological significance of necessity does not solely consist in being the mode of occurring for the absolutely contingent or the finality of the symbolic. Does the subject not contain any capacity beyond exercising a certain flexibility in identity and resiliency?[15] Victims of trauma suffer, this is incontestable, and I wonder how we can ask the questions about how to repair and heal multiple manifestations of wounds without asking what they are suffering from and by what means they are responding to the losses and pains? In part, this question concerns the therapeutic dimension. But it runs deep into the messianic structure, and exposes its ideological tendency of sorting what is permitted to return for response and what is properly speaking, a response.

Derrida knows perfectly well that response must first entail knowing what something is about. In ethics and politics, knowing, he elucidates in "Ethics and Politics Today," brings to light the paradoxical nature of the structure of urgency. There can be no responsibility taken up or a decision made without encountering one's own limit of knowledge in the determinate inquiry into knowing. This interruption is what constitutes the structure of urgency. As Derrida explains, "*Différance* and urgency are the same thing, they have always been the same thing. Thus there can be no responsibility without a structure of deliberation being regulated by a double rule, theoretical and practical: (1) Knowing what it's about, and in what way and how to act accordingly. (2) Which practical laws[,] . . . which principles, the principles to which . . . one must address one's respect in one's actions."[16]

Let me situate these comments alongside another passage. In the subsection titled "Savoir-penser: Inheriting 'The Critical Mission of Philosophy,'" which appears in "As If It Were Possible," Derrida explains that what *différance* announces is that the originality of the thought of the eternal return depends on the trace that it leaves in itself of the one who thinks it. It reveals the alliance between the loop of the eternal return of the same and the singular life that is utterly astonished by it. Derrida's *différance* also showed that Nietzsche's eternal return of the same was the radicalization of the thought of difference.

> Without being a "program" in the least, what does *différance* "say" or "do"? (It is neither a word nor a concept . . . in obvious

> denegation, but whose traces remain, in some sense—to the point of making denegation of denegation as legitimate as it is inoperative . . .). What announced itself thus as *difference* had this singular quality: that it simultaneously welcomed, but without dialectical facility, the same and the other, the economy of analogy . . . absolute heterology. Yet one could also, in this context, re-treat this question of *différance* as a question of legacy.[17]

These very interesting comments about *différance* as a question of legacy reiterate that it also reveals the duality of the loops of the ontological and the autobiographical.[18] To the extent that the question of what announces itself as *différance* is a question of legacy, it is also then a question of (its own) childhood. This question invites a reflection on the meaning of descendent, the sequence of filiation, on processes of education, and on the engendering of heritage by the inheritor into something that is given. *Différance* cannot then avoid the ambiguity between filiation and abjection that negatively reveals its selection and affirmation of what will, must, or can return. If the infinite return of the same is a process that ensures its own difference and thus the operation of its differentiation as the source of any formative process, then it automatically regulates that which does and does not return. Although Derrida insists that *différance* is not a program in the sense that it is an instrument that obeys a program, it is nevertheless a principle of selection that produces its own criteria for the conditions for identity as it operates, creating its norms and orders in the process—no matter how radical its approach is to undermining and overcoming order as such. It is indeed a program that programs life into multiple modes of the living being that expresses itself as forms of finite existence. How can we ignore that becoming, which is so abundant in differences, begins to looks like a series of the normalization of life and the living being? This is a question put to *différance* by posterity.

The problem, to my mind, is that we are required to admit that this mode of the coming of and to finality is nondialectical and that the double rule and the traversing of its inscriptions occur without any resistances that would place its mechanisms in check; the living being is stripped in advance of its capacity to do anything but unfold into preformed patterns of knowing that controls and disciplines the subject. What chance, then, is really left to the subject?

Without getting into the detail of Freud's argument regarding the intellectual gesture of judgment and the interplay of the instinctual impulses as it is laid out in "Negation," it suffices to say that he shows negation to be a particular way of freeing repression by "taking cognizance of what is repressed" without accepting it.[19] What Freud shows is that negation is not a simple matter of "yes" and "no" in the unconscious; there is always a process of engendering the negation in a negative formula, by which "thinking frees itself from the restrictions of repression and enriches itself with material that is indispensable to its proper functioning."[20] Denegation therefore does not have a simple opposite, which is why Freud says that in analysis we can never actually "discover a 'no' in the unconscious."[21] It at once admits what is repressed by asserting it and does not admit what is repressed. The simple point here is that denegation reveals two logics of affective and intellectual negation that are not one and the same and that the results of their dialectical relation are articulated differently in both the unconscious and the ego. *Différance* affirms this dialectical denegation to the extent that, in its very movements, it operates upon its possibility for a return like a scalpel that cuts it out in advance so that it cannot return. This dialectical difference is dissolved by difference as pure negation as the modality for the necessity of coimplication.

The structure of the universal urgency of memory, which is also the structure of deliberation, suffers from these debilitating interruptions that suppress and occult what returns to the living by selecting the ontological range of spectral hauntings, thereby affirming the vitality of positive, creative destruction. However, to affirm that nothing of death returns to the living is to affirm yet again that not everything returns in the eternal return, which is to say that the thought of the interminable return of the same can maintain its fidelity to itself as primarily linked to plenitude. The source redoubles itself. It seems as though deconstruction can only uphold the category of difference as differentiation by maintaining itself as a principle of ontological selection that makes the division between what can and what cannot be experienced. It reproduces its own criteria as it operates on the living, regenerating, in the process, norms of the subject and subjectivity. As a result, and for all that *différance* is an indispensable move, it cannot by itself produce posterity or pure novelty.

What, I wonder, is the actual result of negotiations whose underlying self-deconstructive movement imminent to the real yields preeminent, ghostly appearances of dialectical abjections and filiations that are constrained to a range? To re-treat *différance* as a question of legacy, which is also necessarily a question of the transference and inheritance of "the critical mission of philosophy," requires that we modify the exhausted expressions of the fragility of life, the secret, and of what is most incorporeal to the living being. For responsibility to begin life anew, and to apprehend it in today's geopolitical contexts means that we admit the fact that offspring can start from a non-disseminatory difference. To think and judge duty and response would no longer be the repetitive stereotyped character of the results of the transmission of the seminal reason. What then would responsibility really look like? To begin to answer this question would require that we start by involving the unstable ground of *a priori* irreducibility and necessity.

An important political lesson of the 1947 Partition of India is that the border—the interaction between the geographic, cultural, social, linguistic, and psychic—is organized and indicated in different ways at each time of its historical occurrences. The border is an unallocatable, unstable place that has no proper destination. In trauma, the limit between what is more material or what is more incorporeal to subjectivity is erased. The border is itself not a fixed determination but a fundamental shifting that is a productive movement that borrows from the encounters between the contingencies of necessity and the necessities of contingency. The outlines of the structure and shape of a particular state of things cannot be fully settled in advance.

Now, the critical task of philosophy must include its own incapacity to prove, by means of philosophical reason alone, the absolute legitimacy of its structures of knowledge about the subject. This would loosen the structure of response and open it to the interactions between determinisms and liberties, and thus give the *a posteriori* the chance for the generation and development of logical structures that modify the causal value and status of purely formal structures or logical forms. Now, the new globalized form of violence requires that we elaborate the transformability of the relationship to otherness and responsibility.

Between the traumatic event and the self, it is the sense of the other that is uprooted, dislocated, and released. To think trauma is, in a way, to apprehend otherness and pure novelty from within the structure of the living being but without needing to transgress life. In one way or another, the movements and processes of life borrow from the experiences of irreversible changes in structures that we call the psyche, finitude, the messianic, the border, promise, or the horizon. So long held to be invariant, these structures are themselves fragile and not completely invulnerable to their own destruction.

That completely surprising events can and do happen remains true. The point here is not to cut transiency, finitude, and time to the quick. However, it seems incontestable that the geopolitical changes in cruelty and suffering challenge messianic structures to the extent that new concepts of event, trauma, wound, and necessity are now necessary. What is the reason to continue conceiving of the event as the advent—as the "absolute" appropriating event—absolute hospitality, absolute arrival, absolute rupture, absolute otherness—and as utterly irreducible to any material determination of what constitutes the surprising? In this idea of the event, there is nothing beyond the horizon of anticipation that is originarily opened by the originary temporalization of time. There is nothing but the ways we relate to the question of the exposure to one's own of death, and to the abyssal play of life and death. The event is the very structure of finitude since it designates at once the slit of the other in time and the other in being. It is the immutable hermeneutic horizon of meaning within which beings appear as they are, as the very structure of finitude. Consequently, we are always already doomed to be coming from the event, merely realizing the very end that is at once the vanishing and accomplishment of the finite as excess, and thereby living under the order of succession and the law of the reversibility of difference. We are left to wonder again, what chance is left to childhood, to the chance to follow along with one's own life?

In a time when everything seems to be allocated, including psychic suffering (even in its designation as unheard or unhearable), precisely what is the valid conceptual path? To start answering this question and the others that have been raised in the process, I have attempted to think trauma as a concept of the material event that does not envisage the priority of the need to separate the self from itself. I have also tried to think the traumatic event without promise and without expectation. My answers are no doubt especially vulnerable given the obvious links to ethics and politics. To take seriously the idea of the absence of expectation does not mean that we abnegate responsibility. Rather, it means that we do not regard as probable a causal system of events as that which finally gives shape and meaning to our encounters with the other's pain and suffering. It means that we protect, without first any kind of reflective gesture, the other's suffering by restoring back to the other their losses, and leaving them the chance to go.

People are indeed resilient. However, in our encounters with today's new, globalized forms of violence there is something that has forced a transformation and has arrived to break the expectation of a definite character. Trauma does not just invent its subject; the critical posterity of trauma invents and transforms its relations to that which comes before it. Trauma, or else life begins life anew. This trembling, open form of life is quickly swept up by and kept in the throes of the waves of translation, transcription, appropriation, and possession—of history. Nonetheless, it is our now responsibility to open the places in our theoretical and practical structures where pure novelty can assert itself beyond the familiar modes of recognition. This is the lesson I gathered from the widows I met in Rwanda. Perhaps this task begins with something rather simple: the will to start a new habit in the ways we approach the question of how and by what means the human being constitutes itself in its self-differentiating processes of growth. It is possible to change ontological meaning and significations after the event. Life arrives to interrupt the destiny of trauma's future.

ACKNOWLEDGMENTS

I thank Richard Morrison, my editor, for his patience, kindness, and support of this book. I hope that it will show him the true measure of my sincere gratitude for everything he has done for me.

I thank Deepika Bahri, Cathy Caruth, and Jill Robbins for the perspicacity of their direction during my years as a graduate student, which shaped my academic path in indispensable ways. I am deeply grateful for their guidance and confidence.

Sarah Senk, Mikhal Dekel, Vilashini Cooppan, Beth Bouloukos, Brian McGrath, Omaar Hena, Radhika Mohanram, and Luisa Pèrcopo have extended me their unfailing benevolence, support, and encouragement during particularly challenging periods of my academic life. I would here like to express my enduring respect and friendship to them.

The many wonderful students at Drexel, who likely on the basis of requirement alone stayed in my courses after the first day, have been a source of a sustaining energy. That I have the privilege to witness their processes of growth has me continuously in wonder about my good fortune.

Dan Driscoll granted me the patience, kindness, and encouragement of his reading and listening through the many stages of this book. He is owed more than I can ever fulfill.

I thank my friends and family for their support during the elephantine gestation period in which this book was produced.

Finally, the Nisbet family helped grow me up with a love they were never obligated to give and still give. The very core of my work is beholden to them. I hope they know all that I owe them.

JY

NOTES

PROLOGUE

1. Habit, of course, is not a new concept in philosophy. Though it is not within the scope of this study to elaborate the various philosophical notions of habit, suffice it to say that the concept remains rather ambiguous. The value of habit is widely addressed in philosophy. We see it, for example, in Aristotle's discussion of the necessary role of habit in the making of character, of moral and political virtue in the *Nicomachean Ethics*, in Hume's concept of habit as that which names the necessity of the belief in the necessity of the laws of nature, in Kant's discussion of the character of necessity as that which reveals habit to be a simulation of virtue, and in Deleuze's thinking of habit as pulling something new out of repetition that has been produced by repetition itself. The value of habit is widely addressed. However, whether the value pertains to revealing habit to be a purely senseless routine and or an ontological phenomenon remains unclear.

2. Immanuel Kant, *Critique of Pure Reason*, trans. and ed. Paul Guyer and Allen W. Wood (Cambridge: Cambridge University Press, 1998), 536–539.

INTRODUCTION: THE INTERFACE OF TRAUMA

1. Louis Althusser, "The Underground Current of the Materialism of the Encounter," in *Philosophy of the Encounter: Later Writings, 1978–87*, ed. François Materon and Oliver Corpet, trans. G. M. Goshgarian (London: Verso, 2006), 168.

2. Ibid., 167.

3. Claude Lévi-Strauss, *Introduction to the Work of Marcel Mauss*, trans. Felicity Baker (London: Routledge & Kegan Paul, 1987).

4. It is important to note that in the beginning of the *Introduction to the Work of Marcel Mauss*, Lévi-Strauss contends that what is needed is a symbolic origin of society. According to him, "any culture can be considered as a combination of symbolic systems" (16) because there is a structural identity

between the symbolic and the social and in the way in which human relationships and meanings are distributed. For Lévi-Strauss, the symbolic origin of society is exchange, which is indissoluble from reproduction. This is brought to the fore with his theory of kinship as exchange, which is founded on exogamy and explains the prohibition of incest.

5. Ibid.

6. Ibid.

7. See, e.g., Jill Bennett and Rosanne Kennedy, eds., *World Memory: Personal Trajectories in Global Time* (Houndmills: Palgrave Macmillan, 2003); Gert Buelens, Sam Durrant, and Robert Eaglestone, eds., *The Future of Trauma Theory: Contemporary Literary and Cultural Criticism* (New York: Routledge, 2014); Stef Craps and Gert Buelens, eds., "Postcolonial Trauma Novel," special issue of *Studies in the Novel* 40.1–2 (Spring–Summer 2008); Didier Fassin and Richard Rechtman, *The Empire of Trauma: An Inquiry into the Condition of Victimhood*, trans. Rachel Gomme (Princeton, NJ: Princeton University Press, 2009); and Michael Rothberg, *Multidirectional Memory: Remembering the Holocaust in the Age of Decolonization* (Stanford, CA: Stanford University Press, 2009).

8. Stef Craps, *Postcolonial Witnessing: Trauma Out of Bounds* (Houndmills: Palgrave Macmillan, 2013), 4, 6.

9. Ibid., 1; and see pp. 31–40. Craps pays particular attention to Caruth's formulation of trauma as resituating history "in our understanding," "permitting it to arise where immediate understanding may not" (*Unclaimed Experience* 11). As Craps recounts the development of trauma theory, this thinking laid the groundwork for the ethical imperative to bear witness to the other's trauma. Witnessing, according to Caruth, occurred as "a new mode of reading and listening" (*Unclaimed Experience* 11) that convoked crises of representation manifested on the level of language. "In a catastrophic age," writes Caruth, "trauma itself may provide the very link between cultures: not as a simple understanding of the pasts of others but rather, within the traumas of contemporary history, as our ability to listen though the departures we have all taken from ourselves" (*Trauma: Explorations in Memory* 11). For Craps, the idea that typological schemas of aporia are the necessary mode of occurring for witnessing the other's trauma problematically assumes an uncritical transmissibility of the theory of trauma across non-Western histories and cultures to the extent that it fails in its promise to foster cross-cultural solidarity.

Cathy Caruth, Introduction to *Trauma: Explorations in Memory*, ed. Cathy Caruth (Baltimore, MD: Johns Hopkins University Press, 1995); and Cathy Caruth, *Unclaimed Experience: Trauma, Narrative, and History* (Baltimore, MD: Johns Hopkins University Press, 1996).

In reference to the work of the other scholars Craps addresses, see, e.g., Shoshana Felman and Dori Laub, *Testimony: Crises of Witnessing in Literature, Psychoanalysis, and History* (New York: Routledge, 1992); Geoffrey H. Hartman, *The Longest Shadow: In the Aftermath of the Holocaust* (Bloomington, IN: Indiana University Press, 1996); Dominick LaCapra, *History and Memory after Auschwitz* (Ithaca, NY: Cornell University Press,

1998); and Dominick LaCapra, *Representing the Holocaust: History, Theory, Trauma* (Ithaca, NY: Cornell University Press, 1994).

10. Craps, *Postcolonial Witnessing*, 4, 6.

11. Jenny Edkins, *Trauma and the Memory of Politics* (Cambridge: Cambridge University Press, 2003), 9–10; Ann Kaplan, *Trauma Culture: The Politics of Terror and Loss in Media and Literature* (New Brunswick, NJ: Rutgers University Press, 2005); Anne Whitehead, *Trauma Fiction* (Edinburgh: Edinburgh University Press, 2004).

12. Ruth Leys, *Trauma: A Genealogy* (Chicago, IL: University of Chicago Press, 2000); and Roger Luckhurst, *The Trauma Question* (New York: Routledge, 2008).

13. See also Warwick Anderson, Deborah Jenson, and Richard C. Keller, eds., *Unconscious Dominions: Psychoanalysis, Colonial Trauma, and Global Sovereignties* (Durham, NC: Duke University Press, 2011); and Mark S. Micale and Paul Lerner, eds., *Traumatic Pasts: History, Psychiatry, and Trauma in the Modern Age, 1870–1930* (Cambridge: Cambridge University Press, 2001).

14. Allan Young, *The Harmony of Illusions: Inventing Post-Traumatic Stress Disorder* (Princeton, NJ: Princeton University Press, 1995), 5. For more on PTSD and the history and the validity of the efficacies of the PTSD diagnosis, see Judith Herman, *Trauma and Recovery: The Aftermath of Violence—from Domestic Abuse to Political Terror* (New York: Basic Books, 1992); Mardi J. Horowitz, *Stress Response Syndromes*, 4th ed. (New York: Jason Aronson, 2001); Leys, *Trauma: A Genealogy*; and Claire Stocks, "Trauma Theory and the Singular Self: Rethinking Extreme Experiences in the Light of Cross Cultural Identity," *Textual Practice* 21.1 (2007): 71–92; Bessel A. van der Kolk, Lars Weisaeth, and Onno van der Hart, eds., *Traumatic Stress: The Effects of Overwhelming Experience on Mind, Body, and Society* (New York: Guilford Press, 1996).

15. Didier Fassin, "Ethnopsychiatry and the Postcolonial Encounter: A French Psychopolitics of Otherness," in *Unconscious Dominions*, 244. See also Richard C. Keller's contribution in the same volume, titled "Colonial Madness and the Poetics of Suffering: Structural Violence and Kateb Yacine." He offers a very interesting account of how the practice of medicine is complicit in the structure of colonial violence and thus often the source of suffering and trauma.

16. Rothberg cites "hyper-particularism" as an "inverse risk" of the critiques that seek to deconstruct the "homogenizing geo-cultural regions" (228). Michael Rothberg, "Decolonizing Trauma Studies: A Response," in Craps and Buelens, "Postcolonial Trauma Novel," 224–234.

17. Rothberg's concept of multidirectional memory designates the character of the relation between collective memory and what he calls "group identity" (5). The logic of multidirectional memory works to reveal a "countertradition" that consists in the production of unexpected intersections between Holocaust remembrance and the regimes of transmission of memory and inheritance in colonialism and processes of decolonization (*Multidirectional Memory* 21).

18. Benita Parry, *Postcolonial Studies: A Materialist Critique* (London: Routledge, 2004), 82.

19. Ibid., 76. In the "The Ends of Man," in *Margins of Philosophy*, trans. Alan Bass (Chicago, IL: University of Chicago Press, 1982), 111–136, Derrida shows the links between Sartre's humanism and the thinking of the concept of the human in Hegel, Heidegger, and Husserl.

20. Althusser, "The Underground Current," 200. Unless indicated otherwise, all emphases appear in the original.

21. Derrida, "The Ends of Man."

22. Caruth, *Unclaimed Experience*, 87; and Cathy Caruth, *Literature in the Ashes of History* (Baltimore, MD: Johns Hopkins University Press, 2013), 16.

23. Caruth, *Literature in the Ashes of History*, 9.

24. Ibid., 81.

25. Sigmund Freud, *The Standard Edition of the Complete Psychological Works of Sigmund Freud*, ed. and trans. James Strachey (London: Vintage, 2001), 19:38. Hereafter *SE*, followed by volume and page(s).

26. Ibid., 36.

27. In "The Ends of Man," Derrida presents a very brief but interesting reading of Nietzsche's notion of *aktive Vergesslichkeit*, which he translates as "active forgetting," as conveying the idea of man as beyond, always on his way, as it were, to himself (136). In the English translations of *Genealogy of Morals*, in which the concept appears in his discussion of the capacity to make consciousness available for responsibility, it is translated as "active forgetfulness" (58). But I retain Derrida's translation since it conveys the willfulness of will that I aim to invoke and discuss at length in the latter part of this study.

Friedrich Nietzsche, *On the Genealogy of Morals and Ecce Homo*, trans. Walter Kaufmann (New York: Vintage Press: 1989).

28. Nietzsche, *On the Genealogy of Morals and Ecce Homo*, 58.

CHAPTER 1: THE PROBLEM OF TRAUMA

1. Freud, *SE*, 18:14–15.

2. Ibid., 14.

3. Ibid. 7.

4. Ibid.

5. Ibid. 7, 11.

6. Ibid. 11.

7. Ibid., 12.

8. Ibid., 16.

9. In Caruth's reading of *fort/da* in *Unclaimed Experience*, she pays particular attention to the game's "symbolized pattern of departure and return" as exemplifying how the individual experience of trauma and wider historical experience are coextensive experiences of departure without return (65–66). In her recent book, she offers an updated reading of the fort/da game that operates around the game "as an act of creation" that distinguishes

between life and death and "creates a history by precisely departing toward survival" (*Literature in the Ashes of History* 8). Whereas in her early work, the game offered a symbolized pattern of trauma as a departure without return," the more recent interpretation pays attention to how the creative act of language exemplifies trauma as a "departure into life," that reclaims and generates history by bearing witness to the parting from history (*Literature in the Ashes of History* 9). Cathy Caruth, *Literature in the Ashes of History*, and *Unclaimed Experience: Trauma, Narrative, and History.*

10. Freud, *SE*, 18:29.

11. Ibid., 30. The concept of "bound" excitations is evident throughout all of Freud's writings. The most detailed discussion occurs in section I of part 3 in *Project for a Scientific Psychology.* In that section, he distinguishes between "bound" or "quiescent" psychic energy and "free" or "mobile" (unbounded) psychic energy. This distinction appears in later writings, in chapter 7 of *The Interpretation of Dreams*, for example, and in *Group Psychology and the Analysis of the Ego* during Freud's discussion of the ambivalence of libidinal bonds in the section titled "A Differentiating Grade in the Ego." Freud however, credits the distinction between bounded and unbounded excitations to Breuer, who published his ideas in his contributions to their coauthored *Studies in Hysteria.* One can also read the implications of this concept in Freud's discourse on temporality and morality in his essays "Timely Reflections on War and Death" and "On Transience," as well in the difference between the experience of mourning and the condition of melancholia as detailed in "Mourning and Melancholia."

12. Freud, *SE*, 18:38–40.

13. Ibid., 40.

14. Ibid., 33.

15. Ibid., 32.

16. Ibid., 33.

17. Ibid., 36.

18. Ibid., 62.

19. Ibid.; emphasis added. See also *Project for a Scientific Psychology* in which Freud discusses at length pleasure and unpleasure as economic outcomes relatable to the amount of excitation in the mind that is *not yet bound*; the psyche aims to keep excitation quantities present in it at a minimum or at the very least at a constant (Freud, *SE*, 1:363–371).

20. Catherine Malabou presents the only elaborated exception to this trend in which she argues for the fundamental ambiguity of repetition. Catherine Malabou, *The New Wounded: From Neurosis to Brain Damage*, trans. Steven Miller (New York: Fordham University Press, 2012), 189–202.

21. Freud, *SE*, 18:12.

22. Jacques Lacan, *The Seminar of Jacques Lacan, Book XI: The Four Fundamental Concepts of Psychoanalysis*, trans. Alan Sheridan (New York, NY: Norton, 1992), 53–54.

23. Ibid., 38.

24. Freud, *SE*, 22:59.

25. Ibid., 12. Herman Oppenheim first introduced the term "traumatic neurosis" in an 1889 treatise, which asserted that psychological trauma caused organic changes that gave rise to psychic neuroses. Herman Oppenheim, *Die Traumatischen Neurosen*, 2nd ed. (Berlin: August Hirschwald, 1892).

26. Freud, *SE*, 18:12. It is important to note that Freud undertook this task with the aim of accounting for types of trauma other than childhood traumas that were linked to sexuality.

27. Ibid., 29.

28. In the *Four Fundamental Concepts of Psychoanalysis*, Lacan draws upon the Aristotelian division of chance to develop how we can read our experience of the Real in two, interrelated ways. First, we can read it as a subject's experience in which the conscious experience of accidental events necessarily submits to the organizing functions of the unconscious Other's automaticity. Or second, we may read it as an analytic experience in which the analyst connects the subjective chance (*tuché*), which is the encounter with the Real, in interpreting the Symbolic milieu of unconscious meanings (*automaton*). Lacan interprets *tuché* as the impossible Real in the character of the sudden, forcible time of the unanticipated event. In contrast, *automaton* is the effect whereby the unconscious immediately integrates the Real into the Symbolic (the signifier).

29. Freud, *SE*, 6:191. See the entirety of the chapters "Symptomatic and Chance Actions" and "Determinism, Belief in Chance, and Superstition—Some Points of View" for more.

30. In the beginning of *The Psychopathology of Everyday Life*, Freud becomes involved in a conversation with a traveling companion about the forgetting of an event as a pure "chance event," as *Ereignis* (*SE*, 6:4). Freud recalls the event of his own forgetting of the name of the artist who painted "The Four Last Things [Death, Judgment, Hell, and Heaven] in the Oriveto Cathedral" (2). In forgetting the name Signorelli, he remembers two other familiar names, Botticelli and Boltraffio, both of which he immediately recognizes as being incorrect. It is not until another person says the correct name that he recognizes Signorelli as being immediately correct. This leads him to examine the phenomena of temporal forgetfulness as part of the way the analyst conceives of the nature of symptomatic acts in relation to chance.

For more on Freud's thinking of *Ereignis* and its relation to Heidegger's notion of *Ereignis* see Ned Luckacher, *Primal Scenes: Literature, Philosophy, Psychoanalysis* (Ithaca, NY: Cornell University Press, 1986) and "Chiasmic Reading, Aporetic History: Freud's Macbeth," in *Reading Freud Reading*, ed. Sander L. Gilman, Jutta Birmele, Jay Geller, and Valerie D. Greenberg (New York, NY: New York University Press, 1994), 152–179.

31. From *Studies in Hysteria* onward, Freud maintains that as much as an event that may rightly be called traumatic, the memory of the force of the event and its "aftershock" is just as important and has value as its own scene of occurrence. The first scene becomes, in Freud's assessment, pathogenic within memory since it causes its own overwhelming influx of excitations. In the end, Freud advances the idea that the efficacy of external events is derived

from the fantasies that they activate and then from the excitations that these fantasies trigger. So fantasy comes to name the manner in which accident is elaborated in the psyche while establishing their originary unity. Thus it becomes the conjunction between the internal surge of the psyche's confrontation with the unexpected accident and its internal hermeneutic process. We see this idea of fantasy at work in Freud's distinction between "psychical reality" and "material reality" in *The Interpretation of Dreams* in which the former is a "particular form of existence not to be confused with" the latter (Freud, *SE*, 14:17–18). Something that happens in material reality can trigger a disturbance in the psyche, which causes psychic damage, without necessarily being the cause. The phantasmatic accident translates the materially real event from being a trigger into a precipitating cause. I discuss this in greater detail in the second chapter.

32. Freud, *SE*, 17:137. Sexuality was among the set of few constants throughout Freud's evolving equations for psychic life. He was always clear in stating that sexuality was to be understood in "the extended sense in which it is used in psychoanalysis and is not to be confused with the narrower concept of 'genitality'" (Freud, *SE*, 17:208). Freud designates sexuality as the connection between external events and internal events, psychic events, and thus between contingency and signification. For him, it is a site of convergence, the place where the signification of one event is converted into another. It is the conjoining of the external and internal events. Because of its fundamentally divided nature and construction, Freud never really wavered on the etiology of sexuality and sexual pathology, that is, on the nature of its agents and agitators, of its psychic disturbances. Its own differentiated structure establishes the logic of its functioning. Even in the case of unanticipated fright related to mechanical accidents, for example, there is still, in Freud's assessment, an occurrence of sexual excitation (*SE*, 18:33). We also see this conclusion in Freud's discussion of train travel in "Three Essays on the Theory of Sexuality." There is only trauma when the factor of surprise produces a sexual excitation, which cannot be mastered and awakens a prior conflict by its own violence. For Freud, then, the dualism of the drives and the libido theory pivot around sexuality. For more on this, see Laplanche's assessment of sexuality in relation to *Nachträglichkeit* in "Sexuality and the Vital Order in Psychical Conflict," in *Life and Death in Psychoanalysis*, trans. Jeffrey Mehlman (Baltimore, MD: Johns Hopkins University Press, 1976). See as well Malabou's *The New Wounded* for an especially incisive rethinking of the etiology of sexuality in Freud's work in the context of trauma. For another interesting perspective, see Michael S. Roth's "Hysterical Remembering," *Modernism/Modernity* 3.2 (1996): 1–30.

33. Adrian Johnston, *Time Driven: Metapsychology and the Splitting of the Drive* (Evanston, IL: Northwestern University Press, 2005), 175. Johnston is right to suggest that the model of the drives in the 1915 essay "Drives and Their Vicissitudes" speaks to something internal to the essence of the drives. However, this something is not an inconsistency. It is precisely the opposite: a consistency in the essential transformability of the drives.

34. In her trenchant reassessment of the dualism of the drives and the etiological power of sexuality as the other of sexuality, Malabou designates the libido theory as the "theory of *the partition of energy*" (*The New Wounded* 104).

35. In several places, Freud relies upon the metaphor of libido as a constant flow, like a river, running through interconnected canals. See, for example, "Three Essays on Sexuality," in which Freud states that the "various channels along which the libido passes are related to each other from the very first like inter-communicating pipes" (Freud, *SE*, 7:151). In his brief encyclopedia entry, "The Libido Theory," Freud distinguishes between sublimation, in which both object and aim are changed, and narcissism, which refers to the collateral flow and output of instinct that take the subject's ego as its object (Freud, *SE*, 18:256–257).

36. Freud, *SE*, 14:76.

37. Ibid., 77.

38. Freud, *SE*, 17:209.

39. Ibid., 210–211.

40. Ibid., 209.

41. Freud, *SE*, 14:83.

42. Freud, *SE*, 18:12.

43. Ibid., 31–33.

44. Ibid., 33; emphasis added.

45. Ibid., 26–27.

46. Ibid., 31.

47. Ibid., 130.

48. Ibid., 62.

49. Ibid.

50. Ibid., 49; emphasis added.

51. Freud, *SE*, 18:50.

52. Ibid. Freud reiterates this idea in his essay "The Two Classes of Instincts": "It appears that, as a result of the combination of unicellular organisms into a multicellular forms of life, the death instinct of the single cell can successfully be neutralized and the destructive impulses be diverted on to the external world through the instrumentality of a special organ" (Freud, *SE*, 19:41).

53. Freud, *SE*, 19:42–43. Freud develops the same idea in the encyclopedia article "The Libido Theory":

> The other set of instincts would be those which are better known to us in analysis—the libidinal, sexual or life instincts, which are best comprised under the name of *Eros*; their purpose would be to form living substance into ever greater unities, so that life may be prolonged and brought into higher development (253).

Again in *An Outline of Psychoanalysis*:

> The aim of [Eros] is to establish even greater unities and to preserve them thus—in short, to bind together; the aim of the [destructive

> instinct] is, on the contrary, to undo connections and so to destroy things. In this case of the destructive drive we may suppose that its final aim is to lead what is living into an inorganic state. For this reason we also call it the *death drive*. (Freud, *SE*, 23:148)

And then in *Civilization and Its Discontents*:

> Starting from speculations on the beginning of life and from biological parallels, I drew conclusions that, besides the drive to preserve living substance and to join it into ever larger units, there must exist another, contrary drive seeking to dissolve those units and to bring them back to their primaeval, inorganic state. That is to say, as well as Eros there was a drive of death. The phenomena of life could be explained from the concurrent or mutually opposing actions of these two drives. (Freud, *SE*, 21:118–119)

54. Freud, *SE*, 23:148.

55. Freud, *SE*, 19:41.

56. Freud, *SE*, 18:258. As Freud writes in *Beyond the Pleasure Principle*, "The attributes of life were at some time evoked in inanimate matter by the action of a force of whose nature we can form no conception. . . . The tension which then arose in what had hitherto been an inanimate substance endeavored to cancel itself out. In this way the first instinct came into being: the drive to return to the inanimate state" (38).

57. Ibid., 259. On the plasticity of the libido, see Malabou's *The New Wounded*.

58. Freud, *SE*, 1:296–297.

59. Ibid. "With an [increasing] complexity of the interior [of the organism], the nervous system receives stimuli from the somatic element itself—endogenous stimuli—which equally have to be discharged. . . . From these the organism cannot withdraw as it does from external stimuli; it cannot employ their Q [quantity] for flight from stimulus" (296–297).

60. "Let us recall, then, that from the first the nervous system had two functions: the reception of stimuli *from outside* and the discharge of stimuli of *endogenous* origin. . . . We might then conjecture that it might actually be our systems Φ and ψ each of which had assumed one of these primary obligations. The system Φ would be the group of neurons which the external stimuli reach, the system ψ would contain the neurons which receive the endogenous stimuli" (ibid., 303).

61. Ibid., 307–310.

62. Freud, *SE*, 14:118.

63. Freud, *SE*, 18:38.

64. Ibid. Lacan clarifies that the "inanimate state" that Freud refers to as the point of cathexis for the death drive (in the sense of death as the explicit aim or object of the drive) is not present as an element in the unconscious. It is not a literal fixation upon death per se. Lacan reads it more as a metaphor, or a crack as he calls it, of a drive that operates beyond life. It is inscribed in the movement of life itself. He writes, "In man, there is already a crack, a profound perturbation of the regulation of life. That's the importance of

the notion introduced by Freud of the death drive" (37). Jacques Lacan, *The Seminar of Jacques Lacan, Book II: The Ego in Freud's Theory and in the Technique of Psychoanalysis*, 1954–55, ed. Jacques-Alain Miller, trans. Sylvana Tomaselli (New York: Norton, 1991).

65. Jean Laplanche and Jean-Baptiste Pontalis, *The Language of Psychoanalysis*, trans. Donald Nicholson-Smith (New York: Norton, 1973), 364. Or as Michel de Certeau puts it: "The operations which order representation by articulation through the psychic system are in effect rhetorical: metaphors, metonymies, synecdoches, paranomasia, etc." (*Heterologies*, 22–23). Michel de Certeau, *Heterologies: Discourses on the Other*, trans. Brian Massumi (Minneapolis, MN: University of Minnesota Press, 1986).

66. In "Repression," Freud refers to the proportion of psychic energy and affect as a "definitive quantum of psychical energy" and a "quantum of affect" (Freud, *SE*, 14:152).

67. Freud, *SE*, 14:177.

68. Ibid., 38.

69. Freud, *SE*, 18:8.

70. Ibid., 55–56; emphasis added.

71. Freud, *SE*, 19:160.

72. In the *Project*, Freud discusses the principle of constancy as the principle of inertia, the primary aim of discharging excess stimuli. In his early discussion of memory, he notes that "*memory is represented by the differences in the facilitations between the ψ* [psi] *neurones*." (*SE*, 1:300). Following the general laws of motion, Freud describes the operative power of memory according to wave mechanics. He writes, "The memory of an experience (that is, its continuing operative power) depends on a factor which is called the magnitude of the impression and on the frequency with which the same impression is repeated" (*SE*, 1:300) Taken together, magnitude and frequency of repetition constitute facilitations. Under the persistent exigencies of life, the nervous system is forced to keep a constant reserve of cathected energy in order to maintain its primary endeavor of liquidation and maintaining an inert state. Accordingly, facilitations step in to fulfill the primary function of the nervous system since the more primitive mode of discharging external excitations is no longer possible. So the repetition of the memory becomes a homeostatic process.

73. Martin Hägglund, *Dying for Time: Proust, Woolf, Nabokov* (Cambridge, MA: Harvard University Press, 2012), 126–129.

74. In the rubric of stricture, there can be no essential opposition between the reality principle and the pleasure principle because anything given is necessarily bound to its other. The reality principle binds and at the same time limits the possibility of pleasure within an economy of gain and loss because it must bind itself to something other than itself in order to make pleasure possible in the first place. Derrida's reading focuses intently on Freud's concluding thoughts about binding as a preparatory act in *Beyond the Pleasure Principle* because in his assessment, it reveals how binding makes pleasure possible in the first place and imbues it with unpleasure while also restricting it. Derrida's critical point is that binding is the condition for pleasure

and unpleasure; the reality principle and the pleasure principle are not the conditions for the binding of excitation. Put otherwise, pleasure and unpleasure are not intrinsic conditions in themselves but are instead known only as a relation that is given by binding. The opposition between pleasure and unpleasure, as Derrida emphasizes, is internally limited by pleasure itself. He writes, "There is only pleasure which itself limits itself, only pain which itself limits itself, with all the differences of force, intensity, and quality that a set, a corpus, a 'body' can bear or give 'itself,' let itself be given" (*The Post Card* 401). In "Freud and the Scene of Writing," Derrida puts the same argument somewhat differently when he claims that "the difference between the pleasure principle and the reality principle, for example, is not uniquely, nor primarily, a distinction, an exteriority, but rather the original possibility, within life, of the deferral (*Aufschub*) and the original possibility of the economy of death" (*Writing and Difference* 198). For more, see also Geoffrey Bennington's discussion of binding in "Derridabase," in *Jacques Derrida* (Chicago, IL: University of Chicago Press, 1993). Taking his cue from Derrida's reading of *Beyond the Pleasure Principle*, Martin Hägglund also argues that binding is the condition of possibility for the pleasure principle. See his chapter titled "Reading: Freud, Lacan, Derrida," in *Dying for Time.*

Jacques Derrida, *Writing and Difference*, trans. Alan Bass (Chicago, IL: University of Chicago Press, 1978); and *The Post Card: From Socrates to Freud and Beyond*, trans. Alan Bass (Chicago: University of Chicago Press, 1987).

75. Freud, *SE*, 18:62.

76. Ibid.

77. Ibid., 14.

78. Ibid.

79. Ibid., 14–15.

80. Ibid.

81. Ibid., 16. In "To Speculate—On 'Freud,'" Derrida comments on Sophie's death. In his letters, Freud insists that *Beyond the Pleasure Principle* was mostly written before her death. Even though he resists the idea that the text refers to her death in the strict sense, it can be said that the footnote supports the interpretation that her death haunts the text.

82. Ibid., 15.

83. Ibid. Interestingly, Freud does not explicitly recount the child's expression of the sound "a-a-a-a" as the word *da*. Unlike his telling of the sound "o-o-o-o," he passes by the sound of the 'da' in favor of his interpretation of its translation. See Derrida's reading of the *fort/da* game in *The Post Card*, in which he addresses the movement from sound to word.

84. Freud, *SE*, 18:15. Freud follows this assertion with the interpretation that, in recently having confronted the reality of his mother's own disappearance and return, the game was in fact a reenactment of the mother's departures and returns. Despite his significant attachment to his mother, the child displaces his feeling about her leaving to a game with toys, thereby enabling him to stage and repeat the mother's disappearance and return. Freud emphasizes that the first act, that of *fort*, is "staged as a game in itself

and far more frequently than the episode in its entirety" (16). That the play emphasizes the repetition of the disappearance, as opposed to the more joyful return, inspires Freud to question how the game can adhere to the pleasure principle especially when the mother's disappearance "cannot possibly" have been felt as anything but "distressing" (15). Freud seems to resolve this problem by arguing that the game translates the child's "*passive* situation," which was brought about by the overpowering experience of the mother's departure, into a more "*active* part" that willingly sends his mother away in order to master the experience of that loss as an event *he occasions* (16). The toys thus cathect the impulse of revenge into play, and the boy displaces his feelings of abandonment to the game itself and its objects.

The factor of the mother's disappearance is critical because it compels Freud to question whether the child's compulsion to reenact the unpleasurable experience of his mother's departure adheres to the pleasure principle or is evidence of the death drive. In his narrative, Freud persistently wavers on the answer to this question even though he firmly concludes that the game enables the child to translate himself into an active player who wills the disappearance of the mother.

To elaborate a bit further upon an earlier note, in *Unclaimed Experience*, Caruth focuses on the wavering structure of Freud's account, arguing that the relation between his writing and the story of the child's game formulates an indissoluble link between individual traumatic experience and wider historical experience. "If this game is resonant in *Beyond the Pleasure Principle*," Caruth writes, "it is not only because . . . the symbolized pattern of departure and return brings into prominent view a larger conception of historical experience" (66). The pattern of departure and return becomes a broader historical pattern that forms the basis of the story of the history of the Jews in *Moses and Monotheism*. Caruth's formulation posits individual trauma as an inassimilable experience of departure that is necessarily the arrival into a collective, transgenerational history. This does not assume a direct parallel between the individual and history, but rather that individual trauma presupposes a wider, collective experience. In *Literature in the Ashes of History*, Caruth reads the wavering nature of Freud's account as indicative of his own puzzlement. In her assessment, at the heart of this perplexing experience for Freud is his inability to comprehend the boy's unique narrative. Caruth thereby links repetition in trauma to the creative act of invention, and claims that the act itself witnesses trauma's perplexing nature.

85. Freud, *SE*, 18:39.

86. Ibid.

CHAPTER 2: THE EVENTALITY OF TRAUMA

1. Freud, *SE*, 14: 305.

2. Ibid., 289.

3. Gilles Deleuze, *Difference and Repetition*, trans. Paul Patton (New York, NY: Columbia University Press, 1994), 114.

4. In distinction to other studies that take up the Freudian conception of time, such as Adrian Johnston's excellent book *Time Driven*, Martin Hägglund presents the boldest assertion that Freud effectively fails to think finitude in his book *Dying for Time*.

Adrian Johnston, *Time Driven: Metapsychology and the Splitting of the Drive*; Martin Hägglund, *Dying for Time: Proust, Woolf, Nabokov.*

5. Freud, *SE*, 14: 187.

6. Ibid.

7. In Laplanche's assessment of the deferred action of hysterical trauma, Freud's abandonment of the seduction theory is a significant error since it fails to take into full account the interiorized externality of the psyche. Generally speaking, Laplanche's notion of seduction is much broader than Freud's. For him, they are not just obvious sexual advances made by adults towards children; they are not, in other words, events rendered as distinct traumas locàtable in time. Instead, Laplanche posits these unconscious sexual kernels as "enigmatic signifiers" (*Life and Death in Psychoanalysis* 41), a term he borrows directly from Lacan. See Lacan, "The Instance of the Letter in the Unconscious, or Reason Since Freud," in *Écrits*, trans. Bruce Fink (New York: Norton, 2002), 412–441.

Trauma is not, then, for Laplanche, a psychic property among others. It is the essence of the psyche, constituting its structure and accordingly its functioning and dynamic movements. Psychic trauma also becomes the centralized connection among the different registers, processes, and symptoms of the psyche—it is the structural axis point around which the whole of psychic life orbits. Traumatic kernels that are implanted in the psyche are thereby retroactively activated by later instances that are associated with the initial engraving of the primal scene of trauma. These kernels are mnemic traces laden with evocations of foreign, "seductive" desires, and as such become the fixed points around which the labors of the unconscious continuously revolve in the attempt to answer the questions raised by these enigmas.

Like the Lacanian Real, around which the Symbolic perpetually orbits in the attempt to incorporate the effects of its impossible presence, enigmatic signifiers become determinate points of inquiry upon which the unconscious is always fixed. Laplanche understands dreams, fantasies, and symptoms as translations of perceived but not understood alien desires of others as being part of the sexualized world of adults—a world that traumatically trespasses into the young child's presexual universe. Enigmatic signifiers are thus perpetually capable of receiving fresh elaborations while also demanding repeated associational translations in the belated attempt to answer the always unresolved inquiries posed from the beginning by these enigmas. The persistent attempt to translate enigmatic signifiers opens up a temporal dynamic, which enables the dialecticized interaction between past and present; that is, the labors of the unconscious introduce the temporal dimension that repudiates the conscious, experiential present as mere repetition and instead formulates a conscious, heuristic present.

As Laplanche puts it:

> Between determinism and hermeneutics, what is the contribution of the concept of the enigmatic message and the correlative concept of translation? With the *message*, there is the idea that an existing, pre-existing sense is offered to the subject, of which, however, he is not the master and of which he can become the master only by submitting to it. With the concept of *enigma*, a break in determinism appears: to the extent that the originator of the enigmatic message is unaware of most of what he means, and to the extent that the child possesses only inadequate and imperfect ways to configure or theorize about what is communicated to him, there can be no linear causality between the parental unconscious and discourse on the one hand and what the child does with these on the other. (*Essays on Otherness* 160)

Given that Laplanche's version of the unconscious is also past-oriented, fixated upon enigmatic points of inquiry from which dreams, fantasies, and symptoms issue forth, it is interesting that he criticizes Freud for what he sees as an undialecticized role of the past within the present and thus for advancing a determinist model of time in which the repressed past regulates the conscious, heuristic present. Even though Laplanche's critiques of Freud's relegation of temporality to a linear model of conscious time are evident throughout his writings, one may turn to "The Kent Seminar," in *Jean Laplanche: Seduction, Translation, Drives*, for some particularly insightful comments on the matter. In any case, Laplanche's figuration of psychic trauma as the psyche's "veritable spine" (*Life and Death in Psychoanalysis* 42) offers a compelling thought of trauma as the foundational structural element that determines the whole of psychic life.

Despite his own occasional affirmation of the timeless Freudian unconscious, Lacan's ideas about the "temporal pulsation" and the "closing of the unconscious" offer important insights into the structural relation between time and trauma that Laplanche is expanding. In his engagement with Freud's thinking of the role of conscious daytime fantasies in dream analysis, Lacan argues that these daytime residues operate like an "'open sesame' of the unconscious" ("The Position of the Unconscious" 267). In his argument about daytime residues, Lacan focuses especially on how infantile wishes are incapable of making themselves apparent as daytime fantasies without more current mnemic traces that bear associational connections to older cathected elements. Despite their seeming immunity to time, infantile wishes nevertheless rely upon recent mnemic traces to provide timely openings in which they may make themselves manifest.

The phenomena of hysterical trauma, like daytime residues, is exemplary of the opening and closing of the unconscious and thus of a "higher order" temporal structure:

> One notices that it is the closing of the unconscious which provides the key to its space—namely the impropriety of trying to turn it into an inside. That closing also demonstrates the core of a reversible time, quite

> necessarily introduced if we are to grasp something I have been emphasizing for a long time: the retroactive effect of meaning in sentences, meaning requiring the last word of a sentence to be sealed [*se boucler*]. *Nachträglichkeit* (remember that I was first to extract it from Freud's texts), *Nachträglichkeit* or deferred action [*après-coup*], by which trauma becomes involved in symptoms, reveals a temporal structure of a higher order. ("The Position of the Unconscious" 267–268)

Lacan never resolves the nature of "higher order" uncovered by *Nachträglichkeit* (i.e., whether, in following suit with Lacan's Saussurian inspired structuralist approach to the unconscious, it is synchronic or diachronic). But it does suggest that the *après-coup* of trauma has more to do with the "temporal pulsation" of the unconscious than being an affirmation of the atemporality of the unconscious. The unconscious is timeless insofar as it is defined in part by its incapacity of what Henri Bergson calls *durée*, the notion of duration.

It is worth mentioning that Bergson's notion of duration has been influential in thinking the role of time in psychic life. Bergson claims: "As regards the psychic life unfolding beneath the symbols which conceal it, we readily perceive that time is just the stuff it is made of" (*Creative Evolution* 6). In other words, duration influences conscious experience. In Bergson's assessment, one cannot resolve the existence of a timeless ego and the subject's experience of duration.

Later in his writings from the 1960s, Lacan modifies his argument about the *automaton*. Even though the Symbolic unconscious *automaton* is always working to close in on itself, it is necessarily impacted by the effects of Real events. The Symbolic unconscious integrates itself around trauma's residual points of impact, which means that the unconscious exists "in time." A transition in his thinking on time is evident. In the *Four Fundamental Concepts of Psycho-Analysis*, Lacan's conceptualization of unconscious as timeless is particularly clear. His 1946 essay, "Logical Time and the Assertion of Anticipated Certainty," makes clear his conception of temporality as linked to deliberations on "causes." See especially pp. 31–32 in which he talks about the ideas of duration and logical time. Throughout the seminars of the mid-1960s, the Real and the Symbolic serve as the primary poles around which the dichotomy of *tuché/automaton* operates. The notion of *point de capiton* also demonstrates his undecidability on the matter of time in the unconscious.

Henri Bergson, *Creative Evolution*, trans. Arthur Mitchell (New York: Random House, 1944); Jacques Lacan, "Logical Time and the Assertion of Anticipated Certainty: A New Sophism," trans. Bruce Fink and Marc Silver, *Newsletter of the Freudian Field* 2.2 (1988): 4–22; Jacques Lacan, *The Seminar of Jacques Lacan, Book XI: The Four Fundamental Concepts of Psychoanalysis*; Jacques Lacan, "The Position of the Unconscioius," in *Reading Seminar XI: Lacan's Four Fundamental Concepts of Psychoanalysis*, ed. Richard Feldstein, Bruce Fink, and Marie Jaanus (Albany, NY: State University of New York Press, 1995); Jean Laplanche, *Essays on Otherness*, ed. John Fletcher, trans. Luke Thurston (New York: Routledge, 1999); Jean

Laplanche, "The Kent Seminar," in *Jean Laplanche: Seduction, Translation, Drives*, ed. John Fletcher and Martin Stanton (London: Institute of Contemporary Arts, 1992); Jean Laplanche, *Life and Death in Psychoanalysis.*

8. Johnston, *Time Driven*, 128–143.

9. Freud writes in *Beyond the Pleasure Principle*: "We have learnt that unconscious mental processes are in themselves 'timeless'. This means in the first place that they are not ordered temporally, that time does not change them in any way and that the idea of time cannot be applied to them. These are negative characteristics which can only be clearly understood if a comparison is made with conscious mental processes" (*SE*, 18:28).

In his essay "Freud and the Scene of Writing," Derrida elaborates on Freud's assertion regarding the negative characteristics of the atemporal nature of the unconscious. He argues that "the timelessness of the unconscious is no doubt determined only in opposition to a common concept of time[;] . . . the unconscious is no doubt timeless only from the standpoint of a vulgar conception of time" (215). In Derrida's assessment, the principle of noncontradiction, which formulates the self-presence of presence as given in itself as a unified wholeness conceives of time in a straightforward correspondence with selfhood (ipseity). This principle relies upon a notion of time that is conceptualized on the basis of presence, and thus as a homogeneity of the temporal medium that stabilizes primordial time (time prior to the possibility of being) and forms a living world time that becomes the existence of the object and subject. This is the vulgar or ordinary concept of time. In *Of Grammatology*, Derrida also speaks of a "vulgar concept of writing" (60), which is linked, by the same logic, to the principle of noncontradiction. Jacques Derrida, *Of Grammatology*, trans. Gayatri Chakravorty Spivak (Baltimore, MD: Johns Hopkins University Press, 1976).

10. Freud, *SE*, 1:297.

11. Freud, *SE*, 14:118.

12. Freud, *SE*, 1:295.

13. Ibid., 309.

14. Ibid., 309–310.

15. Ibid., 310.

16. Ibid., 299.

17. Ibid., 309.

18. Ibid., 309–310.

19. Ibid., 310; emphasis added.

20. Ibid., 310; emphasis added.

21. Jacques Lacan, *The Seminar of Jacques Lacan, Book VII: The Ethics of Psychoanalysis, 1959–1960*, ed. Jacques-Alain Miller, trans. Dennis Porter (New York: Norton, 1992), 62, 71.

22. In the *Project*, Freud states: "A psychological theory deserving any consideration must furnish an explanation of 'memory'" (*SE* 1:299). As his work develops, however, it becomes clear that his more obstinate problem is providing an account of the emergence of consciousness that does completely

transcend the problem of quantity posed by the nervous system since the system *Pcpt.-Cs.* is the structure and functioning of the protective shield.

23. Freud, *SE*, 18:28.

24. In his 1946 "Logical Time" essay, Lacan argues that "classical logic" works in "a single stroke," that is, in a synchronic fashion:

> It is precisely because our sophism will not tolerate a spatialized conception that it presents itself as an aporia for the forms of classical logic [. . .] these forms never furnish us anything which cannot already *be seen at a single stroke* [*d'un seul coup*]. In complete opposition to this, the coming into play as signifiers of the phenomena contested here makes the temporal, non spatial, structure of the logical process prevail. What the *suspended motions* disclose is not what the subjects see, but rather what they have found positively about *what they do not see* . . . . That which constitutes these suspended motions as signifying is not their direction, but rather their interruption [*temps d'arrêt*]. Their critical value is . . . of a verificatory movement instituted by a logical process in which a subject transforms the three possible combinations into three *times of possibility* (9).

Lacan therefore argues against any opposition between the external synchrony of logic and the transient, diachronic logic of the extralogical. Indeed he sees the work of his new "sophism," the process of which is constituted by the different-in-kind "times of possibility," as contesting the limiting of logic to synchronic, spatial organizations.

Jacques Lacan, "Logical Time and the Assertion of Anticipated Certainty: A New Sophism."

Jacques-Alain Miller offers a useful assessment of Lacan's early approaches to temporality as characterized by the structural relations governed by the Symbolic. He contends, "There is objective, as measured by clocks, and subjective time: time of maintained interest. . . . Lacan doesn't approach subjective time through a description of feelings which cannot be narrated, attempting to grasp the inner feeling of temporality . . . ; he tries to find the logic of subjective time" (12). Jacques-Alain Miller, "An Introduction to Seminars I and II: Lacan's Orientation Prior to 1953 (I)," in *Reading Seminars I and II: Lacan's Return to Freud*, ed. Richard Feldstein, Bruce Fink, and Maire Jaanus (Albany, NY: State University of New York Press, 1996), 3–14.

25. "Cerebral anatomy," he writes, "has no need to consider why, speaking anatomically, consciousness should be lodged on the surface of the brain instead of being safely housed somewhere in its inmost interior." (Freud, *SE*, 18:24).

26. Freud, *SE*, 19:26; emphasis added.

27. Freud, *SE*, 18:26.

28. Freud, *SE*, 23:144–145.

29. In *The New Wounded*, Malabou develops the concept of cerebral auto-affection (29–45). Citing the revelation of the "emotional brain" in neuroscience, Malabou demonstrates how the brain's autonomous mediation of

stimuli that originate from within its own inside and subsequent production of representations of this inside reveal how endogenous excitations of the nervous system do not belong solely to the province of the psyche. To the contrary, the emotional brain affirms how the problem of managing internal excitations is also a neurological problem.

30. Freud, *SE*, 18:25.
31. Ibid.
32. Freud, *SE*, 19:231; emphasis added.
33. Ibid., 26.
34. Ibid.
35. Ibid., 26–27.
36. Ibid., 27.
37. Ibid.
38. Ibid., 28.
39. Freud remarks upon this inversion in *New Introductory Lectures on Psychoanalysis*, noting, "It was not repression that created the anxiety; the anxiety was there earlier; it was the anxiety that made the repression" (*SE*, 22:86).
40. Freud, *SE*, 22:89.
41. Ibid., 85.
42. Ibid., 88.
43. Ibid., 87–88.
44. Freud, *SE*, 20:135.
45. Freud, *SE*, 22: 86.
46. Ibid., 87.
47. Ibid.
48. Freud, *SE*, 18:12.
49. Freud, *SE*, 19:57–58; emphasis added.
50. Phobia, for example, can step in the moment that the danger becomes less defined. As we see in Freud's analysis of the case of "Little Hans," which refers to the famous Wolf Man case, "the castration anxiety is directed to a different object and expressed in a distorted form, so that the patient is afraid, not of being castrated by his father, but of being bitten by a horse or devoured by a wolf" (*SE*, 20:125).
51. Freud, *SE*, 22:89.
52. Ibid.
53. Ibid., 89–90.
54. Freud, *SE*, 17:235; emphasis added.
55. Freud, *SE*, 22:88.
56. Freud, *SE*, 20:166–168.
57. Lacan, *The Seminar of Jacques Lacan, Book VII*, 191.
58. Freud, *SE*, 22:93.
59. Ibid.
60. Ibid., 94; emphasis added.
61. Ibid.
62. Ibid.
63. Freud, *SE*, 18:39.

64. Freud, *SE*, 20:129. In *The New Wounded*, Malabou underscores the sexual etiology of traumatic neuroses.

65. Ibid.

66. Freud, *SE*, 2:5–6.

67. Ibid., 6.

68. Ibid., 4.

69. Ibid., 5–6.

70. In the preface to the first edition, Freud and Breuer cite the necessity of censoring the most convincing evidence in the interest of maintaining patient confidentiality as proof of the primary role of sexuality in hysteria. Even though, as they write, "sexuality seems to play a principal part in the pathogenesis of hysteria as a source of psychical trauma," they are only able to provide incomplete evidence in favor of this view. (*SE*, 2:xxix). In the preface to the second edition, written in 1908, Freud reflects on the evolution of his work over the past thirteen years, noting that though this evolution is far too extensive to append, it comprises the robust realizations of what is approximated in the early work (xxxi). Though Freud does not explicitly name sexuality, his reference to sexuality as the source and governing system of events of hysteria is clear enough. Indeed both prefaces indicate the importance of the role of sexuality as a major component of hysteria. This, however, is a significant point of departure between Freud and Breuer. Almost without exception Breuer did not acknowledge sexuality, whereas Freud elaborates on hysteria and neurosis in general as constituted by sexuality as the source of its causes.

71. Malabou, *The New Wounded*, 5.

72. Freud, *SE*, 2:6.

73. Freud, *SE*, 18:29.

74. Freud, *SE*, 3:149. Before 1897, Freud posits that a wide array of neurotic symptoms emerge from actual childhood experiences with sexual seduction scenarios. To an extent, his patients (analysands) validate this idea because a large number of them reported memories of sexually traumatic experiences with adults (friends, family members, and strangers alike) during their early childhoods. But in the *Project*, Freud calls his hypothesis into question, doubting that sexual traumas actually occur with such high frequency in families. Even though some patients may have in fact experienced early childhood sexual trauma, he modifies his theory to say that some patients conjure fantasies of sexual seduction that are retroactively constructed with the second event. Therefore the traumatic recollection of seduction scenarios is the belated fulfillment of that repressed wish (*SE*, 1:247, 259).

75. Freud, *SE*, 3:200.

76. Ibid., 259; 7:274.

77. The basic thesis of Freud's 1899 "Screen Memories" is that all mnemic materials are retroactively altered traces of a past that can only ever be recovered in a state of alteration. Thus the act of present recollection necessarily alters past memories and compromises their efficacy as pure representations of prior histories.

78. As Freud observes in "On the History of the Psychoanalytic Movement," "If hysterical subjects trace their symptoms to traumas that are fictitious, then the new fact which emerges is precisely that they create such scenes in fantasy, and that this psychical reality requires to be taken alongside practical reality" (*SE*, 14:17–18).

79. Freud, *SE*, 5:260.

80. Freud, *SE*, 17:29. It is interesting to observe that the style and form of Freud's narrative of the Wolf Man's dream analysis is distinctly different from other case study narratives insofar as it stages the analyst/analysand scene.

81. Freud contends that a child does not, when initially experiencing a primal scene as a factual occurrence, comprehend its meaning. However, the scene may be comprehended after the child has gained a greater understanding of sexuality. He writes in "General Theory of Neuroses": "It is perfectly possible for a child, while he is not yet credited with possessing an understanding or a memory, to be a witness of the sexual act between his parents or other grown-up people; and the possibility cannot be rejected that he will be able to understand and react to the impression *in retrospect*" (*SE*, 16:369).

82. Freud, *SE*, 17:97; emphasis added.

83. It was of course Heidegger who emphasized that only Dasein exists in the mode of being-towards-death. At bottom, we here impact upon a very old structure, the paradoxical partitioning of life from itself in the form of stitching together into a structural unity under the order of the succession of events. As Derrida's work brings to light, all of this falls under the jurisdiction of the founding concepts of metaphysics. We recall what is well known from Heidegger's thinking of primordial temporality. The difference between event and being hinges on the finitude of our subjectivity precisely because Dasein's temporality is grounded in the anticipation of and thereby in the accomplishment of its end. Primordial temporality is Dasein's truth as a history of being.

84. Lacan, *The Seminar of Jacques Lacan, Book VII*, 129.

85. Ibid., 71–72.

86. Ibid., 21.

87. Ibid., 118.

88. Ibid., 71.

89. Ibid., 121.

90. In the twelfth seminar, Lacan addresses the inaccuracy of thinking the Real as a materiality. He emphasizes that even though the Real is anterior to any symbolization, it can only be expressed through the Symbolic order. His depiction of the Real body, for example, as a remainder from the process of subjectifying symbolization coheres with this line of thinking.

Jacques Lacan, *The Seminars of Jacques Lacan, Book X: Anxiety, 1962–1963*, trans. Cormac Gallagher, unpublished typescript; and Jacques Lacan, *The Seminars of Jacques Lacan, Book XXII: R.S.I., 1974–1975*, trans. Jack Stone, unpublished typescript.

91. Jacques Lacan, *The Seminar of Jacques Lacan, Book XI*, 53.

92. Ibid.
93. Ibid., 58.
94. Ibid., 53–54.
95. Ibid., 55; emphasis added. For more on the pleasure principle and the automatism of homeostatic regulation, see Jacques Lacan, *The Seminar of Jacques Lacan, Book II*, especially chapter 5, "Homeostasis and Insistence," and chapter 6, "Freud, Hegel, and the Machine."
96. Lacan, *The Seminar of Jacques Lacan, Book XI*, 52.
97. Ibid., 54.
98. Ibid.
99. Ibid.; emphasis added.
100. Ibid., 58.
101. Ibid., 55, 54.
102. Ibid., 59.
103. Ibid., 58–59.
104. Ibid.
105. Ibid., 60; emphasis added.
106. Ibid., 62.
107 Ibid., 54.
108. Ibid., 56.
109. Ibid., 57.
110. Ibid., 58.
111. Ibid., 59.
112. Freud, *SE*, 229.

CHAPTER 3: WHITHER PARTITION?

1. Saadat Hasan Manto, "Toba Tek Singh" (1955), in *Stories about the Partition of India*, ed. Alok Bhalla (New Delhi: HarperCollins India, 1999), 569.
2. Ibid., 571.
3. Ibid., 572.
4. Ibid., 572–573.
5. Ibid, 573.
6. Ibid.
7. This question and thus the title of this chapter derives from a play on the title of the original version of *Spectres of Marx*, which Derrida presented as a lecture titled "Whither Marxism?" at the University of California, Riverside, in 1993. I also play a bit with the terms of the other questions voiced in this ambiguity. In the preface to the text, Derrida draws out the other questions heard in the ambiguity of the title: "under the ambiguous title in which one may hear beneath the question 'Where is Marxism going?' another question: 'Is Marxism dying?'" (xiii). Jacques Derrida, *Spectres of Marx*, trans. Peggy Kamuf (London: Routledge, 1994).
8. See, for example, Jill Didur, *Unsettling Partition: Literature, Gender, Memory* (Toronto: University of Toronto Press, 2006); Sukeshi Kamra,

Bearing Witness: Partition, Independence, End of the Raj (Calgary: University of Calgary Press, 2002); Ramu Nagappan, *Speaking Havoc: Social Suffering and South Asian Narratives* (Seattle, WA: University of Washington Press, 2005); Gyanendra Pandey, "In Defense of the Fragment: Writing about Hindu-Muslim Riots in India Today," *Economic and Political Weekly* 26.11–12 (1991): 559–572; Ian Talbot, "Literature and the Human Drama of the 1947 Partition," *South Asia: Journal of South Asian Studies* 18 (1995): 37–56.

The discussion of the drawing of new borders is ubiquitous in Partition studies. A sustained study of Partition cartography is presented by Lucy P. Chester in her book, *Borders and Conflict in South Asia: The Radcliffe Boundary Commission and the Partition of Punjab* (Manchester: Manchester University Press, 2009). Mian Muhammad Sadullah et al., eds., *The Partition of Punjab—1947*, 4 vols. (Lahore: Sang-e-Meel Publications, 1993), also offers detailed information about how the maps were drawn in relation to factors such as census figures on population distribution and infrastructure elements such as power lines and waterways. Joya Chatterji offers an insightful analysis of the Bengal Boundary Commission in *The Spoils of Partition: Bengal and India, 1947–1967* (Cambridge: Cambridge University Press, 2007), 19–60.

9. Homi Bhabha, *The Location of Culture* (New York: Routledge, 1994), 112.

10. John Welchman, "The Philosophical Brothel," in *Rethinking Borders*, ed. John Welchman (Minneapolis, MN: University of Minnesota Press, 1996), 177–178.

11. That maps are symbols of power, which reveal the unique political character and values of the institutions and societies that create them, and not simply as neutral tools that offer graphic representations of land and related physical features, has long been discussed. Close cartographic analysis of the maps of South Asia can reveal, for example, the evolution of Britain's imperial power and control. According to Matthew H. Edney, maps were long used as a tool for exercising colonial power. He writes: "The British mapping of India was an exercise in discipline. The British surveyed the Indian landscapes in an effort to assess and to improve them. The disciplining of the landscape took place within the scope of the map, within the geographical archive and panopticon. The British sought to bring the landscape into line with their own preconceptions of territorial order" (334). If one studies the maps created by the Survey of India, the primary institution responsible for making the British imperial maps of South Asia, one can capture the cartographic archive as describing and "allowing access to . . . *British* India, a rational and ordered space that could be governed in a rational and ordered manner" (*Mapping an Empire* 34). Matthew H. Edney, *Mapping an Empire: The Geographical Construction of British India, 1765–1843* (Chicago, IL: University of Chicago Press, 1990). For a useful analysis of maps as symbols of power in general, see J. B. Harley, *The New Nature of Maps: Essays in the History of Cartography* (Baltimore, MD: Johns Hopkins University Press, 2001).

12. Gilles Deleuze and Félix Guattari, *A Thousand Plateaus: Capitalism and Schizophrenia*, trans. Brian Massumi (Minneapolis, MN: University of Minnesota Press, 1987); see especially, "1730: Becoming-Intense, Becoming-Animal, Becoming-Imperceptible . . ."

13. Gilles Deleuze and Félix Guattari, *Kafka: Toward a Minor Literature*, trans. Dana Polan (Minneapolis, MN: University of Minnesota Press, 1986), 22.

14. In *Radical Atheism*, Martin Hägglund has argued that the more accurate term would be "ultratranscendental," on the basis of Derrida's assertion of the term "spacing," which designates the logic of coimplication of becoming-time of space and the becoming-space of time as the condition for everything that can be experienced and understood, and thought on the basis on presence, as "the first word of any deconstruction" (*On Touching* 181). It is true that Derrida sometimes used this term. We see, for example, "ultra-transcendental" deployed in the discussion of the originary trace as "contradictory and not acceptable within the logic of identity" in *Of Grammatology* (61). More frequently, however, he employed the term "quasi-transcendental"—and even recanted his early use of ultratranscendental (see esp. p. 173 n. 14 in *Rogues*). Notwithstanding Derrida's own commentary about the term, it is important to recognize two things in order to see why, briefly, ultrametaphysical is for our purposes here the more accurate term. One, we should remember that Derrida's term "deconstruction" is a translation of Heidegger's term "destruction" (*Destruktion*), which he has discussed in some of his correspondences. Second, Heidegger was not precisely a thinker of the transcendental, which is crucial to understanding how the transformability of Being into being is also an unfolding that produces metaphysics in general. Nevertheless, it does seem to be the case that no matter how radical the critique of the transcendental that we see in Heidegger and Derrida, they do seem to retain something of it in their thinking of concepts that enable the real to exist but without which the real could not exist (namely, that an *a priori* synthesis constitutes the ontological horizon within which being is first capable of being experienced as a being in any kind of empirical synthesis). I retain the use of ultrametaphysical.

Jacques Derrida, *On Touching—Jean Luc Nancy*, trans. Christine Irizarry (Stanford, CA: Stanford University Press, 2005); *Rogues*, trans. Pascale-Anne Brault and Michael Naas (Stanford, CA: Stanford University Press, 2005); Jacques Derrida, "Letter to a Japanese Friend," in *Derrida and Différance*, ed. David Wood and Robert Bernasconi (Evanston, IL: Northwestern University Press, 1988); Martin Hägglund, *Radical Atheism: Derrida and the Time of Life* (Stanford, CA: Stanford University Press, 2008).

15. Jacques Derrida, *Dissemination*, trans. Barbara Johnson (Chicago, IL: University of Chicago Press, 1981), 193.

16. Ibid., 4.

17. Derrida also makes this point very clearly in "Letter to a Japanese Friend" (3).

In one of his late interviews, "Others Are Secret Because They Are Other," Derrida remarks on the history of the term "deconstruction," echoing earlier discussions in which he states clearly that deconstruction is not a method:

> There is a history of "deconstruction" in France and abroad, going back more than thirty years. This pathway—I don't say method—has transformed, displaced, complicated definitions, strategies, and styles that themselves vary from one country to another. This variety is essential to deconstruction, which is neither a philosophy, nor a science, nor a method, nor a doctrine, but, as I often say, the *impossible*, and the impossible as *that which comes about* [*arrive*]. (137)

While, as Derrida notes, deconstruction has itself experienced its own translational varietals, it is only possible to come to it in two ways that are coextensive: deconstruction is what occurs, what takes place, and/or it describes what occurs, the taking of place. This is why it is easier, as Derrida himself demonstrates in this response to defining deconstruction in terms of what it is not, because it takes on, from the beginning, the destabilization of the unity of tradition and gathering in general (as opposed to *Destruktion*, which takes on the question of being).

Jacques Derrida, "Others Are Secret Because They Are Other," in *Paper Machine*, trans. Rachel Bowbly (Stanford, CA: Stanford University Press, 2005).

18. Any methodological determination regarding the (non)subject that is the consequence of a deconstructive method, even if that determination is a porosity within a symbolic fabric that exceeds any primacy of the West, does not actually invent anything new. It is just an expression of the general logic in the critique itself. Spivak is especially attuned to this problem, drawing attention to it in her own writings as a "mistake," from which she proceeds according to a critical, translating gesture that does the work of working "at the deconstructive 'new politics of reading'" (*A Critique of Postcolonial Reason* 39, 91). For as indispensable a move this is, it nevertheless serves to confirm what in the philosophical tradition can be called the tradition of rereading, which in its turn, affirms the classical concept of life.

Gayatri Chakravorty Spivak, *A Critique of Postcolonial Reason: Toward a History of the Vanishing Present* (Cambridge, MA: Harvard University Press, 1999).

19. Derrida, *Dissemination*, 193.

20. Homi K. Bhabha, "DissemiNation: Time, Narrative, and the Margins of the Modern Nation," in *Nation and Narration*, ed. Homi K. Bhabha (New York: Routledge, 1990), 302.

21. Ibid., 292, 295.

22. Ibid., 297, 311.

23. Ibid., 297.

24. Ibid.

25. Ibid.

26. Bhabha, *The Location of Culture*, 4, 5.

27. Bhabha, "DissemiNation," 302.

28. Ibid.

29. Benita Parry has provided the most incisive materialist critique of postcolonial studies and of Bhabha's work. In her critique of Bhabha's work,

she writes: "When language is taken as a paradigm of all meaning-creating signifying systems, and human practice is consequently perceived as mimicking writing, the definitive disparities between construing the structure of language and explaining the forms of social and cultural practice are collapsed, the inference being that these latter also operate as an hermetic encoding of discursive differentials within a regime of phrases, and also follow the agonistic and ambivalent movement of writing" (60). However, and I very briefly make this point in the introduction, Parry's approach also assumes a dialectic of materialism that directs the construction and direction of social political forms towards to an exteriority that by necessity cannot be absorbed by the textual representation of politics it is said to organize. In her work, we are thus presented with a deduction that reveals the conditions of possibility for materialism. In other words, materialism itself becomes a kind of idealism. See the chapter, "Liberation Theory: Variations on Themes of Marxism and Modernity."

Benita Parry, *Postcolonial Studies: A Materialist Critique* (London: Routledge, 2004).

30. Bhabha, *The Location of Culture*, 186.

31. Parry, *Postcolonial Studies*, 19.

32. Althusser, "The Underground Current," 262.

33. Ibid., 262.

34. Ibid., 193.

35. Bhabha, *The Location of Culture*, 4.

36. See, for example, Dipesh Chakrabarty, *Provincializing Europe: Postcolonial Thought and Historical Difference* (Princeton, NJ: Princeton University Press, 2000); Francis Fukuyama, *The End of History and the Last Man* (New York: Free Press, 1992); Edward Said, *Orientalism* (New York: Vintage Books, 1978); Amartya Sen, *Development as Freedom* (Oxford: Oxford University Press, 2001); and Spivak, *A Critique of Postcolonial Reason*.

37. The point here is not to explicate the genealogy of the coextensive expansions of the terms "subaltern" and "postcolonial"; rather I aim merely to mark it and acknowledge their complexification as part of a certain historical tendency. However, a note on the matter might offer some further clarification.

Generally speaking, the emergence of postcolonial criticism in the academy in the 1990s drew attention to forms of historical knowledge and consciousness as Eurocentric, arguing that the historiographical enterprise had been characterized by a universalist narrative that perpetuated a history of Western domination in its discourses and authorship of social identities. In his highly influential text *Orientalism*, Edward Said, a founding figure of what has been called postcolonial theory, develops "Orientalism" as a term that conveys the Western study of Eastern cultures and signals the framework through which the West perceives and represents the East. Drawing significantly upon Said's work, the advent of the critical field of postcolonialism effected a radical rethinking and decentralizing of Europe and the West more broadly as the center from and around which notions of the other emerged.

This traces to the collective writings of the Subaltern Studies Group, a group of scholars formed in the 1980s and whose namesake derives from and signals the widening of Antonio Gramsci's writings on the subaltern in the *Prison Notebooks*. At the time, this group of scholars, namely, Ranajit Guha, Partha Chatterjee, Gyanendra Pandey, David Arnold, and Gayatri Chakravorty Spivak, aimed to explore the fractures and discontinuities in Western historical discourses to provide different accounts of the nation and subject formation.

Through new readings of colonial-nationalist archives, the early phase of Subaltern Studies was more precisely interested in rewriting Indian colonial history from the view of the masses of peasants and urban poor. For example, Ranajit Guha's work, which recuperates the peasant from elite and positivist historiography, is a notable example of the early scholarship that uses conventionally neglected sources like previously unused colonial administrative documents to recover an autonomous subaltern consciousness. More contemporary postcolonial historiographical efforts, however, seek to challenge the operative power of Western discourses that have been canonized by conventional Eurocentric historiography, authorized by colonialism, and authenticated by the deployment of the nation-state. Postcolonial historiography today is less animated by the interest in recovering the autonomous consciousness of the subaltern precisely because, as Spivak and Lati Mani's work asserts, such a task is always thwarted by the impossibility of autonomy intrinsic to subalternity. Instead contemporary approaches generally aim to elucidate how historical thinking, knowledge, consciousness, and processes are intrinsically marked by gaps, absences, and silences in the very writing of history. In so doing, the postcolonial schema interrogates Western history as a form of being and knowledge while identifying disjunctive moments of discourse that mark the subaltern's silence in history as the radical reinscription of another form of history writing. As Michel de Certeau rightly underscores in *The Writing of History*, history writing, at once limited and limiting, is always necessarily a displacing operation that problematically constructs the nature and role of history itself. The individual style of the postcolonial is, in a sense, the bringing about of the subaltern figure as a discourse event that challenges the discursive elements of history precisely by reinscribing knowledge itself as a problematic concept that continuously circulates as such within the self-regulating system of signification.

Michel de Certeau, *The Writing of History*, trans. Tom Conley (New York, NY: Columbia University Press, 1988); Antonio Gramsci, *Selections from the Prison Notebooks*, ed. Quintin Hoare and Geoffrey Nowell Smith (New York, NY: International Publishers, 1971); Ranajit Guja, ed., *A Subaltern Studies Reader: 1986–1995* (Minneapolis, MN: University of Minnesota Press, 1997); Lata Mani, *Contentious Traditions: The Debate on Sati in Colonial India* (Berkeley: University of California Press, 1988).

38. Here I have in mind Spivak's very well known assessment of the subaltern woman as the impossible subject. I am also thinking of Sam Durrant's *Postcolonial Narrative and the Work of Mourning* (Albany, NY: State University of New York Press, 2004), which enjoins the two logics of

contradiction in deconstruction and the dialectic into what he calls "inconsolable ethico-political practices" (27).

Gayatri Chakravorty Spivak, "Can the Subaltern Speak?," in *Marxism and the Interpretations of Culture*, ed. Cary Nelson and Lawrence Grossberg (Urbana: University of Illinois Press, 1988), 271–313.

39. Althusser, *Philosophy of the Encounter*, 170.

40. The process of partitioning the British subcontinent began before August. On June 3, Lord Louis Mountbatten and Indian National Congress leaders spoke on All-India Radio to announce that the previous day the relevant constituencies had voted to accept the Mountbatten Plan, which involved the creation of two dominions, that of India and Pakistan, on August 15, 1947. This plan became the basis of the India Independence Act, which was ratified by the British Parliament and Crown on July 18, 1947. A few days earlier, on July 15, the House of Commons announced the decision to divide British India into two independent dominions. For more on this, see Sumit Sarkar, *Modern India: 1885–1947* (Delhi: MacMillan India, 1983).

41. The full text of Nehru's speech is read among numerous sources that are all easily accessed on the Internet. I have chosen to quote the speech as it appears in Salman Rushdie and Elizabeth West's edited collection, *Mirrorwork: 50 Years of Indian Writing 1947–1997* (New York, NY: Henry Holt, 1997), 3.

42. The full text of Jinnah's independence day speech may be accessed at www.columbia.edu/itc/mealac/pritchett/00islamlinks/txt_jinnah_assembly_1947.html.

43. This is an argument that Gyanendra Pandey makes in his book *Remembering Partition: Violence, Nationalism, and History in India* (Cambridge: Cambridge University Press, 2001).

44. For a useful sampling of the vast amount of historical scholarship on the Partition, see Chowdhury Muhammad Ali, *The Emergence of Pakistan* (New York, NY: Columbia University Press, 1967); Judith Brown, *Modern India: The Origins of an Asian Democracy* (New York, NY: Oxford University Press, 1994); Joya Chatterji, *Bengal Divided: Hindu Communalism and Partition, 1932–1947* (Cambridge: Cambridge University Press, 1995); Suranjan Das, *Communal Riots in Bengal: 1905–1947* (Delhi: Oxford University Press, 1991); H. V. Hodson, *The Great Divide: Britain, India, and Pakistan* (London: Oxford University Press, 1969); Leonard Mosley, *The Last Days of the British Raj* (New York: Harcourt, Brace & World, 1962); Pandey, *Remembering Partition*; Ishtiaq Husain Qureshi, *The Muslim Community of the Indo-Pakistan Subcontinent, 610–1947: A Brief Historical Analysis* (Gravenhage: Mouton, 1962); Satya M. Rai, *Partition of the Punjab* (London: Asia Publishing House, 1965); Sumit Sarkar, *Modern India: 1885–1947*; Amrik Singh, ed. *The Partition in Retrospect* (New Delhi: Anamika, 2000); Anita Inder Singh, *The Origins of the Partition of India: 1936–1947* (New Delhi: Oxford University Press, 1987); Ian Talbot, *Freedom's Cry: The Popular Dimension in the Pakistan Movement and Partition Experience in North-West India* (Karachi: Oxford University Press, 1996); and Ian Talbot and Gurharpal Singh, *The Partition of India* (Cambridge: Cambridge University Press, 2009).

It is also important to note the term "Partition" bears different meanings within the Indian subcontinent, which, of course, has not been the only partition in modern history. In Indian historiography, the Partition refers to the 1947 division of the Indian subcontinent—more specifically, the Punjab region—into an independent Pakistan and India. For Pakistanis, the Partition more acutely refers to the independence of Pakistan. After the 1971 Liberation War of Bangladesh, the war that officially separated East Pakistan from West Pakistan, Partition came to be known for those in Bangladesh as 1947, "the year of Partition," which was followed by 1971, "the year of Independence." For an elaboration on the different meanings of Partition, see Pandey, *Remembering Partition*, 13–15.

45. In the years immediately following the 1947 Partition of British India, scholarship tended to be oriented around a discourse that focused on issues of nationalism and the triangulated politics among Britain, India, and Pakistan. For a select sampling, see Hodson, *The Great Divide*; Mosley, *The Last Days of the British Raj*; and Qureshi, *The Muslim Community of the Indo-Pakistan Subcontinent, 610–1947.*

The early accounts were instrumental in forging dialogues about Partition history as a nationalist history that departed from conversations singularly focused on the end of British imperial rule. In the years to come, however, such assessments were scrutinized for their conspicuous silence about the role the unprecedented level of violence played in the formation of India and Pakistan as independent nations. Scholars who address the psychological impact of that divide have made critical interventions in Partition historiography by documenting and addressing the difficult legacy of genocidal violence in the subcontinent while exposing the seemingly official policy of silence that shrouded hegemonic accounts. When the fiftieth anniversary was celebrated in 1997, the silence was openly confronted.

In the commemorative issue of *India International Centre Quarterly* celebrating the fiftieth anniversary of the Partition, Krishna Sobti began to give voice to that silence when she claimed that the Partition was "not so much a happening or historical event as living history." It was, as Sobti continues, "easily the most massive experience of a kind that became an encounter between man and reality" ("Memory and History of the Partition" 55). When Sobti drew more upon the continued experiential dimension than the politics, she evoked a critical intervention in Partition dialogues. Her comments drew attention away from the dominant and impersonal nationalist rhetoric that denied the communal violence its prevalent and indispensable part and towards the personal that could not deny the difficult memories created during the summer of 1947. Krishna Sobti, "Memory and History of the Partition," *India International Centre Quarterly* 24.2–3 (1997): 55–78.

This sparked a resurgence of academic interest in Partition history characterized by the distinct departure from previous conversations. The new discourse that emerged broadened Partition historiography by turning to the traumatic dimensions of individual experiences as centrally defining aspects of that history. The work of Urvashi Butalia and Ritu Menon and Kamla Bhasin, for example, was foundational in arguing for the gendered nature of the violence that erupted in the subcontinent. Their work, which also sought to collect and record testimony from women, has been instrumental in creating a feminist historiography of the Partition that privileges the experience of women as an essential aspect in the historicity of the Partition. See Urvashi Butalia's *The Other Side of Silence: Voices from the Partition of India* (Durham, NC: Duke University Press, 2000); Ritu Menon's edited volume, *No Woman's Land: Women from Pakistan, India, and Bangladesh Write on the Partition of India* (New Delhi: Women Unlimited, 2004); and Ritu Menon and Kamla Bhasin, *Borders and Boundaries: Women in India's Partition* (New Brunswick, NJ: Rutgers University Press, 1998). For more recent work, see Jasodhara Bagchi and Subhoranjan Dasgupta, *The Trauma and the Triumph: Gender and Partition in Eastern India* (Kolkata: Stree, 2003). See as well Sukeshi Kamra, *Bearing Witness: Partition, Independence, End of the Raj*; Ramu Naggapan, *Speaking Havoc: Social Suffering and South Asian Narratives*; and Jill Didur, *Unsettling Partition: Literature, Gender, Memory.*

46. Deleuze, *Difference and Repetition*, 300.

47. On December 29, 1930, Sir Muhammad Iqbal, a Muslim poet, philosopher, and politician, opened his presidential address to the twenty-fifth session of the All-India Muslim League by marking the moment as among the most crucial in the history of Muslim thought and activity in India. A few months before, in May, the Simon Commission published its two-volume report assessing the system of diarchy established by the 1919 Government of India Act. Chief among the commission's recommendations for constitutional reform was the abolition of the diarchy system and the establishment of a representative government in the provinces—of a federal system—that retained separate communal electorates until tensions between Hindus and Muslims had subsided. In response to the increase in tensions and to the opposition against the commission posed by Indian intellectuals, the Labour Government, which had come into power in 1929, initiated a series of Round Table Conferences to be held in London in order to include the Indian National Congress in the deliberations of the future of the constitutional government in India. The first of these conferences convened on November 12, 1930, in spite of the fact that the congress did not participate because many of its leaders were jailed for their participation in Gandhi's Civil Disobedience Movement.

48. Rahmat Ali, "Now or Never: Are We to Live or Perish Forever" (January 28, 1933). The text can be accessed at www.columbia.edu/itc/mealac/pritchett/00islamlinks/txt_rahmatali_1933.html.

49. See Christophe Jaffrelot, ed., *A History of Pakistan and Its Origins* (London: Anthem Press, 2004).

50. Jacques Derrida, "Signature Event Context," in *Margins of Philosophy*, trans. Alan Bass, 307–330; and *On the Name*, trans. David Wood, John P. Leavey Jr., and Ian McLeod (Stanford, CA: Stanford University Press, 1995).

51. For more on Jinnah's demand and the Resolution, see Singh, *The Origins of the Partition of India*, 55–57; and Pandey, *Remembering Partition*, 25–27.

52. As Sumit Sarkar puts it: "Starting with Calcutta on 16–19 August, touching Bombay from 1 September, spreading to Noakhali in east Bengal (10 October), Bihar (25 October), Garmukteswar in U.P. [Uttar Pradesh] (November), and engulfing the Punjab from March 1947 onwards, the whole of the Indian scene was rapidly transformed by communal riots on an unprecedented scale" (*Modern India* 432).

53. Lucy P. Chester, *Borders and Conflict in South Asia,* 55.

54. Ibid., 66–70.

55. For more on the details of Radcliffe's different maps, which were the sketch map, the quarter-inch maps, and the Kasur tehsil map, see Chester, *Borders and Conflict in South Asia*, 93–100.

56. Chester, *Borders and Conflict in South Asia*, 78.

57. Akbar S. Ahmed's *Jinnah, Pakistan and Islamic Identity: The Search for Saladin* (New York: Routledge, 1997) offers an interesting account of Jinnah's politics during the time of the Partition including his reactions to the final decision about the new border.

Radcliffe's line in the Punjab region granted Pakistan approximately 64 percent of the area, which included about 60 percent of the Muslim population, and awarded the remaining portion to India. Indeed one of the most salient features of the new map was that it divided Lahore, once the capital of Punjab and now in Pakistan, and Amritsar, now in India. It also, however, distributed the majority of the Gurdaspur District to India, which Pakistan interpreted as Britain's desire to secure India's land link with the Kashmir region. Furthermore, the new border significantly disrupted Pakistan's irrigation system, whose main water source emerges from the rivers in Kashmir. While Radcliffe had no direct responsibility for the new national identity of the Kashmir region—the Maharajah of Kashmir was allowed to choose between India and Pakistan—the new border nevertheless ignited the ongoing conflict over the Kashmir region, the politics of which continue to plague contemporary Indo-Pakistani relations. Some historians claim that Radcliffe gave portions of northern Punjab to India in order to maintain strategic access to Kashmir. See Alastair Lamb, *Incomplete Partition: The Genesis of the Kashmir Dispute 1947–1948* (Hertingfordbury: Roxford Books, 1997).

58. Joya Chatterji, "The Fashioning of a Frontier: The Radcliffe Line and Bengal's Border Landscape, 1947–52," *Modern Asian Studies* 33.1 (2009): 242.

59. Ibid.

60. Freud, *SE*, 19:76.

61. See "The Ego and the Ego-Ideal," in *The Ego and Id*. Freud, *SE*, 19:38.

62. Freud, *SE*, 19:77–78.

63. See Althusser, *Philosophy of the Encounter*, 169–170.

64. Amitav Ghosh, *The Shadow Lines* (New Delhi: Ravi Dayal Publisher, 1998), 96.

65. Ibid., 152.

66. Ibid.

67. It is of course impossible to have a precise number of casualties during the summer of 1947. One million has become the generally agreed upon number, though it has fluctuated from half a million to two million. In a section titled "The Question of Casualties: A Note on Tertiary Discourse," in *Remembering Partition*, Pandey offers numerous citations for such statistics.

68. Jacques Derrida, "Force and Signification," in *Writing and Difference*, 12.

69. Ibid.

70. Ibid.

71. Ibid., 12–13.

72. Ibid., 13.

73. René Descartes, *The Passions of the Soul*, trans. Stephen Voss (Indianapolis: Hackett Publishing Company, 1989).

74. Jacques Derrida, "Admiration of Nelson Mandela, or The Laws of Reflection," *Law & Literature* 26.1 (2014): 9–30.

75. See Derrida, "The Ends of Man," in which he shows, through his engagements with Hegel's, Husserl's, and Heidegger's critiques of anthropology and humanism, that the idea of man is a contradictory unity intrinsic to the entire metaphysical tradition. So any attempt to critique the notion of the human is but itself the accomplishment of the very concept of the human. Jacques Derrida, "The Ends of Man," in *Margins of Philosophy*.

76. Althusser, *Philosophy of the Encounter*, 193.

77. Jacques Derrida, "On Forgiveness," in *On Cosmopolitanism and Forgiveness*, trans. Mark Dooley and Michael Hughes (London: Routledge, 2001), 28, 57.

78. Ibid., 30–31.

CHAPTER 4: RWANDA TRANSFORMING

1. Survivor testimony contests the French narrative, which claims that the army rescued remaining survivors after the May attack. For more on this and the details of the unique case of resistance in Bisesero, see Christian P. Scherrer, *Genocide and Crisis in Central Africa: Conflict Roots, Mass Violence, and Regional War* (Westport, CT: Praeger, 2002), especially part II.

2. Jacques Derrida, "Faith and Knowledge: The Two Sources of 'Religion' at the Limits of Reason Alone," in *Acts of Religion*, ed. Gil Anidjar, trans. Sam Weber (New York: Routledge, 2010), 66.

3. Ibid., 56.

4. Derrida, "On Forgiveness," 55.

5. Ibid.

6. Ibid., 29.

7. Pierre Nora, "Between Memory and History," *Lieux de Mémoires*, *Representations*, special issue *Memory and Counter-Memory*, no. 26 (Spring 1989): 19. With the use of the term "fluxibility," I also have in mind Henri Bergson's notion pure flux of *durée*. Henri Bergson, *Creative Evolution*.

8. Ibid.

9. Ibid.

10. Some of the relevant texts here are Marita Sturken, *Tangled Memories: The Vietnam War, the AIDS Epidemic, and the Politics of Remembering* (Berkeley, CA: University of California Press, 1997); Marita Sturken, *Tourists of History: Memory, Kitsch, and Consumerism from Oklahoma City to Ground Zero* (Durham, NC: Duke University Press, 2007); James Young, *The Texture of Time: Holocaust Memorials and Meaning* (New Haven, CT: Yale University Press, 1993); James Young, *At Memory's Edge: After-Images of the Holocaust in Contemporary Art and Architecture* (New Haven, CT: Yale University Press, 2000).

See as well Michael Rothberg, *Multidirectional Memory: Remembering the Holocaust in the Age of Decolonization*; and Marianne Hirsch, *The Generation of Postmemory: Writing and Visual Culture after the Holocaust* (New York, NY: Columbia University Press, 2012).

For more on the topic, see Kora Andrieu, "'Sorry for the Genocide': How Public Apologies Can Help Promote National Reconciliation," *Millennium* 38.3 (2010): 3–23; Duncan Bell, ed., *Memory, Trauma, and World Politics: Reflections between Past and Present* (London: Palgrave Macmillan, 2006); and "Memory and Violence," *Millennium* 38.2 (2009): 345–360; Andreas Huyssen, *Twilight Memories: Marking Time in a Culture of Amnesia* (London: Routledge, 1994); Jeffrey Olick, ed., *States of Memory: Continuities, Conflicts, and Transformation in National Retrospective* (Durham, NC: Duke University Press, 2003); Maja Zehfuss, *Wounds of Memory: The Politics of War in Germany* (Cambridge: Cambridge University Press, 2007).

11. We see this especially in Deleuze's discussion of habit and in his development of the doubling economy of death as characterized by the movement of three syntheses of repetition in three schemes of temporalization, which correspond to the three important things, "Death, Time, and No," that are constitutive of the unconscious.

12. This is a central argument in Cathy Caruth's recent study *Literature in the Ashes of History*.

13. On the topic of the politics of memory and the Rwandan genocide, see especially Alexandre Dauge-Roth's very rich study, *Writing and Filming the Genocide of the Tutsis in Rwanda: Disremembering and Remembering Traumatic History* (Lanham, MD: Lexington Books, 2010). See also Peter Hohenhaus, "Commemorating and Commodifying the Rwandan Genocide: Memorial Sites in a Politically Difficult Context," in *Dark Tourism and Place Identity: Managing and Interpreting Dark Places*, ed. Leanne White and Elspeth Frew (London: Routledge, 2013), 142–155.

See also Jessica Auchter, *The Politics of Haunting and Memory in International Relations* (London: Routledge, 2014); and Audrey Small, "The Duty of Memory: A Solidarity of Voices after the Rwandan Genocide," *Paragraph: A Journal of Modern Critical Theory* 30.1 (2007): 85–100.

14. I retain the reference to the Rwandan genocide or the genocide in Rwanda in significant part because it does not semantically elide the fact that politically moderate Hutus were also killed during the genocide. Additionally,

the reference that I retain is the one used in the research and by the international community.

15. Jens Meierhenrich, "The Transformation of Lieux de Mémoires: The Nyabarongo River in Rwanda, 1992–2006," *Anthropology Today* 25 (2009): 13–19.

16. One such example concerns two of the state-regulated memorial sites. In 1995, the government installed a three-phase plan to erect a major memorial in each of the eleven prefectures as well as oversee the consecrated burial of the remains of victims. In its early stage, the government converted the Ntarama and Nyamata churches, both of which were the sites of concentrated mass killings, into two of its official memorial sites by leaving them entirely untouched. Nyamata became notorious for the display of a Tutsi woman who had been impaled on a pike. For many years, her body remained exactly as it had been left by the Hutu militia. In the years immediately following the genocide, many survivors were deeply opposed to sites like Ntarama and Nyamata because they dispossessed the victims of proper burials, which in turn denied family and friends the ritual mourning process. See Donald G. McNeil Jr., "Ntarama Journal: At Church, Testament to Horror," *New York Times*, August 4, 1995.

17. I borrow the term "mythico-historical" from Lisa Malkki, *Purity and Exile: Violence, Memory, and National Cosmology among Hutu Refugees in Tanzania* (Chicago, IL: University of Chicago Press, 1995).

There are a number of excellent studies discussing these complex issues. The germane texts are Alison Des Forges, *"Leave No One to Tell the Story": Genocide in Rwanda* (New York: Human Rights Watch, 1999); Alison Des Forges, "Origins of Rwandan Genocide," *Journal of African History* 46.3 (2005): 550–551; Lee Ann Fuji, *Killing Neighbors: Webs of Violence in Rwanda* (Ithaca, NY: Cornell University Press, 2009); Philip Gourevitch, *We Wish to Inform You That Tomorrow We Will Be Killed with Our Families: Stories from Rwanda* (New York: Picador/Farrar, Straus and Giroux, 1998); René Lemarchand, *Rwanda and Burundi* (London: Pall Mall Press, 1970); Timothy Longman, *Christianity and Genocide in Rwanda* (Cambridge: Cambridge University Press, 2010); Mahmood Mamdani, *When Victims Become Killers: Colonialism, Nativism, and the Genocide in Rwanda* (Princeton, NJ: Princeton University Press, 2001); Gérard Prunier, *The Rwanda Crisis: History of a Genocide* (New York, NY: Columbia University Press, 1997); Josias Semujanga, *Origins of Rwandan Genocide* (New York: Humanity Books, 2003); Scherrer, *Genocide and Crisis in Central Africa*; and Scott Straus, *The Order of Genocide: Race, Power, and War in Rwanda* (Ithaca, NY: Cornell University Press, 2006).

18. See Jessica Auchter, *The Politics of Haunting and Memory in International Relations.*

19. For more on this triad, see Jennie E. Burnet, *Genocide Lives in Us: Women, Memory, and Silence in Rwanda* (Madison, WI: University of Wisconsin Press, 2012). On the concept of "chosen amnesia" in postgenocide Rwanda, see Susanne Buckley-Zistel, "Remembering to Forget: Chosen Amnesia as a Strategy for Local Coexistence in PostGenocide Rwanda,"

Africa 76.2 (May 2006): 131–150. For more on the legacies of the genocide in Rwanda, see Dauge-Roth, *Writing and Filming the Genocide of the Tutsis in Rwanda*; and Small, "The Duty of Memory."

20. The memorial was originally named the Kigali Memorial Centre.

21. See www.cnlg.gov.rw/home/.

22. The official website for the Kigali Genocide Memorial offers information about the building of the museum as well as its scope and aim. See www.genocidearchiverwanda.org.rw/. For a useful survey of memorial museums around the world and a meditation on the unique scope and aims of the memorial museum, see Paul Williams, *Memorial Museums: The Global Rush to Commemorate Atrocities* (Oxford: Berg Publishers, 2007).

23. The government adopted *gacaca* courts, a community-based system of justice convened by the individual parties to arbitrate a civil dispute, to try perpetrators of the genocide. In 2001, the parliament passed legislation that established the jurisdictions of the *gacaca* courts and organized prosecutions for offenses committed between October 1, 1990, and December 31, 1994, that constituted crimes against humanity and genocide. Critiques of the *gacaca* court trial process for perpetrators have discussed their lack of adherence to international human rights standards, corruption, failure to facilitate reconciliation, false portrayals of being a mode of establishing the truth of the genocide, failures to achieve stated aims of transitional justice goals, and destabilization of communities. Especially disturbing, however, was the rise in violence against genocide survivors who testified as witnesses in *gacaca* court trials, many of whom were killed in ways that echoed the methods employed during the genocide.

Though much has been written about the *gacaca* courts, the material has been in the form of short of articles. Paul Christoph Bornkamm's study, *Rwanda's Gacaca Courts: Between Retribution and Reparation* (Oxford: Oxford University Press, 2012), is the only (to the best of my knowledge) monograph that offers a devoted analysis of the legislation, practice, and assessment of the *gacaca* courts from the perspective of international law. Other useful texts on the matter include Burnet, "Reconciliation, Justice, and Amplified Silence," in *Genocide Lives in Us;* Christina Carroll, "An Assessment of the Role and Effectiveness of the International Criminal Tribunal for Rwanda and the Rwandan National Justice System in Dealing with the Mass Atrocities of 1994," *Boston University International Law Journal* 18.2 (2000): 163–200; and Alexander Laban Hinton, "Introduction: Toward an Anthropology of Transnational Justice," in *Transnational Justice: Global Mechanisms and Local Realities after Genocide and Mass Violence*, ed. Alexander Laban Hinton (New Brunswick, NJ: Rutgers University Press, 2010), 1–24.

24. In commemoration of the twentieth anniversary, the Memorial expanded to include the Global Centre for Humanity, an international institute aimed at collecting witness testimony, documenting mass atrocities, and conducting research on mass atrocity prevention. See www.

genocidearchiverwanda.org.rw/. The Centre was announced during the twentieth anniversary in April 2014 but officially opened its doors in February 2015.

The twentieth anniversary ceremony took place in a newly constructed amphitheater (finished only days before) and formally inaugurated on April 8, 2014, at the Kigali Genocide Memorial. The amphitheater, which was carved into the landscape and has since been used for a range of festivals and events, marked the completion of the first phase of a multiphase master plan to expand the Memorial grounds into a memorial environment. In the most straightforward regard, the Kigali Genocide Memorial is a dynamic, transforming space, what has been called a "memoryscape." See Shannon Davis and Jacky Bowring, "Connecting with Tragedy through Landscapes of Memory: Memorial Design, Tourism, and the Post-Genocide Memoryscapes of Cambodia, Rwanda, and Germany," *Memory Connection* 1.1 (2011): 377–391.

25. The pursuit of a comprehensive account of the history of Rwanda and the genocide extends beyond the scope of the current project.

26. In 1926, the Belgians introduced a classification system that employed mandatory identification cards to all Rwandans based on the following organization: those in possession of ten or more cows were classified as Tutsi; those with fewer than ten cows were classified as Hutu.

27. Estimates regarding how many people died during the genocide vary widely. Based on a study by the demographer William Seltzer, a report from Human Rights Watch produced the most conservative estimate of "at least a half a million" (Des Forges, *"Leave No One To Tell the Story"* 15). A UN expert estimated that 800,000 Rwandans died between April and June 1994, but this estimate included those who died of causes unrelated to the genocide (Des Forges, *"Leave No One To Tell the Story"* 15). Prunier, in *The Rwanda Crisis*, also estimates that 800,000 Tutsis died between April and June 1994, but he attributes those deaths solely to the genocide. In 2001, the Rwandan Ministry of Local Affairs and Social Affairs conducted its own census of victims and concluded that more than one million were killed in massacres and the genocide between October 1, 1991, and December 3, 1994. Although the report estimates that 97.3 percent of these victims were Tutsi (thus about 1.4 million), it is likely that the figure is high given that a 1991 census showed the Tutsi population to be approximately 700,000 (www.irinnews.org/report/29236/rwanda-government-puts-genocide-victims-at-1–07-million).

28. Drawing on the work of Nora and scholarship in the field of trauma studies, Sarah Steele argues that the Kigali Genocide Memorial is a site that encourages "metamorphosis in the present and the future" and "re-bonding, both by victims and Rwandans more widely" (2, 11). Sarah Steele, "Memorialisation and the Land of the Eternal Spring: Performative Practices of Memory on the Rwandan Genocide," retrieved from www.law.unimelb.edu.au/cmcl.

29. Mona Friedrich and Tony Johnston, "Beauty versus Tragedy: Thanatourism and the Memorialisation of the 1994 Rwandan Genocide," *Journal of Tourism and Cultural Change* 11.4 (2013): 304. See also Hohenhaus, "Commemorating and Commodifying the Rwandan Genocide."

30. Young, *The Texture of Memory*, 27.

31. Bunkers featuring stacked bones and complete skeletons are also a prominent feature at the Nyamata Church Memorial Site. The Murambi Memorial Site also features the remains of victims lying en masse, but there the display is more controversial than at other sites. In 1994, Murambi was a vocational school in the process of being built. During the genocide, Tutsis who were hiding in local churches were encouraged to gather there instead. Estimates vary, but approximately 40,000 to 55,000 Tutsis from the southern province, where the school is located, gathered at Murambi. Because of its isolated location on top of a hill, it was relatively easy for the militia to kill the vast numbers of Tutsis seeking safety. It is said that fewer than 20 survivors remain from the massacres at Murambi. When I visited in December 2013, Emmanuel Murangira, one of the few survivors, was my guide (as far as I know, he is still a guide). Like most of the memorial sites, there are mass graves at Murambi. Because so many bodies had been buried in one grave, tightly packed against each other, many of them did not decompose. The National Museum in Rwanda decided to preserve these 848 bodies in lime. They are on display on wooden cots in dormitory rooms—one of which is dedicated exclusively to infants and young children—where the sight and distinct smell stops one short. Interestingly, only a few of the many rooms are actually open to the public for viewing. The bodies are frozen in contorted positions of pain, fear, and violence. Among some, arms and hands are still covering heads and faces, in the attempt to shield themselves from the imminent machete strikes. On other bodies, pieces of clothes and hair peek through the white calcification as splashes of color that seem like horrendous non-sequiturs. Evidence of deep gashes on heels—a common practice—also catch the eye. The display of these bodies remains controversial in the local survivor community. Nicki Hitchcott, "Writing on Bones: Commemorating Genocide in Boubacar Boris Diop's Murambi," *Research in African Literatures* 40.3 (2009): 48–61, offers a reading of the bodies at Murambi as "forever trapped in the horror of experiencing their own deaths" (45). In *The Politics of Haunting and Memory in International Relations*, Jessica Auchter argues that Murambi—as well as the other national memorial sites—adheres to the logic of Derrida's notion of hauntology, claiming that the preserved bodies blur "the ontological line between life and death through haunting" (65).

32. Freud, *SE*, 21:69.

33. Ibid.

34. Ibid., 68.

35. For Freud, the primitive is also the savage, or prehistoric man, that subsists in everyone. I mean here, however, as much as possible, to use primitivity as convoking the earliest state of things, which includes the prehuman. This would not then include the concept of the uncivilized savage upon which colonial and imperial rhetoric and power turned.

36. Freud, *SE*, 21:71.

37. "There must come a point at which the analogy between an auxiliary apparatus of this kind and the organ which is its prototype will cease to

apply." Freud, *SE*, 19:230. I also have in mind here Gregory Bateson's concept of the ecology of the mind, which opposes the indestructibility of the Freudian unconscious. Gregory Bateson, *Steps to an Ecology of Mind* (Chicago, IL: University of Chicago Press, 1972).

38. Mamdani, *When Victims Become Killers*, 9, 14.

39. Ibid., 14.

40. Ibid.

41. Ibid.

42. Althusser, *Philosophy of the Encounter*, 187.

43. For more on the policy of "ethnic equilibrium," see John Corry, "A Formula for Genocide," *American Spectator* 31.9 (1998): 22–27; Prunier, *The Rwanda Crisis*; and Kenneth R. White, "Scourge of Racism Genocide in Rwanda," *Journal of Black Studies* 39.3 (2009): 471–481. See as well Timothy Longman, "Rwanda: Democratization and Disorder: Political Transformation and Social Deterioration," in *Political Reform in Francophone Africa*, ed. John F. Clark and David E. Gardinier (Boulder, CO: Lynne Rienner, 1997), 75–92; and Catherine Newbury, "Rwanda: Recent Debates over Governance and Rural Development," in *Governance and Politics in Africa*, ed. Goran Hyden and Michael Bratton (Boulder, CO: Lynne Rienner, 1992), 193–219, for more on the widespread ethnic discrimination against Tutsis during the Habyarimana regime.

44. Mamdani, *When Victims Become Killers*, 277.

45. Mamdani's thinking here might be seen as aligned with Étienne Balibar's concept of the form of the nation as necessarily presented "in the form of a narrative which attributes to these entities the continuity of a subject" (86). While Mamdani does not directly address the general structure of writing, except to say that Western historiography has been complicit in the imperialist project of "*naturalizing* political identities" (*When Victims Become Killers* xiii), his concluding comments are nonetheless manifestly interested in moving away from explaining postgenocide Rwanda as somehow mimicking prior narratives.

Étienne Balibar, "The Nation Form: History and Ideology," in Balibar and Immanuel Wallerstein, *Race, Nation, Class: Ambiguous Identities*, trans. Christ Turner (New York: Verso, 1991), 86.

46. Bill Ashcroft, *On Post-Colonial Futures: Transformations of Colonial Culture* (London: Continuum, 2001), 44.

47. Ibid., 45.

48. Ibid., 53.

49. Ibid.

50. Ibid.

51. Indeed Ashcroft's argument regarding the capacity of the postcolonial to subvert and transform colonial power into its own futures irreducible to colonialism itself is precisely that the postcolonial is a doubling excess. See especially the chapter titled "Post-Colonial Excess and Colonial Transformation," in *On Post-Colonial Futures*.

52. Gilles Deleuze, *Difference and Repetition*.

53. We see this, of course, as a fundamental aspect in Derrida's and Levinas's work. It is also evident throughout the humanities-based field of trauma studies. We can think here of the work of Cathy Caruth, Shoshana Felman, and Dori Laub, as well as of the work on PTSD by Bessel van Der Kolk, all of which insists on the transmissibility of the unspoken and unspeakable in trauma. Here are some of the seminal texts: Shoshana Felman, *The Juridical Unconscious: Trials and Traumas in the Twentieth Century* (Cambridge, MA: Harvard University Press, 1992); Shoshana Felman and Dori Laub, *Testimony: Crises of Witnessing in Literature, Psychoanalysis, and History*; Cathy Caruth, *Unclaimed Experience: Trauma, Narrative, and History*; Bessel A. van Der Kolk, Alexander C. McFarlane, and Lars Weisath, *Traumatic Stress: The Effects of Overwhelming Experience on Mind, Body, and Society.*

Françoise Davoine and Jean-Max Gaudillière challenge the classical psychoanalytic structure of transference by demonstrating its clinical variations when especially confronted with patients who are utterly disaffected to the point that they cannot in any capacity "transmit their position as subject affectively with regard to certain elementary oppositions" (50). Françoise Davoine and Jean-Max Gaudillière, *History Beyond Trauma: Whereof One Cannot Speak, Thereof One Cannot Remain Silent*, trans. Susan Fairfield (New York: Other Press, 2004).

54. Nietzsche, *On the Genealogy of Morals and Ecce Homo*, 58.

55. See Prunier, "Aftermath or New Beginning? (22 August–31 December)," in *The Rwanda Crisis*; and Mamdani, "Tutsi Power in Rwanda and the Citizenship Crisis in Eastern Congo," in *When Victims Become Killers.*

56. Here one can easily see the refugee problem as affirming Balibar's thinking on the general movements of immigration as an intensification of the "heritage of colonialism" as a "fluctuating combination of continued exteriorization and 'internal exclusion'" ("Racism and Nationalism" 43). However, Balibar's argument hinges on a continuity of subjectivity that extends as modes of being. The excess of fluxibility and reification owes to an essential continuity of being that flows into predetermined molds of power, to which my general thinking of transformation is opposed.

57. I hesitate with the term "globalized form of trauma" because I think the global also requires a rethinking along the lines of the new notion of life as not irremediably divided between the symbolic and the material that I have been attempting to formulate in this study. Such a concept of global would not be precisely the same 'global' that we see in global warming, which concerns the earth, or in globalization, which concerns the world, for example.

58. For more see Burnett, *Genocide Lives in Us.*

AFTER WORD

1. Jacques Derrida, "Geopsychoanalysis . . . 'and the Rest of the World,'" in *The Psychoanalysis of Race*, ed. Christopher Lane (New York, NY: Columbia University Press, 1998), 65.

2. Ibid., 66–68.

3. Ibid., 67.
4. Ibid., 68.
5. Ibid.
6. Jacques Derrida, "Psychoanalysis Searches the State of Its Soul: The Impossible Beyond of a Sovereign Cruelty," in *Without Alibi*, trans. Peggy Kamuf (Stanford, CA: Stanford University Press, 2002), 244.
7. Ibid.
8. Ibid., 245.
9. Ibid., 244.
10. Ibid., 243.
11. Ibid., 244.
12. Ibid., 239.
13. Ibid., 244, 257.
14. Ibid., 245.
15. In her discussion of the double structure of mimesis and antimimesis (with the latter exemplified in the therapist's demand for the subject's capacity to distance himself critically from the scene of trauma) in the thinking of trauma, Ruth Leys describes how the subject has no value in the psychic elaboration of trauma. The subject is entirely and blindly regulated by trauma through and through (35–40). Ruth Leys, *Trauma: A Genealogy.*
16. Jacques Derrida, *Negotiations: Interventions and Interviews 1971–2001*, ed. and trans. Elizabeth Rottenberg (Stanford, CA: Stanford University Press, 2002), 299.
17. Ibid., 365–366.
18. See Jacques Derrida, "Otobiographies," in *The Ear of the Other: Otobiography, Transference, Translation*, trans. Peggy Kamuf and Avital Ronell (Lincoln, NE: University of Nebraska Press, 1988).
19. Freud, *SE*, 19:235–239.
20. Ibid., 236.
21. Ibid., 239.

INDEX